HYMNS OLD & NEW

HYMNS OLD & NEW

NEW ANGLICAN EDITION

Kevin Mayhew

First published in Great Britain in 1996 by
KEVIN MAYHEW LIMITED
Rattlesden
Bury St Edmunds
Suffolk IP30 0SZ

The following editions are available

Words Only (hardback)	ISBN	0 86209 805 X
	Catalogue No.	1413021
Full Music (hardback)	ISBN	0 86209 806 8
	Catalogue No.	1413024

Front cover design by Graham Johnstone
Printed and bound in Great Britain

Foreword

Hymns Old & New was first published in 1986. The decade that followed has seen what can only be described as an explosion of new hymns and worship songs. For that *Deo gratias*, for surely this is a sign that God is blessing his Church with an abundance of creativity in its worship. Clearly, though, the time had come for a thorough and far-reaching revision of the book.

The new *Hymns Old & New* here presented is at once traditional and radical. The radical aspects will be self-evident in what follows and in the texts of some of the new hymns we have included. It is traditional partly because a large number of the texts have stood the test of time; and it is 'traditional' in another sense, for the process of critical scrutiny and rewriting of established texts has itself a long and honourable history. Throughout the time hymns have been in use they have been reviewed, adapted and rewritten; many of the hymns now regarded as classics are in reality very different from the original texts.

This is the tradition in which we, as an editorial panel, felt ourselves to be placed, and we sought to discharge our responsibilities as faithfully as we were able. We were a diverse group of people, both denominationally and doctrinally: a diversity which was vital to the breadth and richness of the hymnody we were considering. Yet there were some basic principles upon which we were absolutely of common mind.

We wanted the overall tone of the book to be positive: to bear witness to the abundant grace and unconditional love of God; to enable the Church to sing of the *Good News* of salvation; to celebrate humanity as God's creation, fallen though we are, and affirm the essential goodness of the world which he has made and to which he has shown himself to be committed even unto death. Of course, we recognise the reality of sin and evil, and we would not for a moment deny that the world can be a dark and fearful place, but as Christians we believe we are called to point to the light that is never overcome; the darkness of the *background* to that is then self-evident.

We were also concerned that the book should use positive and appropriate images, and decided that militarism and triumphalism were, therefore, not appropriate. We recognise that military imagery is used in the Bible, but history, including current events, shows only too clearly the misuse to which those images are open. All too often, in the Christian and other religions, texts advocating *spiritual* warfare are used to justify the self-serving ambitions behind *temporal* conflicts. Christian 'triumph' is the triumph of love which 'is not envious or boastful or arrogant' (1 Corinthians 13:4): the triumph of the cross.

Another fundamental principle was the use of inclusive language in referring to the human race. Rare exceptions were only made for very clear reasons and after much deliberation. Non-copyright texts were amended by members of the editorial panel while those by living authors were referred back. We are grateful to the authors concerned for their willingness to co-operate.

Some traditional hymns have been difficult for congregations to sing effectively because of variations in metre from verse to verse. Most of these, except for those few which are so well-known that it would be counterproductive, have now been adapted so that the words fit easily and consistently to the tune. A classic example, of course, is *God is working his purpose out:* a deservedly well-loved hymn which is now much easier to sing well and therefore more enjoyable for all concerned.

We were also aware that a number of hymns which have served well down the ages are now being seriously questioned. Some hymns are clearly manipulative, often written by adults for children and trying to impose values which were in reality more social and cultural than religious. In other cases we felt that God was being pushed out of this world at times when we should be looking to find him within it. In cases such as this, we attempted to redress the emphasis by rewriting, rather than by deleting well-loved hymns from the book. Whether that has been worthily done will be for the churches to decide as they use the texts.

In applying our criteria, we inevitably encountered a problem: there are a number of hymns which, however doubtful the text, are rightly loved for their music; and music is an essential part of our glorifying God in worship. We then had to establish another final criterion: ultimately, what we say to and about God and each other matters, and no dubious text would be included solely because of its tune. The solution we found was, in certain cases, to commission new texts to be sung to those tunes, hence such new hymns as *Stand up, stand up for Jesus, God is our strength from days of old* and *Onward, Christian pilgrims*.

While thus occupied with the classic texts we were also aware of the enormous number of new hymns and worship songs of recent years. Jesus said that being involved in the kingdom of heaven means treasuring things both old and new, and so we turned our attention to the new. Here we found an almost bewildering diversity. As well as the offerings of communities such as Taizé and Iona, we took into account a wide range of new hymns and songs, from texts using traditional metres to the freely expressive styles with which the Church has been blessed through the renewal movement. Through these modern texts we restate the ancient traditions of the faith, explore new insights, proclaim hope, protest, express solidarity with the poor, call ourselves and others to penitence and faith; and in all that we celebrate the eternal Mystery who surrounds, embraces and permeates creation. In other words, we do what hymns have always done.

The tunes in *Hymns Old & New* are no less eclectic than the texts. We hope that our attempt to be generous and broad in our selection will be self-evident, with much-loved traditional tunes rubbing shoulders with equally revered modern compositions and worship songs.

The singing of hymns and psalms in worship pre-dates Christianity. It is something that Jesus himself would have been familiar with in the temple, and he certainly sang at the Last Supper – 'After psalms had been sung they left for the Mount of Olives,' writes Matthew. What a wonderful tradition we share!

We hope that in this diverse and approachable collection of hymns we have sown some seeds; that is all we can do. It is in the worship of the churches that those seeds must be brought to glorious flower.

GEOFFREY MOORE
Compiler and General Editor

SUSAN SAYERS
Liturgical Adviser

MICHAEL FORSTER
Theological Editor

KEVIN MAYHEW
Publisher

HYMNS OLD & NEW

1

1. A brighter dawn is breaking,
   and earth with praise is waking;
   for thou, O King most highest,
   the pow'r of death defiest.

2. And thou hast come victorious,
   with risen body glorious,
   who now for ever livest,
   and life abundant givest.

3. O free the world from blindness,
   and fill the earth with kindness,
   give sinners resurrection,
   bring striving to perfection.

4. In sickness give us healing,
   in doubt thy clear revealing,
   that praise to thee be given
   in earth as in thy heaven.

   Percy Dearmer (1867-1936)

2

1. A great and mighty wonder,
   a full and holy cure!
   The Virgin bears the infant
   with virgin-honour pure:

   Repeat the hymn again!
   'To God on high be glory,
   and peace on earth shall reign.'

2. The Word becomes incarnate,
   and yet remains on high;
   and cherubim sing anthems
   to shepherds from the sky:

3. While thus they sing your monarch,
   those bright angelic bands,
   rejoice, ye vales and mountains,
   ye oceans, clap your hands:

4. Since all he comes to ransom
   by all be he adored,
   the infant born in Bethl'em,
   the Saviour and the Lord:

   St. Germanus (c. 634-c. 734) trans.
   John Mason Neale (1818-1866) alt.

3

1. A man there lived in Galilee
   like none who lived before,
   for he alone from first to last
   our flesh unsullied wore;
   a perfect life of perfect deeds
   once to the world was shown,
   that people all might mark his steps
   and in them plant their own.

2. A man there died on Calvary
   above all others brave;
   the human race he saved and blessed,
   himself he scorned to save.
   No thought can gauge the weight
     of woe
   on him, the sinless, laid;
   we only know that with his blood
   our ransom price was paid.

3. A man there reigns in glory now,
   divine, yet human still;
   that human which is all divine
   death sought in vain to kill.
   All pow'r is his; supreme he rules
   the realms of time and space;
   yet still our human cares and needs
   find in his heart a place.

   Somerset Corry Lowry (1855-1932)

4

A new commandment
I give unto you:
that you love one another
as I have loved you,
that you love one another
as I have loved you.

1. By this shall all know
   that you are my disciples
   if you have love one for another.
   By this shall all know
   that you are my disciples
   if you have love one for another.

2. You are my friends
   if you do what I command you.
   Without my help you can do nothing.
   You are my friends
   if you do what I command you.
   Without my help you can do nothing.

3. I am the true vine,
   my Father is the gard'ner.
   Abide in me: I will be with you.
   I am the true vine,
   my Father is the gard'ner.
   Abide in me: I will be with you.

4. True love is patient,
   not arrogant or boastful;
   love bears all things, love is eternal.
   True love is patient,
   not arrogant or boastful;
   love bears all things, love is eternal.

v. 1: unknown, based on John 13:34-35
vs. 2-4: Aniceto Nazareth, based on John 15
and 1 Corinthians 13

5

Abba, Father, let me be
yours and yours alone.
May my will for ever be
more and more your own.
Never let my heart grow cold,
never let me go.
Abba, Father, let me be
yours and yours alone.

Dave Bilbrough
© 1977 Kingsway's Thankyou Music

6

1. Abide with me,
   fast falls the eventide;
   the darkness deepens;
   Lord, with me abide:
   when other helpers fail,
   and comforts flee,
   help of the helpless,
   O abide with me.

2. Swift to its close
   ebbs out life's little day;
   earth's joys grow dim,
   its glories pass away;
   change and decay
   in all around I see;
   O thou who changest not,
   abide with me.

3. I need thy presence
   ev'ry passing hour;
   what but thy grace can foil
   the tempter's pow'r?
   Who like thyself my guide
   and stay can be?
   Through cloud and sunshine,
   Lord, abide with me.

4. I fear no foe
   with thee at hand to bless;
   ills have no weight,
   and tears no bitterness.
   Where is death's sting?
   Where, grave, thy victory?
   I triumph still,
   if thou abide with me.

5. Hold thou thy cross
   before my closing eyes;
   shine through the gloom,
   and point me to the skies;
   heav'n's morning breaks,
   and earth's vain shadows flee;
   in life, in death, O Lord,
   abide with me.

   Henry Francis Lyte (1793-1847)

7

Adoramus te, Domine.

1. With the angels and archangels:

2. With the patriarchs and prophets:

3. With the Virgin Mary,
   mother of God:

4. With the apostles and evangelists:

5. With all the martyrs of Christ:

6. With all who witness
   to the Gospel of the Lord:

7. With all your people
   of the Church throughout the world:

   Taizé Community

8

1. Ah, holy Jesu,
   how hast thou offended,
   that so to judge thee
   mortals have pretended?
   By foes derided,
   by thine own rejected,
   O most afflicted.

2. Who was the guilty?
   Who brought this upon thee?
   Alas, O Lord,
   my treason hath undone thee.
   'Twas I, Lord Jesu,
   I it was denied thee:
   I crucified thee.

3. Lo, the good shepherd
   for the sheep is offered;
   the slave hath sinnèd,
   and the Son hath suffered;
   for our atonement
   Christ himself is pleading,
   still interceding.

4. For me, kind Jesu,
   was thy incarnation,
   thy mortal sorrow,
   and thy life's oblation;
   thy death of anguish
   and thy bitter passion,
   for my salvation.

5. Therefore, kind Jesu,
   since I cannot pay thee,
   I do adore thee,
   and will ever pray thee,
   think on thy pity
   and thy love unswerving,
   not my deserving.

   Robert Bridges (1844-1930)
   from J. Heerman (1585-1647) alt.
   based on an 11th century Latin meditation

9

1. All creatures of our God and King,
lift up your voice and with us sing
alleluia, alleluia!
Thou burning sun with golden beam,
thou silver moon with softer gleam:

O praise him, O praise him,
alleluia, alleluia, alleluia.

2. Thou rushing wind that art so strong,
ye clouds that sail in heav'n along,
O praise him, alleluia!
Thou rising morn, in praise rejoice,
ye lights of evening, find a voice:

3. Thou flowing water, pure and clear,
make music for thy Lord to hear,
alleluia, alleluia!
Thou fire so masterful and bright,
that givest us both warmth and light:

4. Dear mother earth, who day by day
unfoldest blessings on our way,
O praise him, alleluia!
The flow'rs and fruits that in thee grow,
let them his glory also show.

5. All you with mercy in your heart,
forgiving others, take your part,
O sing ye, alleluia!
Ye who long pain and sorrow bear,
praise God and on him cast your care:

6. And thou, most kind and gentle death,
waiting to hush our latest breath,
O praise him, alleluia!
Thou leadest home the child of God,
and Christ our Lord the way hath trod:

7. Let all things their Creator bless,
and worship him in humbleness,
O praise him, alleluia!
Praise, praise the Father,
praise the Son,
and praise the Spirit, Three in One.

William Henry Draper (1855-1933) alt.
based on the 'Cantico di Frate Sole' of
St. Francis of Assisi (1182-1226)

10

1. All for Jesus! All for Jesus!
This our song shall ever be;
for we have no hope nor Saviour
if we have not hope in thee.

2. All for Jesus! thou wilt give us
strength to serve thee hour by hour:
none can move us from thy presence
while we trust thy love and pow'r.

3. All for Jesus! at thine altar
thou dost give us sweet content;
there, dear Saviour, we receive thee
in thy holy sacrament.

4. All for Jesus! thou hast loved us,
all for Jesus! thou hast died,
all for Jesus! thou art with us,
all for Jesus, glorified!

5. All for Jesus! All for Jesus!
This the Church's song shall be,
till at last the flock is gathered
one in love, and one in thee.

William John Sparrow-Simpson (1859-1952) alt.

11

All glory, laud and honour,
to thee, Redeemer King,
to whom the lips of children
made sweet hosannas ring.

1. Thou art the King of Israel,
   thou David's royal Son,
   who in the Lord's name comest,
   the king and blessed one.

2. The company of angels
   are praising thee on high,
   and mortals, joined with all things
   created, make reply.

3. The people of the Hebrews
   with palms before thee went:
   our praise and prayer and anthems
   before thee we present.

4. To thee before thy passion
   they sang their hymns of praise:
   to thee now high exalted
   our melody we raise.

5. Thou didst accept their praises,
   accept the prayers we bring,
   who in all good delightest,
   thou good and gracious king.

St. Theodulph of Orleans (d. 821)
trans. John Mason Neale (1818-1866) alt.

12

1. All hail and welcome, holy child,
   you poor babe in the manger.
   So happy and rich it is you are
   tonight inside your castle.

2. God bless you, Jesus, once again!
   Your life in its young body,
   your face more lovely than the sun
   – a thousand welcomes, baby!

3. Tonight we greet you in the flesh;
   my heart adores my young king.
   You came to us in human form –
   I bring you a kiss and a greeting.

Aodh Mac Cathmhaoil (1571-1626)
trans. George Otto Simms (1910-1991)

13

When the tune 'Miles Lane' is used.

1. All hail the pow'r of Jesus' name!
   let angels prostrate fall;
   bring forth the royal diadem
   and crown him,
   crown him, crown him,
   crown him Lord of all.

2. Crown him, ye martyrs of your God,
   who from his altar call;
   praise him whose way of pain ye trod
   and crown him,
   crown him, crown him,
   crown him Lord of all.

3. Ye prophets who our freedom won,
   ye searchers, great and small,
   by whom the work of truth is done,
   now crown him,
   crown him, crown him,
   crown him Lord of all.

4. Ye seed of Israel's chosen race
   ye ransomed of the fall,
   hail him who saves you by his grace,
   and crown him,
   crown him, crown him,
   crown him Lord of all.

Continued overleaf

5. Let ev'ry tribe and ev'ry tongue
   to him their hearts enthral:
   lift high the universal song
   and crown him,
   crown him, crown him,
   crown him Lord of all.

   Edward Perronet (1726-1792)

When the tune 'Diadem' is used.

1. All hail the pow'r of Jesus' name!
   let angels prostrate fall,
   let angels prostrate fall,
   bring forth the royal diadem,
   and crown him, crown him,
   crown him, crown him,
   and crown him Lord of all.

2. Crown him, ye martyrs of your God,
   who from his altar call,
   who from his altar call;
   praise him whose way of pain ye trod,
   and crown him, crown him,
   crown him, crown him,
   and crown him Lord of all.

3. Ye prophets who our freedom won,
   ye searchers, great and small,
   ye searchers, great and small;
   by whom the work of truth is done,
   now crown him, crown him,
   crown him, crown him,
   now crown him Lord of all.

4. Ye seed of Israel's chosen race
   ye ransomed of the fall,
   ye ransomed of the fall,
   hail him who saves you by his grace,
   and crown him, crown him,
   crown him, crown him,
   and crown him Lord of all.

5. Let ev'ry tribe and ev'ry tongue
   to him their hearts enthral,
   to him their hearts enthral;
   lift high the universal song,
   and crown him, crown him,
   crown him, crown him,
   and crown him Lord of all.

   Edward Perronet (1726-1792)

14

1. All heav'n declares
   the glory of the risen Lord.
   Who can compare
   with the beauty of the Lord?
   For ever he will be
   the Lamb upon the throne.
   I gladly bow the knee
   and worship him alone.

2. I will proclaim
   the glory of the risen Lord,
   who once was slain
   to reconcile us to God.
   For ever you will be
   the Lamb upon the throne;
   I gladly bow the knee,
   and worship you alone.

   Noel and Tricia Richards
   © 1987 Kingsway's Thankyou Music

15

1. All my hope on God is founded;
   he doth still my trust renew.
   Me through change and chance
      he guideth,
   only good and only true.
   God unknown,
   he alone
   calls my heart to be his own.

2. Human pride and earthly glory,
   sword and crown betray his trust;
   what with care and toil he buildeth,
   tow'r and temple, fall to dust.
   But God's pow'r,
   hour by hour,
   is my temple and my tow'r.

3. God's great goodness aye endureth,
   deep his wisdom, passing thought:
   splendour, light and life attend him,
   beauty springeth out of naught.
   Evermore,
   from his store
   new-born worlds rise and adore.

4. Still from earth to God eternal
   sacrifice of praise be done,
   high above all praises praising
   for the gift of Christ his Son.
   Christ doth call
   one and all:
   ye who follow shall not fall.

   Robert Bridges (1844-1930) alt.
   based on the German of Joachim Neander
   (1650-1680)

16

1. All over the world
   the Spirit is moving,
   all over the world,
   as the prophets said it would be.
   All over the world
   there's a mighty revelation
   of the glory of the Lord,
   as the waters cover the sea.

2. All over this land
   the Spirit is moving,
   all over this land,
   as the prophets said it would be.
   All over this land
   there's a mighty revelation
   of the glory of the Lord,
   as the waters cover the sea.

3. All over the Church
   the Spirit is moving,
   all over the Church,
   as the prophets said it would be.
   All over the Church
   there's a mighty revelation
   of the glory of the Lord,
   as the waters cover the sea.

4. All over us all
   the Spirit is moving,
   all over us all,
   as the prophets said it would be.
   All over us all
   there's a mighty revelation
   of the glory of the Lord,
   as the waters cover the sea.

5. Deep down in my heart
   the Spirit is moving,
   deep down in my heart,
   as the prophets said it would be.
   Deep down in my heart
   there's a mighty revelation
   of the glory of the Lord,
   as the waters cover the sea.

   Roy Turner (b. 1940)
   © 1984 Kingsway's Thankyou Music

17

1. All people that on earth do dwell,
   sing to the Lord with cheerful voice;
   him serve with fear, his praise forth tell,
   come ye before him and rejoice.

2. The Lord, ye know, is God indeed,
   without our aid he did us make;
   we are his folk, he doth us feed,
   and for his sheep he doth us take.

3. O enter then his gates with praise,
   approach with joy his courts unto;
   praise, laud and bless his name always,
   for it is seemly so to do.

4. For why, the Lord our God is good:
   his mercy is for ever sure;
   his truth at all times firmly stood,
   and shall from age to age endure.

5. To Father, Son and Holy Ghost,
   the God whom heav'n and earth adore,
   from us and from the angel-host
   be praise and glory evermore.

William Kethe (d. 1594) from
'Day's Psalter' (1560) alt.

2. Thou cam'st to us
   in lowliness of thought;
   by thee the outcast
   and the poor were sought,
   and by thy death
   was God's salvation wrought:
   Alleluia.

3. Let this mind be in us
   which was in thee,
   who wast a servant
   that we might be free,
   humbling thyself
   to death on Calvary:
   Alleluia.

4. Wherefore, by God's
   eternal purpose,
   thou art high exalted
   o'er all creatures now,
   and giv'n the name to which
   all knees shall bow:
   Alleluia.

5. Let ev'ry tongue confess
   with one accord
   in heav'n and earth
   that Jesus Christ is Lord;
   and God the Father
   be by all adored:
   Alleluia.

Francis Bland Tucker (1895-1984)
based on Philippians 2:5-11

18

1. All praise to thee,
   for thou, O King divine,
   didst yield the glory
   that of right was thine,
   that in our darkened hearts
   thy grace might shine:
   Alleluia.

19

1. All that I am, all that I do,
   all that I'll ever have I offer now to you.
   Take and sanctify these gifts
   for your honour, Lord.
   Knowing that I love and serve you
   is enough reward.
   All that I am, all that I do,
   all that I'll ever have I offer now to you.

2. All that I dream, all that I pray,
   all that I'll ever make I give to you
   today.
   Take and sanctify these gifts
   for your honour, Lord.
   Knowing that I love and serve you
   is enough reward.
   All that I am, all that I do,
   all that I'll ever have I offer now to you.

Sebastian Temple (b. 1928)
© 1967 OCP Publications

20

All the nations of the earth,
praise the Lord who brings to birth
the greatest star, the smallest flow'r.
Alleluia.

1. Let the heavens praise the Lord,
   alleluia.
   Moon and stars, praise the Lord,
   alleluia.

2. Snow-capped mountains, praise
     the Lord,
   alleluia.
   Rolling hills, praise the Lord,
   alleluia.

3. Deep sea water, praise the Lord,
   alleluia.
   Gentle rain, praise the Lord,
   alleluia.

4. Roaring lion, praise the Lord,
   alleluia.
   Singing birds, praise the Lord,
   alleluia.

5. Earthly monarchs, praise the Lord,
   alleluia.
   Young and old, praise the Lord,
   alleluia.

Michael Cockett (b. 1938)

21

All things bright and beautiful,
all creatures great and small,
all things wise and wonderful,
the Lord God made them all.

1. Each little flow'r that opens,
   each little bird that sings,
   he made their glowing colours,
   he made their tiny wings.

2. The purple-headed mountain,
   the river running by,
   the sunset and the morning,
   that brightens up the sky.

3. The cold wind in the winter,
   the pleasant summer sun,
   the ripe fruits in the garden,
   he made them ev'ry one.

4. The tall trees in the greenwood,
   the meadows for our play,
   the rushes by the water,
   to gather ev'ry day.

5. He gave us eyes to see them,
   and lips that we may tell
   how great is God Almighty,
   who has made all things well.

Cecil Frances Alexander (1818-1895) alt.

22

1. All ye who seek a comfort sure
   in trouble and distress,
   whatever sorrow vex the mind,
   or guilt the soul oppress:

2. Jesus, who gave himself for you
   upon the cross to die,
   opens to you his sacred heart;
   O, to that heart draw nigh.

3. Ye hear how kindly he invites;
   ye hear his words so blest:
   'All ye that labour, come to me,
   and I will give you rest.'

4. What meeker than the Saviour's heart?
   As on the cross he lay,
   it did his murderers forgive,
   and for their pardon pray.

5. O heart, thou joy of saints on high,
   thou hope of sinners here,
   attracted by those loving words
   to thee I lift my prayer.

6. Wash thou my wounds in that dear
      blood
   which forth from thee doth flow;
   by grace a better hope inspire,
   and risen life bestow.

18th Century Latin trans. Edward Caswall
(1814-1878) alt.

23

1. Alleluia . . .

2. Jesus is Lord . . .

3. And I love him . . .

4. Christ is risen . . .

Additional verses may be composed to suit
the occasion. For example:

5. Send your Spirit . . .

6. Abba, Father . . .

7. Come, Lord Jesus . . .

vs: 1-4 unknown, vs: 5-7 Damian Lundy (b. 1944)

24

Alleluia, alleluia,
give thanks to the risen Lord,
alleluia, alleluia,
give praise to his name.

1. Jesus is Lord of all the earth.
   He is the King of creation.

2. Spread the good news o'er all the earth.
   Jesus has died and is risen.

3. We have been crucified with Christ.
   Now we shall live for ever.

4. God has proclaimed the just reward:
   'Life for us all, alleluia!'

5. Come, let us praise the living God,
   joyfully sing to our Saviour.

Donald Fishel (b. 1950) alt.
© 1973 Word of God Music/CopyCare Ltd

25

1. Alleluia, alleluia,
   hearts to heav'n and voices raise;
   sing to God a hymn of gladness,
   sing to God a hymn of praise:
   he who on the cross a victim
   for the world's salvation bled,
   Jesus Christ, the King of Glory,
   now is risen from the dead.

2. Christ is risen, Christ the first-fruits
   of the holy harvest field,
   which will all its full abundance
   at his second coming yield;
   then the golden ears of harvest
   will their heads before him wave,
   ripened by his glorious sunshine,
   from the furrows of the grave.

3. Christ is risen, we are risen;
   shed upon us heav'nly grace,
   rain, and dew, and gleams of glory
   from the brightness of thy face;
   that we, with our hearts in heaven,
   here on earth may fruitful be,
   and by angel-hands be gathered,
   and be ever, Lord, with thee.

4. Alleluia, alleluia,
   glory be to God on high;
   alleluia to the Saviour,
   who has gained the victory;
   alleluia to the Spirit,
   fount of love and sanctity;
   alleluia, alleluia,
   to the Triune Majesty.

   Christopher Wordsworth (1807-1885)

26

1. Alleluia, sing to Jesus,
   his the sceptre, his the throne;
   alleluia, his the triumph,
   his the victory alone:
   hark the songs of peaceful Sion
   thunder like a mighty flood:
   Jesus, out of ev'ry nation,
   hath redeemed us by his blood.

2. Alleluia, not as orphans
   are we left in sorrow now;
   alleluia, he is near us,
   faith believes, not questions how;
   though the cloud from
      sight received him
   when the forty days were o'er,
   shall our hearts forget his promise,
   'I am with you evermore'?

3. Alleluia, bread of angels,
   thou on earth our food, our stay;
   alleluia, here the sinful
   flee to thee from day to day;
   intercessor, friend of sinners,
   earth's redeemer, plead for me,
   where the songs of all the sinless
   sweep across the crystal sea.

4. Alleluia, King eternal,
   thee the Lord of lords we own;
   alleluia, born of Mary,
   earth thy footstool, heav'n thy throne;
   thou within the veil hast entered
   robed in flesh, our great High Priest;
   thou on earth both priest and victim
   in the Eucharistic Feast.

   William Chatterton Dix (1837-1898)

27

1. Amazing grace! How sweet the sound
that saved a wretch like me.
I once was lost, but now I'm found;
was blind but now I see.

2. 'Twas grace that taught my heart to fear,
and grace my fears relieved.
How precious did that grace appear
the hour I first believed.

3. Through many dangers, toils and snares
I have already come.
'Tis grace hath brought me safe thus far,
and grace will lead me home.

4. The Lord has promised good to me,
his word my hope secures;
he will my shield and portion be
as long as life endures.

5. When we've been there a thousand
years,
bright shining as the sun,
we've no less days to sing God's praise
that when we first begun.

vs. 1-4: John Newton (1725-1807) alt.,
vs. 5: John Rees (1828-1900)

28

1. Among us and before us,
Lord, you stand
with arms outstretched
and bread and wine at hand.
Confronting those
unworthy of a crumb,
you ask that to your table
we should come.

2. Who dare say No,
when such is your resolve
our worst to witness,
suffer and absolve,
our best to raise in lives
by God forgiv'n,
our souls to fill on earth
with food from heav'n?

3. Who dare say No,
when such is your intent
to love the selves
we famish and resent,
to cradle our
uncertainties and fear,
to kindle hope as
you in faith draw near?

4. Who dare say No,
when such is your request
that each around your table
should be guest,
that here the ancient word
should live as new
'Take, eat and drink –
all this is meant for you.'?

5. No more we hesitate
and wonder why;
no more we stand indiff'rent,
scared or shy.
Your invitation leads us
to say Yes,
to meet you where you nourish,
heal and bless.

John L. Bell (b. 1949) and Graham Maule (b. 1958)

29

1. An upper room did our Lord prepare
for those he loved until the end:
and his disciples still gather there,
to celebrate their risen friend.

2. A lasting gift Jesus gave his own:
   to share his bread, his loving cup.
   whatever burdens may bow us down,
   he by his cross shall lift us up.

3. And after supper he washed their feet
   for service, too, is sacrament.
   In him our joy shall be made
      complete –
   sent out to serve, as he was sent.

4. No end there is! We depart in peace,
   he loves beyond our uttermost:
   in ev'ry room in our Father's house
   he will be there, as Lord and host.

   Fred Pratt Green (b. 1903)

4. Long my imprisoned spirit lay
   fast bound in sin and nature's night;
   thine eye diffused a quick'ning ray,
   I woke, the dungeon flamed with light;
   my chains fell off, my heart was free;
   I rose, went forth, and followed thee.

5. No condemnation now I dread;
   Jesus, and all in him, is mine!
   Alive in him, my living Head,
   and clothed in righteousness divine,
   bold I approach the eternal throne,
   and claim the crown, through Christ
      my own.

   Charles Wesley (1707-1788)

30

1. And can it be that I should gain
   an in'trest in the Saviour's blood?
   Died he for me, who caused his pain?
   for me, who him to death pursued?
   Amazing love! How can it be
   that thou, my God, shouldst die
      for me?

2. 'Tis myst'ry all! th'Immortal dies:
   who can explore his strange design?
   In vain the first-born seraph tries
   to sound the depths of love divine!
   'Tis mercy all! Let earth adore,
   let angel minds inquire no more.

3. He left his Father's throne above
   so free, so infinite his grace;
   emptied himself of all but love,
   and bled for Adam's helpless race;
   'tis mercy all, immense and free;
   for, O my God, it found out me.

31

1. And did those feet in ancient time
   walk upon England's mountains
      green?
   And was the holy Lamb of God
   on England's pleasant pastures seen?
   And did the countenance divine
   shine forth upon our clouded hills?
   And was Jerusalem builded here
   among those dark satanic mills?

2. Bring me my bow of burning gold!
   Bring me my arrows of desire!
   Bring me my spear! O clouds unfold!
   Bring me my chariot of fire!
   I will not cease from mental fight,
   nor shall my sword sleep in my hand,
   till we have built Jerusalem
   in England's green and pleasant land.

   William Blake (1757-1827)

32

1. And now, O Father,
   mindful of the love
   that bought us, once for all,
   on Calv'ry's tree,
   and having with us him
   that pleads above,
   we here present,
   we here spread forth to thee
   that only off'ring
   perfect in thine eyes,
   the one true, pure,
   immortal sacrifice.

2. Look, Father,
   look on his anointed face,
   and only look on us
   as found in him;
   look not on our
   misusings of thy grace,
   our prayer so languid,
   and our faith so dim:
   for lo, between our sins
   and their reward
   we set the Passion
   of thy Son our Lord.

3. And then for those,
   our dearest and our best,
   by this prevailing presence
   we appeal:
   O fold them closer
   to they mercy's breast,
   O do thine utmost
   for their souls' true weal;
   from tainting mischief
   keep them pure and clear,
   and crown thy gifts
   with strength to persevere.

4. And so we come:
   O draw us to thy feet,
   most patient Saviour,
   who canst love us still;
   and by this food,
   so aweful and so sweet,
   deliver us from
   ev'ry touch of ill:
   in thine own service
   make us glad and free,
   and grant us never more
   to part with thee.

   William Bright (1824-1901)

33

1. Angel-voices ever singing
   round thy throne of light,
   angel-harps for ever ringing,
   rest not day nor night;
   thousands only live to bless thee,
   and confess thee Lord of might.

2. Thou who art beyond the farthest
   mortal eye can see,
   can it be that thou regardest
   our poor hymnody?
   Yes, we know that thou art near us
   and wilt hear us constantly.

3. Yea, we know that thou rejoicest
   o'er each work of thine;
   thou didst ears and hands and voices
   for thy praise design;
   craftsman's art and music's measure
   for thy pleasure all combine.

4. In thy house, great God, we offer
   of thine own to thee;
   and for thine acceptance proffer
   all unworthily,
   hearts and minds and hands and voices
   in our choicest psalmody.

5. Honour, glory, might and merit,
   thine shall ever be,
   Father, Son and Holy Spirit,
   blessèd Trinity.
   Of the best that thou hast given
   earth and heaven render thee.

   Francis Pott (1832-1909) alt.

4. Saints before the altar bending,
   watching long in hope and fear,
   suddenly the Lord, descending,
   in his temple shall appear:

5. Though an infant now we view him,
   he shall fill his Father's throne,
   gather all the nations to him;
   ev'ry knee shall then bow down:

   James Montgomery (1771-1854)

34

1. Angels from the realms of glory,
   wing your flight o'er all the earth;
   ye who sang creation's story
   now proclaim Messiah's birth:

   Come and worship
   Christ, the new-born King:
   come and worship,
   worship Christ, the new-born King.

2. Shepherds, in the field abiding,
   watching o'er your flocks by night,
   God with us is now residing,
   yonder shines the infant Light:

3. Sages, leave your contemplations;
   brighter visions beam afar:
   seek the great Desire of Nations;
   ye have seen his natal star:

35

1. Around the throne of God a band
   of glorious angels ever stand;
   bright things they see, sweet harps
     they hold,
   and on their heads are crowns of gold.

2. Some wait around him, ready still
   to sing his praise and do his will;
   and some, when he commands
     them, go
   to guard his servants here below.

3. Lord, give thy angels ev'ry day
   command to guide us on our way,
   and bid them ev'ry evening keep
   their watch around us while we sleep.

4. So shall no wicked thing draw near,
   to do us harm or cause us fear;
   and we shall dwell, when life is past,
   with angels round thy throne at last.

   John Mason Neale (1818-1866)

36

1. As Jacob with travel
   was weary one day,
   at night on a stone
   for a pillow he lay;
   he saw in a vision
   a ladder so high
   that its foot was on earth
   and its top in the sky:

   Alleluia to Jesus
   who died on the tree,
   and has raised up a ladder
   of mercy for me,
   and has raised up a ladder
   of mercy for me.

2. This ladder is long,
   it is strong and well-made,
   has stood hundreds of years
   and is not yet decayed;
   many millions have climbed it
   and reached Sion's hill,
   and thousands by faith
   are climbing it still:

3. Come let us ascend!
   all may climb it who will;
   for the angels of Jacob
   are guarding it still:
   and remember, each step
   that by faith we pass o'er,
   some prophet or martyr
   has trod it before:

4. And when we arrive
   at the haven of rest
   we shall hear the glad words,
   'Come up hither, ye blest,
   here are regions of light,
   here are mansions of bliss.'
   O who would not climb
   such a ladder as this?

   18th century

37

1. As now the sun's declining rays
   at eventide descend,
   e'en so our years are sinking down
   to their appointed end.

2. Lord, on the cross thine arms were
      stretched
   to draw the nations nigh;
   O grant us then that cross to love,
   and in those arms to die.

3. To God the Father, God the Son,
   and God the Holy Ghost,
   all glory be from saints on earth
   and from the angel host.

   Charles Coffin (1676-1749)
   trans. John Chandler (1806-1876)

38

1. As pants the hart for cooling streams
   when heated in the chase,
   so longs my soul, O God, for thee,
   and thy refreshing grace.

2. For thee, my God, the living God,
   my thirsty soul doth pine:
   O when shall I behold thy face,
   thou majesty divine?

3. Why restless, why cast down, my soul?
   hope still, and thou shalt sing
   the praise of him who is thy God,
   thy health's eternal spring.

4. To Father, Son and Holy Ghost,
   the God whom we adore,
   be glory, as it was, is now,
   and shall be evermore.

Psalm 42 in 'New Version' (Tate and Brady, 1696)

39

1. As the deer pants for the water
   so my soul longs after you.
   You alone are my heart's desire
   and I long to worship you.

   You alone are my strength, my shield,
   to you alone may my spirit yield.
   You alone are my heart's desire
   and I long to worship you.

2. I want you more than gold or silver,
   only you can satisfy.
   You alone are the real joy-giver
   and the apple of my eye.

3. You're my friend and you are my
      brother,
   even though you are a king.
   I love you more than any other,
   so much more than anything.

Martin Nystrom, based on Psalm 42:1-2
© 1983 Restoration Music Ltd/
Sovereign Lifestyle Music Ltd

40

As we are gathered, Jesus is here,
one with each other, Jesus is here,
joined by the Spirit, washed in the blood,
part of the Body, the Church of God.
As we are gathered, Jesus is here,
one with each other, Jesus is here.

John Daniels
© 1979 Springtide/Word Music (UK)/CopyCare Ltd

41

1. As with gladness men of old
   did the guiding star behold,
   as with joy they hailed its light,
   leading onward, beaming bright;
   so, most gracious Lord, may we
   evermore be led to thee.

2. As with joyful steps they sped,
   to that lowly manger-bed,
   there to bend the knee before
   him whom heav'n and earth adore,
   so may we with willing feet
   ever seek thy mercy-seat.

3. As their precious gifts they laid,
   at thy manger roughly made,
   so may we with holy joy,
   pure, and free from sin's alloy,
   all our costliest treasures bring,
   Christ, to thee, our heav'nly King.

4. Holy Jesu, ev'ry day
   keep us in the narrow way;
   and, when earthly things are past,
   bring our ransomed souls at last
   where they need no star to guide,
   where no clouds thy glory hide.

Continued overleaf

5. In the heav'nly country bright
   need they no created light;
   thou its light, its joy, its crown,
   thou its sun which goes not down;
   there for ever may we sing
   alleluias to our King.

   William Chatterton Dix (1837-1898) alt.

42

Ascribe greatness to our God, the rock,
his work is perfect and all his ways are just.
A God of faithfulness
and without injustice;
good and upright is he.

Peter West, Mary Lou Locke & Mary Kirkbride
© 1979 Peter West/Integrity's Hosanna! Music/
Kingsway's Thankyou Music

43

1. At even, ere the sun was set,
   the sick, O Lord, around thee lay;
   O in what divers pains they met!
   O with what joy they went away!

2. Once more 'tis eventide, and we
   oppressed with various ills draw near;
   what if thy form we cannot see?
   We know and feel that thou art here.

3. O Saviour Christ, our woes dispel;
   for some are sick, and some are sad,
   and some have never loved thee well,
   and some have lost the love they had.

4. And some have found the world is vain,
   yet from the world they break not free;
   and some have friends who give them
      pain,
   yet have not sought a friend in thee.

5. And none, O Lord, has perfect rest,
   for none is wholly free from sin;
   and they who fain would serve thee best
   are conscious most of wrong within.

6. O Christ, thou hast been human too,
   thou hast been troubled, tempted, tried;
   thy kind but searching glance can view
   the very wounds that shame would hide.

7. Thy touch has still its ancient pow'r;
   no word from thee can fruitless fall:
   hear, in this solemn evening hour,
   and in thy mercy heal us all.

   Henry Twells (1823-1900) alt.

44

1. At the cross her station keeping,
   stood the mournful mother weeping,
   where he hung, the dying Lord.

2. For her soul, of joy bereavèd,
   bowed with anguish, deeply grievèd,
   felt the sharp and piercing sword.

3. O, how sad and sore distressèd
   now was she, that mother blessèd,
   of the sole-begotten one!

4. Deep the woe of her affliction,
   when she saw the crucifixion
   of her ever-glorious Son.

5. Who, on Christ's dear mother gazing,
   pierced by anguish so amazing,
   born of woman, would not weep?

6. Who, on Christ's dear mother thinking,
   such a cup of sorrow drinking,
   would not share her sorrows deep?

7. For his people's sins chastisèd,
   she beheld her Son despisèd,
   scourged, and crowned with thorns
      entwined.

8. Saw him then from judgement taken,
   and in death by all forsaken,
   till his spirit he resigned.

9. O good Jesu, let me borrow
   something of thy mother's sorrow,
   fount of love, Redeemer kind.

10. That my heart fresh ardour gaining,
    and a purer love attaining,
    may with thee acceptance find.

   ascribed to Jacopone da Todi (d. 1306)
   trans. Edward Caswall (1814-1878)

3. Mighty victim from above,
   conqu'ring by the pow'r of love;
   thou hast triumphed in the fight,
   thou hast brought us life and light.
   Now no more can death appal,
   now no more the grave enthral:
   thou hast opened paradise,
   and in thee thy saints shall rise.

4. Easter triumph, Easter joy,
   nothing now can this destroy;
   from sin's pow'r do thou set free
   souls new-born, O Lord, in thee.
   Hymns of glory and of praise,
   risen Lord, to thee we raise;
   holy Father, praise to thee,
   with the Spirit, ever be.

   Latin trans. Robert Campbell (1814-1868)

45

1. At the Lamb's high feast we sing
   praise to our victorious King,
   who hath washed us in the tide
   flowing from his piercèd side;
   praise we him, whose love divine
   gives his sacred blood for wine,
   gives his body for the feast,
   Christ the victim, Christ the priest.

2. Where the paschal blood is poured,
   death's dark angel sheathes his sword;
   faithful hosts triumphant go
   through the wave that drowns the foe.
   Praise we Christ, whose blood was
      shed,
   paschal victim, paschal bread;
   with sincerity and love
   eat we manna from above.

46

1. At the name of Jesus
   ev'ry knee shall bow,
   ev'ry tongue confess him
   King of glory now;
   'tis the Father's pleasure
   we should call him Lord,
   who, from the beginning,
   was the mighty Word.

2. At his voice creation
   sprang at once to sight,
   all the angels' faces,
   all the hosts of light,
   thrones and dominations,
   stars upon their way,
   all the heav'nly orders
   in their great array.

Continued overleaf

3. Humbled for a season,
to receive a name
from the lips of sinners
unto whom he came,
faithfully he bore it,
spotless to the last,
brought it back victorious
when from death he passed.

4. Bore it up triumphant,
with its human light,
through all ranks of creatures
to the central height,
to the throne of Godhead,
to the Father's breast,
filled it with the glory
of that perfect rest.

5. All creation, name him,
with love as strong as death;
but with awe and wonder,
and with bated breath.
He is God the Saviour,
he is Christ the Lord,
ever to be worshipped,
trusted and adored.

6. In your hearts enthrone him;
there let him subdue
all that is not holy,
all that is not true;
crown him as your captain
in temptation's hour;
let his will enfold you
in its light and pow'r.

7. Truly, this Lord Jesus
shall return again,
with his Father's glory,
with his angel train;
for all wreaths of empire
meet upon his brow,
and our hearts confess him
King of glory now.

Caroline Maria Noel (1817-1877) alt.

47

At this time of giving,
gladly now we bring
gifts of goodness and mercy
from a heav'nly King.

1. Earth could not contain the treasures
heaven holds for you,
perfect joy and lasting pleasures,
love so strong and true.

2. May his tender love surround you
at this Christmas time;
may you see his smiling face
that in the darkness shines.

3. But the many gifts he gives
are all poured out from one;
come, receive the greatest gift,
the gift of God's own Son.

Last two choruses and verses:
Lai, lai, lai . . . *(Accelerating with each*
verse)

Graham Kendrick (b. 1950)
© 1988 Make Way Music Ltd

48

1. Author of life divine,
who hast a table spread,
furnished with mystic wine
and everlasting bread,
preserve the life thyself hast giv'n,
and feed and train us up for heav'n.

2. Our needy souls sustain
with fresh supplies of love,
till all thy life we gain,
and all thy fulness prove,
and, strengthened by thy perfect grace,
behold without a veil thy face.

Charles Wesley (1707-1788)

49

1. Awake, awake: fling off the night!
   for God has sent his glorious light;
   and we who live in Christ's new day
   must works of darkness put away.

2. Awake and rise, in Christ renewed,
   and with the Spirit's pow'r endued.
   The light of life in us must glow,
   and fruits of truth and goodness show.

3. Let in the light; all sin expose
   to Christ, whose life no darkness
     knows.
   Before his cross for guidance kneel;
   his light will judge and, judging, heal.

4. Awake, and rise up from the dead,
   and Christ his light on you will shed.
   Its pow'r will wrong desires destroy,
   and your whole nature fill with joy.

5. Then sing for joy, and use each day;
   give thanks for everything alway.
   Lift up your hearts; with one accord
   praise God through Jesus Christ our
     Lord.

John Raphael Peacey (1896-1971)
based on Ephesians 5:6-20 alt.

50

1. Awake, my soul, and with the sun
   thy daily stage of duty run;
   shake off dull sloth, and joyful rise
   to pay thy morning sacrifice.

2. Redeem thy mis-spent time that's past,
   and live this day as if thy last;
   improve thy talent with due care;
   for the great day thyself prepare.

3. Let all thy converse be sincere,
   thy conscience as the noon-day clear;
   think how all-seeing God thy ways
   and all thy secret thoughts surveys.

4. Wake, and lift up thyself, my heart,
   and with the angels bear thy part,
   who all night long unwearied sing
   high praise to the eternal King.

PART TWO

5. Glory to thee, who safe hast kept
   and hast refreshed me whilst I slept;
   grant, Lord, when I from death shall
     wake,
   I may of endless light partake.

6. Lord, I my vows to thee renew;
   disperse my sins as morning dew;
   guard my first springs of thought
     and will,
   and with thyself my spirit fill.

7. Direct, control, suggest, this day,
   all I design or do or say;
   that all my pow'rs, with all their might,
   in thy sole glory may unite.

This Doxology is sung after either part

8. Praise God, from whom all blessings
     flow,
   praise him, all creatures here below,
   praise him above, angelic host,
   praise Father, Son and Holy Ghost.

Thomas Ken (1637-1711) alt.

51

1. Away in a manger,
   no crib for a bed,
   the little Lord Jesus
   laid down his sweet head.
   The stars in the bright sky
   looked down where he lay,
   the little Lord Jesus,
   asleep on the hay.

2. The cattle are lowing,
   the baby awakes,
   but little Lord Jesus
   no crying he makes.
   I love thee, Lord Jesus!
   Look down from the sky,
   and stay by my side
   until morning is nigh.

3. Be near me, Lord Jesus;
   I ask thee to stay
   close by me for ever,
   and love me, I pray.
   Bless all the dear children
   in thy tender care,
   and fit us for heaven,
   to live with thee there.

An alternative version

1. Away in a manger,
   no crib for a bed,
   the little Lord Jesus
   laid down his sweet head.
   The stars in the bright sky
   looked down where he lay,
   the little Lord Jesus,
   asleep on the hay.

2. The cattle are lowing,
   they also adore
   the little Lord Jesus
   who lies in the straw.
   I love you, Lord Jesus,
   I know you are near
   to love and protect me
   till morning is here.

3. Be near me, Lord Jesus;
   I ask you to stay
   close by me for ever,
   and love me, I pray.
   Bless all the dear children
   in your tender care,
   prepare us for heaven,
   to live with you there.

Original text: William James Kirkpatrick (1838-1921)
Alternative text, vs. 2 & 3: Michael Forster (b. 1946)

52

1. Be still and know that I am God.
   Be still and know that I am God.
   Be still and know that I am God.

2. I am the Lord that healeth thee.
   I am the Lord that healeth thee.
   I am the Lord that healeth thee.

3. In thee, O Lord, I put my trust.
   In thee, O Lord, I put my trust.
   In thee, O Lord, I put my trust.

Unknown, based on Psalm 46

53

1. Be still, for the presence of the Lord,
   the Holy One, is here;
   come, bow before him now,
   with reverence and fear.
   In him no sin is found,
   we stand on holy ground.
   Be still, for the presence of the Lord,
   the Holy One, is here.

2. Be still, for the glory of the Lord
   is shining all around;
   he burns with holy fire,
   with splendour he is crowned.
   How awesome is the sight,
   our radiant King of Light!
   Be still, for the glory of the Lord
   is shining all around.

3. Be still, for the power of the Lord
   is moving in this place,
   he comes to cleanse and heal,
   to minister his grace.
   No work too hard for him,
   in faith receive from him;
   be still, for the power of the Lord
   is moving in this place.

David J. Evans (b. 1957)
© 1986 Kingsway's Thankyou Music

54

1. Be still, my soul:
   the Lord is at your side;
   bear patiently the cross
   of grief and pain;
   leave to your God
   to order and provide;
   in ev'ry change
   he faithful will remain.
   Be still, my soul:
   your best, your heav'nly friend,
   through thorny ways,
   leads to a joyful end.

2. Be still, my soul:
   your God will undertake
   to guide the future
   as he has the past.
   Your hope, your confidence
   let nothing shake,
   all now mysterious
   shall be clear at last.
   Be still, my soul:
   the tempests still obey
   his voice, who ruled them
   once on Galilee.

3. Be still, my soul:
   the hour is hastening on
   when we shall be for ever
   with the Lord,
   when disappointment,
   grief and fear are gone,
   sorrow forgotten,
   love's pure joy restored.
   Be still, my soul:
   when change and tears are past,
   all safe and blessèd
   we shall meet at last.

Katharina Von Schlegal (b. 1697)
trans. Jane L. Borthwick alt.

55

1. Be thou my guardian and my guide,
   and hear me when I call;
   let not my slipp'ry footsteps slide,
   and hold me lest I fall.

2. The world, the flesh, and Satan dwell
   around the path I tread;
   O save me from the snares of hell,
   thou quick'ner of the dead.

3. And if I tempted am to sin,
   and outward things are strong,
   do thou, O Lord, keep watch within,
   and save my soul from wrong.

4. Still let me ever watch and pray,
   and feel that I am frail;
   that if the tempter cross my way,
   yet he may not prevail.

   Isaac Williams (1802-1865)

56

1. Be thou my vision,
   O Lord of my heart,
   naught be all else to me
   save that thou art;
   thou my best thought
   in the day and the night,
   waking or sleeping,
   thy presence my light.

2. Be thou my wisdom,
   be thou my true word,
   I ever with thee
   and thou with me, Lord;
   thou my great Father,
   and I thy true heir;
   thou in me dwelling,
   and I in thy care.

3. Be thou my breastplate,
   my sword for the fight,
   be thou my armour,
   and be thou my might,
   thou my soul's shelter,
   and thou my high tow'r,
   raise thou me heav'nward,
   O Pow'r of my pow'r.

4. Riches I need not,
   nor all the world's praise,
   thou mine inheritance
   through all my days;
   thou, and thou only,
   the first in my heart,
   high King of heaven,
   my treasure thou art!

5. High King of heaven
   when battle is done,
   grant heaven's joy to me,
   O bright heav'n's sun;
   Christ of my own heart,
   whatever befall,
   still be my vision,
   O Ruler of all.

   Irish (c. 8th century) trans. Mary Byrne (1880-1931)
   and Eleanor Hull (1860-1935)

57

1. Before the ending of the day,
   Creator of the world, we pray,
   that with thy wonted favour thou
   wouldst be our guard and keeper now.

2. From all ill dreams defend our eyes,
   from nightly fears and fantasies;
   tread under foot our ghostly foe,
   that no pollution we may know.

3. O Father, that we ask be done,
   through Jesus Christ thine only Son,
   who, with the Holy Ghost and thee,
   doth live and reign eternally. Amen.

'Te lucis ante terminum' (pre 8th century)
trans. John Mason Neale (1818-1866)

58

1. Behold, the great Creator makes
   himself a house of clay,
   a robe of virgin flesh he takes
   which he will wear for ay.

2. Hark, hark! the wise eternal Word
   like a weak infant cries;
   in form of servant is the Lord,
   and God in cradle lies.

3. This wonder struck the world amazed,
   it shook the starry frame;
   squadrons of angels stood and gazed,
   then down in troops they came.

4. Glad shepherds run to view this sight;
   a choir of angels sings,
   and eastern sages with delight
   adore this King of kings.

5. Join then, all hearts that are not stone,
   and all our voices prove;
   to celebrate this Holy One,
   the God of peace and love.

Thomas Pestel (1585-1659) alt.

59

1. Beneath the cross of Jesus
   I fain would take my stand,
   the shadow of a mighty rock
   within a weary land;
   a home within a wilderness,
   a rest upon the way,
   from burning heat at noontide and
   the burden of the day.

2. O safe and happy shelter!
   O refuge tried and sweet!
   O trysting place where heaven's love
   and heaven's justice meet!
   As to the holy patriarch
   that wondrous dream was giv'n,
   so seems my Saviour's cross to me
   a ladder up to heav'n.

3. There lies, beneath its shadow,
   but on the farther side,
   the darkness of an awful grave
   that gapes both deep and wide;
   and there between us stands the cross,
   two arms outstretched to save;
   a watchman set to guard the way
   from that eternal grave.

4. Upon that cross of Jesus
   mine eye at times can see
   the very dying form of One
   who suffered there for me;
   and from my stricken heart, with tears,
   two wonders I confess –
   the wonders of redeeming love,
   and my unworthiness.

5. I take, O cross, thy shadow
   for my abiding place!
   I ask no other sunshine than
   the sunshine of his face;
   content to let the world go by,
   to reckon gain as loss –
   my sinful self, my only shame,
   my glory all – the cross.

Elizabeth C. Clephane (1830-1869) alt.

60

Bind us together, Lord,
bind us together with cords
that cannot be broken.
Bind us together, Lord,
bind us together, Lord,
bind us together in love.

1. There is only one God,
   there is only one King.
   There is only Body,
   that is why we sing:

2. Fit for the glory of God,
   purchased by his precious Blood,
   born with the right to be free:
   Jesus the vict'ry has won.

3. We are the fam'ly of God,
   we are his promise divine,
   we are his chosen desire,
   we are the glorious new wine.

Bob Gillman
© 1977 Kingsway's Thankyou Music

61

Bless the Lord, my soul,
and bless God's holy name.
Bless the Lord, my soul,
who leads me into life.

Taizé Community, from Psalm 103

62

1. Blessed assurance, Jesus is mine:
   O what a foretaste of glory divine!
   Heir of salvation, purchase of God;
   born of his Spirit, washed in his blood

This is my story, this is my song,
praising my Saviour all the day long.
This is my story, this is my song,
praising my Saviour all the day long.

2. Perfect submission, perfect delight,
   visions of rapture burst on my sight;
   angels descending, bring from above
   echoes of mercy, whispers of love.

3. Perfect submission, all is at rest,
   I in my Saviour am happy and blest;
   watching and waiting, looking above,
   filled with his goodness, lost in his love.

Frances Jane van Alstyne
(Fanny J. Crosby) (1820-1915)

63

1. Blest are the pure in heart,
   for they shall see our God;
   the secret of the Lord is theirs,
   their soul is Christ's abode.

2. The Lord who left the heav'ns
   our life and peace to bring,
   to dwell in lowliness with us,
   our pattern and our King.

3. Still to the lowly soul
   he doth himself impart,
   and for his dwelling and his throne
   chooseth the pure in heart.

4. Lord, we thy presence seek;
   may ours this blessing be:
   give us a pure and lowly heart,
   a temple meet for thee.

vs. 1, 3: John Keble (1792-1866)
vs. 2, 4: William John Hall's 'Psalms & Hymns'
(1836) alt.

64

1. Blest Creator of the light,
   making day with radiance bright,
   thou didst o'er the forming earth
   give the golden light its birth.

2. Thou didst mark the night from day
   with the dawn's first piercing ray;
   darkness now is drawing nigh;
   listen to our humble cry.

3. May we ne'er by guilt depressed
   lose the way to endless rest;
   nor with idle thoughts and vain
   bind our souls to earth again.

4. Rather may we heav'nward rise
   where eternal treasure lies;
   purified by grace within,
   hating ev'ry deed of sin.

5. Holy Father, hear our cry
   through thy Son our Lord most high,
   whom our thankful hearts adore
   with the Spirit evermore.

'Lucis Creator Optime' trans. unknown

65

1. Born in the night,
   Mary's child,
   a long way from your home;
   coming in need,
   Mary's child,
   born in a borrowed room.

2. Clear shining light,
   Mary's child,
   your face lights up our way;
   light of the world,
   Mary's child,
   dawn on our darkened day.

3. Truth of our life,
   Mary's child,
   you tell us God is good;
   prove it is true,
   Mary's child,
   go to your cross of wood.

4. Hope of the world,
   Mary's child,
   you're coming soon to reign:
   King of the earth,
   Mary's child,
   walk in our streets again.

Geoffrey Ainger (b. 1925)

66

1. Bread is blessed and broken,
   wine is blessed and poured:
   take this and remember
   Christ the Lord.

2. Share the food of heaven
   earth cannot afford.
   Here is grace in essence –
   Christ the Lord.

3. Know yourself forgiven,
   find yourself restored,
   meet a friend for ever –
   Christ the Lord.

4. God has kept his promise
   sealed by sign and word:
   here, for those who want him –
   Christ the Lord.

John L. Bell (b. 1949) and Graham Maule (b. 1958)
©1978 Sovereign Music UK

67

1. Bread of heav'n, on thee we feed,
   for thy flesh is meat indeed;
   ever may our souls be fed
   with this true and living bread;
   day by day with strength supplied
   through the life of him who died.

2. Vine of heav'n, thy blood supplies
   this blest cup of sacrifice;
   Lord, thy wounds our healing give,
   to thy cross we look and live:
   Jesus, may we ever be
   grafted, rooted, built in thee.

   Josiah Conder (1789-1855)

68

1. Bread of the world in mercy broken,
   wine of the soul in mercy shed,
   by whom the words of life were spoken,
   and in whose death our sins are dead.

2. Look on the heart by sorrows broken,
   look on the tears by sinners shed;
   and be thy feast to us the token
   that by thy grace our souls are fed.

   Reginald Heber (1783-1826)

69

1. Breathe on me, Breath of God,
   fill me with life anew,
   that I may love what thou dost love
   and do what thou wouldst do.

2. Breathe on me, Breath of God,
   until my heart is pure:
   until with thee I have one will
   to do and to endure.

3. Breathe on me, Breath of God,
   till I am wholly thine,
   until this earthly part of me
   glows with thy fire divine.

4. Breathe on me, Breath of God,
   so shall I never die,
   but live with thee the perfect life
   of thine eternity.

   Edwin Hatch (1835-1889)

70

1. Bright the vision that delighted
   once the sight of Judah's seer;
   sweet the countless tongues united
   to entrance the prophet's ear.

2. Round the Lord in glory seated
   cherubim and seraphim
   filled his temple, and repeated
   each to each the alternate hymn:

3. 'Lord, thy glory fills the heaven;
   earth is with its fulness stored;
   unto thee be glory given,
   holy, holy, holy, Lord.'

4. Heav'n is still with glory ringing,
   earth takes up the angels' cry,
   'Holy, holy, holy,' singing,
   'Lord of hosts, the Lord most high.'

5. With his seraph train before him,
   with his holy Church below,
   thus unite we to adore him,
   bid we thus our anthem flow:

6. 'Lord, thy glory fills the heaven;
   earth is with its fulness stored;
   unto thee be glory given,
   holy, holy, holy, Lord.'

   Richard Mant (1776-1848)

4. Vainly we offer
   each humble oblation,
   vainly with gifts
   would his favour secure:
   richer by far
   is the heart's adoration,
   dearer to God
   are the prayers of the poor.

   Reginald Heber (1783-1826)

71

1. Brightest and best
   of the suns of the morning,
   dawn on our darkness
   and lend us thine aid;
   star of the east,
   the horizon adorning,
   guide where our infant
   Redeemer is laid.

2. Cold on his cradle
   the dew-drops are shining;
   low lies his head
   with the beasts of the stall;
   angels adore him
   in slumber reclining,
   Maker and Monarch
   and Saviour of all.

3. Say, shall we yield him,
   in costly devotion,
   odours of Edom,
   and off'rings divine,
   gems of the mountain,
   and pearls of the ocean,
   myrrh from the forest,
   or gold from the mine?

72

Broken for me,
broken for you,
the body of Jesus
broken for us.

1. He offered his body,
   he poured out his soul;
   Jesus was broken
   that we might be whole.

2. Come to my table
   and with me dine;
   eat of my bread
   and drink of my wine.

3. This is my body
   given for you;
   eat it, rememb'ring
   I died for you.

4. This is my blood
   I shed for you,
   for your forgiveness,
   making you new.

   Janet Lunt
   © 1978 Sovereign Music UK

73

1. Brother, sister, let me serve you,
   let me be as Christ to you;
   pray that I may have the grace to
   let you be my servant, too.

2. We are pilgrims on a journey,
   fellow trav'llers on the road;
   we are here to help each other
   walk the mile and bear the load.

3. I will hold the Christlight for you
   in the night-time of your fear;
   I will hold my hand out to you,
   speak the peace you long to hear.

4. I will weep when you are weeping;
   when you laugh I'll laugh with you.
   I will share your joy and sorrow
   till we've seen this journey through.

5. When we sing to God in heaven
   we shall find such harmony,
   born of all we've known together
   of Christ's love and agony.

6. Brother, sister, let me serve you,
   let me be as Christ to you;
   pray that I may have the grace to
   let you be my servant, too.

Richard Gillard
© 1977 Scripture in Song/CopyCare Ltd

74

By your side I would stay;
in your arms I would lay.
Jesus, lover of my soul,
nothing from you I withhold.
Lord, I love you, and adore you;
what more can I say?
You cause my love to grow stronger
with ev'ry passing day.

Noel and Tricia Richards.
© 1989 Kingsway's Thankyou Music

75

1. Child in the manger, infant of Mary;
   outcast and stranger, Lord of all;
   child who inherits all our transgressions,
   all our demerits on him fall.

2. Once the most holy child of salvation
   gently and lowly lived below;
   now as our glorious mighty Redeemer,
   see him victorious o'er each foe.

3. Prophets foretold him, infant of wonder;
   angels behold him on his throne;
   worthy our Saviour of all their praises;
   happy for ever are his own.

Mary MacDonald (1817-1890)
trans. Lachlan MacBean (1853-1931)

76

1. Christ is made the sure foundation,
   Christ the head and cornerstone,
   chosen of the Lord, and precious,
   binding all the Church in one,
   holy Sion's help for ever,
   and her confidence alone.

2. To this temple, where we gather,
   come, O Lord of Hosts, today;
   with thy wonted loving-kindness,
   hear thy servants as they pray,
   and thy fullest benediction
   shed within its walls alway.

3. Here vouchsafe to all thy servants
   what they ask of thee to gain,
   what they gain from thee for ever
   with the blessèd to retain,
   and hereafter in thy glory
   evermore with thee to reign.

4. Praise and honour to the Father,
   praise and honour to the Son,
   praise and honour to the Spirit,
   ever Three and ever One,
   consubstantial, co-eternal,
   while unending ages run.

   'Urbs beata Jerusalem' (c. 7th century)
   trans. John Mason Neale (1818-1866) alt.

77

1. Christ is our cornerstone,
   on him alone we build;
   with his true saints alone
   the courts of heav'n are filled:
   on his great love our hopes we place
   of present grace and joys above.

2. O then with hymns of praise
   these hallowed courts shall ring;
   our voices we will raise
   the Three in One to sing;
   and thus proclaim in joyful song,
   both loud and long, that glorious name.

3. Here, gracious God, do thou
   for evermore draw nigh;
   accept each faithful vow,
   and mark each suppliant sigh;
   in copious show'r on all who pray
   each holy day thy blessings pour.

4. Here may we gain from heav'n
   the grace which we implore;
   and may that grace, once giv'n,
   be with us evermore,
   until that day when all the blest
   to endless rest are called away.

   Latin (before 9th century)
   trans. John Chandler (1806-1876)

78

1. Christ is the world's true light,
   its captain of salvation,
   the daystar clear and bright
   of ev'ry race and nation;
   new life, new hope awakes,
   where'er we own his sway:
   freedom her bondage breaks,
   and night is turned to day.

2. In Christ all races meet,
   their ancient feuds forgetting,
   the whole round world complete,
   from sunrise to its setting:
   when Christ is throned as Lord,
   all shall forsake their fear,
   to ploughshare beat the sword,
   to pruning-hook the spear.

3. One Lord, in one great name
   unite us all who own thee;
   cast out our pride and shame
   that hinder to enthrone thee;
   the world has waited long,
   has travailed long in pain;
   to heal its ancient wrong,
   come, Prince of Peace, and reign!

   George Wallace Briggs (1875-1959)

79

1. Christ, the fair glory
   of the holy angels,
   thou who hast made us,
   thou who o'er us rulest,
   grant of thy mercy,
   unto us thy servants
   steps up to heaven.

2. Send thy archangel,
   Michael, to our succour;
   peacemaker blessèd,
   may he banish from us
   striving and hatred,
   so that for the peaceful
   all things may prosper.

3. Send thy archangel,
   Gabriel, the mighty;
   herald of heaven,
   may he from us mortals
   spurn the old serpent,
   watching o'er the temples
   where thou art worshipped.

4. Send thy archangel,
   Raphael, the restorer
   of the misguided ways
   of those who wander,
   who at thy bidding
   strengthens soul and body
   with thine anointing.

5. May the blest Mother
   of our God and Saviour,
   may the assembly
   of the saints in glory,
   may the celestial
   companies of angels
   ever assist us.

6. Father Almighty,
   Son and Holy Spirit,
   God ever blessèd,
   be thou our preserver;
   thine is the glory
   which the angels worship,
   veiling their faces.

Latin, ascribed to Rabanus Maurus (776-856)
trans. Athelstan Riley (1858-1945)

80

1. Christ the Lord is ris'n again,
   Christ hath broken ev'ry chain.
   Hark, angelic voices cry,
   singing evermore on high,
   Alleluia.

2. He who gave for us his life,
   who for us endured the strife,
   is our paschal Lamb today;
   we too sing for joy, and say:
   Alleluia.

3. He who bore all pain and loss
   comfortless upon the cross,
   lives in glory now on high,
   pleads for us, and hears our cry:
   Alleluia.

4. He whose path no records tell,
   who descended into hell,
   who the strongest arm hath bound,
   now in highest heav'n is crowned.
   Alleluia.

5. He who slumbered in the grave
   is exalted now to save;
   now through Christendom it rings
   that the Lamb is King of kings.
   Alleluia.

6. Now he bids us tell abroad
   how the lost may be restored,
   how the penitent forgiv'n,
   how we too may enter heav'n.
   Alleluia.

7. Thou, our paschal Lamb indeed,
   Christ, thy ransomed people feed;
   take our sins and guilt away;
   let us sing by night and day:
   Alleluia.

Michael Weisse (c. 1480-1534)
trans. Catherine Winkworth (1827-1878) alt.

81

1. Christ triumphant, ever reigning,
   Saviour, Master, King,
   Lord of heav'n, our lives sustaining,
   hear us as we sing:

   Yours the glory and the crown,
   the high renown, the eternal name.

2. Word incarnate, truth revealing,
   Son of Man on earth!
   Pow'r and majesty concealing
   by your humble birth:

3. Suff'ring servant, scorned, ill-treated,
   victim crucified!
   Death is through the cross defeated,
   sinners justified:

4. Priestly King, enthroned for ever
   high in heav'n above!
   Sin and death and hell shall never
   stifle hymns of love:

5. So, our hearts and voices raising
   through the ages long,
   ceaselessly upon you gazing,
   this shall be our song:

Michael Saward (b. 1932)

82

1. Christ, whose glory fills the skies,
   Christ, the true, the only light,
   Sun of Righteousness arise,
   triumph o'er the shades of night;
   Dayspring from on high, be near;
   Daystar, in my heart appear.

2. Dark and cheerless is the morn
   unaccompanied by thee;
   joyless is the day's return,
   till thy mercy's beams I see,
   till they inward light impart,
   glad my eyes, and warm my heart.

3. Visit then this soul of mine,
   pierce the gloom of sin and grief;
   fill me, radiancy divine,
   scatter all my unbelief;
   more and more thyself display,
   shining to the perfect day.

Charles Wesley (1707-1788)

83

1. Christ's is the world in which we move,
   Christ's are the folk we're summoned
   to love,
   Christ's is the voice which calls us to
   care,
   and Christ is the one who meets us
   here.

   To the lost Christ shows his face;
   to the unloved he gives his embrace;
   to those who cry in pain or disgrace,
   Christ makes with his friends a touching
   place.

Continued overleaf

2. Feel for the people we most avoid,
   strange or bereaved or never employed;
   feel for the women, and feel for the men
   who fear that their living is all in vain.

   To the lost Christ shows his face;
   to the unloved he gives his embrace;
   to those who cry in pain or disgrace,
   Christ makes with his friends a touching
     place.

3. Feel for the parents who've lost their
     child,
   feel for the women whom men have
     defiled,
   feel for the baby for whom there's no
     breast,
   and feel for the weary who find no rest.

4. Feel for the lives by life confused,
   riddled with doubt, in loving abused;
   feel for the lonely heart, conscious of sin,
   which longs to be pure but fears to
     begin.

   John L. Bell (b. 1949) and Graham Maule (b. 1958)

84

1. Christians, awake!
   salute the happy morn,
   whereon the Saviour
   of the world was born;
   rise to adore the mystery of love,
   which hosts of angels
   chanted from above:
   with them the joyful
   tidings first begun
   of God incarnate
   and the virgin's Son.

2. Then to the watchful
   shepherds it was told,
   who heard th' angelic
   herald's voice, 'Behold,
   I bring good tidings
   of a Saviour's birth
   to you and all the
   nations on the earth:
   this day hath God
   fulfilled his promised word,
   this day is born a Saviour,
   Christ the Lord.'

3. He spake; and straightway
   the celestial choir
   in hymns of joy,
   unknown before, conspire;
   the praises of redeeming
   love they sang,
   and heav'n's whole orb
   with alleluias rang:
   God's highest glory
   was their anthem still,
   peace on the earth,
   in ev'ry heart good will.

4. To Bethl'em straight
   th'enlightened shepherds ran,
   to see, unfolding,
   God's eternal plan,
   and found, with Joseph
   and the blessèd maid,
   her Son, the Saviour,
   in a manger laid:
   then to their flocks,
   still praising God, return,
   and their glad hearts
   with holy rapture burn.

5. O may we keep
and ponder in our mind
God's wondrous love
in saving lost mankind;
trace we the babe,
who hath retrieved our loss,
from his poor manger
to his bitter cross;
tread in his steps
assisted by his grace,
till our first heav'nly state
again takes place.

6. Then may we hope,
th'angelic hosts among,
to sing, redeemed,
a glad triumphal song:
he that was born
upon this joyful day
around us all
his glory shall display;
saved by his love,
incessant we shall sing
eternal praise to heav'n's
almighty King.

John Byrom (1692-1763) alt.

85

1. City of God, how broad and far
outspread thy walls sublime!
Thy free and loyal people are
of ev'ry age and clime.

2. One holy Church, one mighty throng,
one steadfast, high intent;
one working band, one harvest-song,
one King omnipotent.

3. How purely hath thy speech come
down
from earth's primeval youth!
How grandly hath thine empire grown
of freedom, love and truth!

4. How gleam thy watch-fires through
the night
with never-fainting ray!
How rise thy tow'rs, serene and bright,
to meet the dawning day!

5. In vain the surge's angry shock,
in vain the drifting sands;
unharmed upon th'eternal Rock
th'eternal city stands.

Samuel Johnson (1822-1882) alt.

86

Cloth for the cradle,
cradle for the child,
the child for our ev'ry joy and sorrow;
find him a shawl that's woven by us all
to welcome the Lord
of each tomorrow.

1. Darkness and light
and all that's known by sight,
silence and echo fading,
weave into one a welcome for the Son,
set earth its own maker serenading.

2. Claimant and queen,
wage earners in between,
trader and travelling preacher,
weave into one a welcome for the Son,
whose word brings new life to ev'ry
creature.

3. Hungry and poor,
the sick and the unsure,
wealthy, whose needs are stranger,
weave into one a welcome for the Son,
leave excess and want beneath the
manger.

Continued overleaf

Cloth for the cradle,
cradle for the child,
the child for our ev'ry joy and sorrow;
find him a shawl that's woven by us all
to welcome the Lord
of each tomorrow.

4. Wrinkled or fair,
   carefree or full of care,
   searchers of all the ages,
   weave into one a welcome for the Son,
   the Saviour of shepherds and of sages.

John L. Bell (b. 1949) and Graham Maule (b. 1958)

87

1. Colours of day dawn into the mind,
   the sun has come up,
   the night is behind.
   Go down in the city, into the street,
   and let's give the message
   to the people we meet.

   So light up the fire
   and let the flame burn,
   open the door, let Jesus return,
   take seeds of his Spirit,
   let the fruit grow,
   tell the people of Jesus,
   let his love show.

2. Go through the park, on into the town;
   the sun still shines on;
   it never goes down.
   The light of the world is risen again;
   the people of darkness
   are needing our friend.

3. Open your eyes, look into the sky,
   the darkness has come,
   the sun came to die.
   The evening draws on,
      the sun disappears,
   but Jesus is living,
   and his Spirit is near.

Sue McClellan (b. 1951), John Paculabo (b.1946)
and Keith Ryecroft (b. 1949)
© 1974 Kingsway's Thankyou Music

88

1. Come and see, come and see,
   come and see the King of love;
   see the purple robe
   and crown of thorns he wears.
   Soldiers mock, rulers sneer
   as he lifts the cruel cross;
   lone and friendless now,
   he climbs towards the hill.

   We worship at your feet,
   where wrath and mercy meet,
   and a guilty world is washed
   by love's pure stream.
   For us he was made sin
   – oh, help me take it in.
   Deep wounds of love cry out 'Father,
   *   forgive'.*
   I worship, I worship the Lamb
   who was slain.

2. Come and weep, come and mourn
   for your sin that pierced him there;
   so much deeper than
   the wounds of thorn and nail.
   All our pride, all our greed,
   all our fallenness and shame;
   and the Lord has laid
   the punishment on him.

3. Man of heav'n, born to earth
   to restore us to your heav'n;
   here we bow in awe
   beneath your searching eyes.
   From your tears comes our joy,
   from your death our life shall spring;
   by your resurrection power
   we shall rise.

Graham Kendrick (b. 1950)
© 1989 Make Way Music Ltd

89

Come, come, come to the manger,
children, come to the children's King;
sing, sing, chorus of angels,
star of morning o'er Bethlehem sing.

1. He lies 'mid the beasts of the stall,
   who is maker and Lord of us all;
   the wintry wind blows cold and dreary,
   see, he weeps, the world is weary;
   Lord, have pity and mercy on me!

2. He leaves all his glory behind,
   to be born and to die for mankind,
   with grateful beasts his cradle chooses,
   thankless world his love refuses;
   Lord, have pity and mercy on me!

3. To the manger of Bethlehem come,
   to the Saviour Emmanuel's home;
   the heav'nly hosts above are singing,
   set the Christmas bells a-ringing;
   Lord, have pity and mercy on me!

Unknown, alt.

90

1. Come down, O Love divine,
   seek thou this soul of mine,
   and visit it with
   thine own ardour glowing;
   O Comforter, draw near,
   within my heart appear,
   and kindle it,
   thy holy flame bestowing.

2. O let it freely burn,
   till earthly passions turn
   to dust and ashes
   in its heat consuming;
   and let thy glorious light
   shine ever on my sight,
   and clothe me round,
   the while my path illuming.

3. Let holy charity
   mine outward vesture be,
   and lowliness become
   mine inner clothing;
   true lowliness of heart,
   which takes the humbler part,
   and o'er its own shortcomings
   weeps with loathing.

4. And so the yearning strong,
   with which the soul will long,
   shall far outpass
   the pow'r of human telling;
   nor can we guess its grace,
   till we become the place
   wherein the Holy Spirit
   makes his dwelling.

Bianco da Siena (d. 1434) trans. Richard F. Littledale
(1833-1890) alt.

91

1. Come, Holy Ghost, our hearts inspire,
   let us thine influence prove;
   source of the old prophetic fire,
   fountain of life and love.

2. Come, Holy Ghost – for, moved by
      thee,
   thy prophets wrote and spoke –
   unlock the truth, thyself the key,
   unseal the sacred book.

3. Expand thy wings, celestial Dove,
   brood o'er our nature's night;
   on our disordered spirits move,
   and let there now be light.

4. God, through himself, we then shall
      know,
   if thou within us shine;
   and sound, with all thy saints below,
   the depths of love divine.

   Charles Wesley (1707-1788)

92

1. Come, Holy Ghost, our souls inspire,
   and lighten with celestial fire;
   thou the anointing Spirit art,
   who dost thy sev'nfold gifts impart.

2. Thy blessèd unction from above
   is comfort, life, and fire of love;
   enable with perpetual light
   the dullness of our blinded sight.

3. Anoint and cheer our soilèd face
   with the abundance of thy grace:
   keep far our foes, give peace at home;
   where thou art guide no ill can come.

4. Show us the Father and the Son,
   in thee and with thee, ever one.
   Then through the ages all along,
   this shall be our unending song.

5. 'Praise to thy eternal merit,
   Father, Son and Holy Spirit.'
   Amen.

   vs. 1-3, 5: John Cosin (1594-1672)
   after Rabanus Maurus (c. 776-856) alt.
   v. 4: Michael Forster (b. 1946)

93

1. Come, Holy, Spirit, come!
   inflame our souls with love,
   transforming ev'ry heart and home
   with wisdom from above.
   O let us not despise
   the humble path Christ trod,
   but choose, to shame the worldly wise,
   the foolishness of God.

2. All-knowing Spirit, prove
   the poverty of pride,
   by knowledge of the Father's love
   in Jesus crucified.
   And grant us faith to know
   the glory of that sign,
   and in our very lives to show
   the marks of love divine.

3. Come with the gift to heal
   the wounds of guilt and fear,
   and to oppression's face reveal
   the kingdom drawing near.
   Where chaos longs to reign,
   descend, O holy Dove,
   and free us all to work again
   the miracles of love.

4. Spirit of truth, arise;
   inspire the prophet's voice:
   expose to scorn the tyrant's lies,
   and bid the poor rejoice.
   O Spirit, clear our sight,
   all prejudice remove,
   and help us to discern the right,
   and covet only love.

5. Give us the tongues to speak,
   in ev'ry time and place,
   to rich and poor, to strong and weak,
   the word of love and grace.
   Enable us to hear
   the words that others bring,
   interpreting with open ear
   the special song they sing.

6. Come, Holy Spirit, dance
   within our hearts today,
   our earthbound spirits to entrance,
   our mortal fears allay.
   And teach us to desire,
   all other things above,
   that self-consuming holy fire,
   the perfect gift of love!

Michael Forster (b.1946) based on 1 Corinthians 12

94

1. Come, let us join our cheerful songs
   with angels round the throne;
   ten thousand thousand are their
       tongues,
   but all their joys are one.

2. 'Worthy the Lamb that died,' they cry,
   'to be exalted thus.'
   'Worthy the Lamb,' our lips reply,
   'for he was slain for us.'

3. Jesus is worthy to receive
   honour and pow'r divine;
   and blessings, more than we can give,
   be, Lord, for ever thine.

4. Let all creation join in one
   to bless the sacred name
   of him that sits upon the throne,
   and to adore the Lamb.

Isaac Watts (1674-1748) alt.

95

Come on and celebrate!
His gift of love we will celebrate –
the Son of God,
who loved us and gave us life.
We'll shout your praise, O King:
you give us joy nothing else can bring;
we'll give to you our offering
in celebration praise.
Come on and celebrate,
celebrate, celebrate and sing,
celebrate and sing to the King:

Repeat the last three lines.

Patricia Morgan
© 1984 Kingsway's Thankyou Music

96

1. Come, risen Lord,
   and deign to be our guest;
   nay, let us be thy guests;
   the feast is thine;
   thyself at thine own board
   make manifest,
   in thine own sacrament
   of bread and wine.

Continued overleaf

2. We meet, as in
   that upper room they met;
   thou at thy table,
   blessing, yet dost stand:
   'This is my body'
   – so thou givest yet;
   faith still receives the cup
   as from thy hand.

3. One body we,
   one body who partake,
   one Church united
   in communion blest;
   one name we bear,
   one bread of life we break,
   with all thy saints on earth
   and saints at rest.

4. One with each other,
   Lord, for one in thee,
   who art one Saviour
   and one living Head;
   then open thou our eyes,
   that we may see:
   be known to us
   in breaking of the bread.

George Wallace Briggs (1875-1959)

97

1. Come, thou Holy Spirit, come,
   and from thy celestial home
   shed a ray of light divine;
   come, thou Father of the poor,
   come, thou source of all our store,
   come, within our bosoms shine.

2. Thou of comforters the best,
   thou the soul's most welcome guest,
   sweet refreshment here below;
   in our labour rest most sweet,
   grateful coolness in the heat,
   solace in the midst of woe.

3. O most blessèd Light divine,
   shine within these hearts of thine,
   and our inmost being fill;
   where thou art not, we have naught,
   nothing good in deed or thought,
   nothing free from taint of ill.

4. Heal our wounds; our strength renew;
   on our dryness pour thy dew;
   wash the stains of guilt away;
   bend the stubborn heart and will;
   melt the frozen, warm the chill;
   guide the steps that go astray.

5. On the faithful, who adore
   and confess thee, evermore
   in thy sev'nfold gifts descend:
   give them virtue's sure reward,
   give them thy salvation, Lord,
   give them joys that never end.

Stephen Langton (d. 1228)
trans Edward Caswall (1814-1878) alt.

98

1. Come, thou long expected Jesus,
   born to set thy people free;
   from our fears and sins release us;
   let us find our rest in thee.

2. Israel's strength and consolation,
   hope of all the earth thou art;
   dear desire of ev'ry nation,
   joy of ev'ry longing heart.

3. Born thy people to deliver;
   born a child and yet a king;
   born to reign in us for ever;
   now thy gracious kingdom bring.

4. By thine own eternal Spirit,
   rule in all our hearts alone:
   by thine all-sufficient merit,
   raise us to thy glorious throne.

Charles Wesley (1707-1788)

99

1. Come, ye faithful, raise the anthem,
   cleave the skies with shouts of praise;
   sing to him who found the ransom,
   Ancient of eternal days,
   God of God, the Word incarnate,
   whom the heav'n of heav'n obeys.

2. Ere he raised the lofty mountains,
   formed the seas or built the sky,
   love eternal, free and boundless,
   moved the Lord of Life to die,
   fore-ordained the Prince of princes
   for the throne of Calvary.

3. There, for us and our redemption,
   see him all his life-blood pour!
   There he wins our full salvation,
   dies that we may die no more;
   then arising, lives for ever,
   reigning where he was before.

4. High on yon celestial mountains
   stands his sapphire throne, all bright,
   midst unending alleluias
   bursting from the saints in light;
   Sion's people tell his praises,
   victor after hard-won fight.

5. Bring your harps, and bring your
         incense,
   sweep the string and pour the lay;
   let the earth proclaim his wonders,
   King of that celestial day;
   he the Lamb once slain is worthy,
   who was dead and lives for ay.

6. Laud and honour to the Father,
   laud and honour to the Son,
   laud and honour to the Spirit,
   ever Three and ever One,
   consubstantial, co-eternal,
   while unending ages run.

Job Hupton (1762-1849)
and John Mason Neale (1818-1866) alt.

100

1. Come, ye faithful, raise the strain
   of triumphant gladness!
   God hath brought his Israel
   into joy from sadness;
   loosed from Pharaoh's bitter yoke
   Jacob's sons and daughters;
   led them with unmoistened foot
   through the Red Sea waters.

2. 'Tis the spring of souls today;
   Christ hath burst his prison,
   and from three days' sleep in death
   as a sun hath risen:
   all the winter of our sins,
   long and dark, is flying
   from his light, to whom we give
   laud and praise undying.

3. Now the queen of seasons, bright
   with the day of splendour,
   with the royal feast of feasts,
   comes its joy to render;
   comes to glad Jerusalem,
   who with true affection
   welcomes in unwearied strains
   Jesu's resurrection.

4. Alleluia now we cry
   to our King immortal,
   who triumphant burst the bars
   of the tomb's dark portal;
   Alleluia, with the Son,
   God the Father praising;
   Alleluia yet again
   to the Spirit raising.

St. John of Damascus (d. c. 754)
trans. John Mason Neale (1816-1866) alt.

101

1. Come, ye thankful people, come,
   raise the song of harvest-home!
   All is safely gathered in,
   ere the winter storms begin;
   God, our maker, doth provide
   for our wants to be supplied;
   come to God's own temple, come;
   raise the song of harvest-home!

2. We ourselves are God's own field,
   fruit unto his praise to yield;
   wheat and tares together sown,
   unto joy or sorrow grown;
   first the blade and then the ear,
   then the full corn shall appear:
   grant, O harvest Lord, that we
   wholesome grain and pure may be.

3. For the Lord our God shall come,
   and shall take his harvest home,
   from his field shall purge away
   all that doth offend, that day;
   give his angels charge at last
   in the fire the tares to cast,
   but the fruitful ears to store
   in his garner evermore.

4. Then, thou Church triumphant, come,
   raise the song of harvest-home;
   all be safely gathered in,
   free from sorrow, free from sin,
   there for ever purified
   in God's garner to abide:
   come, ten thousand angels, come,
   raise the glorious harvest-home!

   Henry Alford (1810-1871)

102

1. Creator of the starry height,
   thy people's everlasting light,
   Jesu, redeemer of us all,
   hear thou thy servants when they call.

2. Thou, grieving at the helpless cry
   of all creation doomed to die,
   didst come to save our fallen race
   by healing gifts of heav'nly grace.

3. When earth was near its evening hour,
   thou didst, in love's redeeming pow'r,
   like bridegroom from his chamber,
      come
   forth from a Virgin-mother's womb.

4. At thy great name, exalted now,
   all knees in lowly homage bow;
   all things in heav'n and earth adore,
   and own thee King for evermore.

5. To thee, O Holy One, we pray,
   our judge in that tremendous day,
   ward off, while yet we dwell below,
   the weapons of our crafty foe.

6. To God the Father, God the Son
   and God the Spirit, Three in One,
   praise, honour, might and glory be
   from age to age eternally.
   (Amen.)

   7th century trans. John Mason Neale (1818-1866) alt.

103

1. Crown him with many crowns,
   the Lamb upon his throne;
   hark, how the heav'nly anthem drowns
   all music but its own;
   awake, my soul, and sing
   of him who died for thee,
   and hail him as thy matchless King
   through all eternity.

2. Crown him the Virgin's Son,
the God incarnate born,
whose arm those crimson trophies won
which now his brow adorn;
fruit of the mystic Rose,
as of that Rose the Stem,
the Root, whence mercy ever flows,
the Babe of Bethlehem.

3. Crown him the Lord of love;
behold his hands and side,
rich wounds, yet visible above,
in beauty glorified:
no angel in the sky
can fully bear that sight,
but downward bends each burning eye
at mysteries so bright.

4. Crown him the Lord of peace,
whose pow'r a sceptre sways
from pole to pole, that wars may cease,
absorbed in prayer and praise:
his reign shall know no end,
and round his piercèd feet
fair flow'rs of paradise extend
their fragrance ever sweet.

5. Crown him the Lord of years,
the Potentate of time,
Creator of the rolling spheres,
ineffably sublime.
All hail, Redeemer, hail!
for thou hast died for me;
thy praise shall never, never fail
throughout eternity.

Matthew Bridges (1800-1894)

104

1. Cry 'Freedom!' in the name of God
and let the cry resound;
proclaim for all that freedom
which in Jesus Christ is found,
for none of us is truly free
while anyone is bound.

Cry 'Freedom!' cry 'Freedom!'
in God's name!
Cry 'Freedom!' cry 'Freedom!'
in God's name!

2. Cry 'Freedom!' for the victims
of the earthquake and the rain:
where wealthy folk find shelter
and the poor must bear the pain;
where weapons claim resources
while the famine strikes again.

3. Cry 'Freedom!' for dictators
in their fortresses confined,
who hide behind their bodyguards
and fear the open mind,
and bid them find true freedom
in the good of humankind.

4. Cry 'Freedom!' in the church when
honest doubts are met with fear;
when vacuum-packed theology
makes questions disappear;
when journeys end before they start
and mystery is clear!

5. Cry 'Freedom!' when we find ourselves
imprisoned in our greed,
to live in free relationship
and meet each other's need.
From self released for others' good
we should be free indeed!

Michael Forster (b. 1946)

105

Dance and sing, all the earth,
gracious is the hand that tends you:
love and care ev'rywhere,
God on purpose sends you.

1. Shooting star and sunset shape
   the drama of creation;
   lightning flash and moonbeam share
   a common derivation.

2. Deserts stretch and torrents roar
   in contrast and confusion;
   treetops shake and mountains soar
   and nothing is illusion.

3. All that flies and swims and crawls
   displays an animation;
   none can emulate or change
   for each has its own station.

4. Brother man and sister woman,
   born of dust and passion,
   praise the one who calls you friends
   and makes you in his fashion.

5. Kiss of life and touch of death
   suggest our imperfection:
   crib and womb and cross and tomb
   cry out for resurrection.

John L. Bell (b. 1949) and Graham Maule (b.1958)

106

1. Dear Lord and Father of mankind,
   forgive our foolish ways!
   Reclothe us in our rightful mind,
   in purer lives thy service find,
   in deeper rev'rence praise,
   in deeper rev'rence praise.

2. In simple trust like theirs who heard,
   beside the Syrian sea,
   the gracious calling of the Lord,
   let us, like them, without a word,
   rise up and follow thee,
   rise up and follow thee.

3. O Sabbath rest by Galilee!
   O calm of hills above,
   where Jesus knelt to share with thee
   the silence of eternity,
   interpreted by love!
   Interpreted by love!

4. Drop thy still dews of quietness,
   till all our strivings cease;
   take from our souls the strain and
        stress,
   and let our ordered lives confess
   the beauty of thy peace,
   the beauty of thy peace.

5. Breathe through the heats of our desire
   thy coolness and thy balm;
   let sense by dumb, let flesh retire;
   speak through the earthquake, wind
        and fire,
   O still small voice of calm!
   O still small voice of calm!

John Greenleaf Whittier (1807-1892)

107

1. Dearest Jesu, we are here,
   at thy call, thy presence owning;
   pleading now in holy fear
   that great sacrifice atoning:
   Word incarnate, much in wonder
   on this myst'ry deep we ponder.

2. Jesu, strong to save – the same
   yesterday, today, for ever –
   make us fear and love thy name,
   serving thee with best endeavour:
   in this life, O ne'er forsake us,
   but to bliss hereafter take us.

   George Ratcliffe Woodward (1848-1934)
   after T. Clausnitzer (1619-1684)

3. Sun, who all my life dost brighten,
   Light, who dost my soul enlighten,
   Joy, which through my spirit floweth,
   Fount, which life and health
       bestoweth,
   at thy feet I cry, my Maker,
   let me be a fit partaker
   of this blessèd food from heaven,
   for our good, thy glory, given.

4. Jesus, Bread of Life, I pray thee,
   let me gladly here obey thee;
   never to my hurt invited,
   be thy love with love requited:
   from this banquet let me measure,
   Lord, how vast and deep its treasure;
   through the gifts thou here dost
       give me,
   as thy guest in heav'n receive me.

   Johann Franck (1618-1677)
   trans. Catherine Winkworth (1827-1878)

108

1. Deck thyself, my soul, with gladness,
   leave the gloomy haunts of sadness;
   come into the daylight's splendour,
   there with joy thy praises render
   unto him whose grace unbounded
   hath this wondrous banquet founded:
   high o'er all the heav'ns he reigneth,
   yet to dwell with thee he deigneth.

2. Now I sink before thee lowly,
   filled with joy most deep and holy,
   as with trembling awe and wonder
   on thy mighty works I ponder:
   how, by mystery surrounded,
   depth no mortal ever sounded,
   none may dare to pierce unbidden
   secrets that with thee are hidden.

109

1. Ding dong! merrily on high,
   in heav'n the bells are ringing;
   ding dong! verily the sky
   is riv'n with angel-singing.

   Gloria, hosanna in excelsis!

2. E'en so here below, below,
   let steeple bells be swungen,
   and io, io, io,
   by priest and people sungen.

3. Pray you, dutifully prime
   your matin chime, ye ringers;
   may you beautifully rhyme
   your evetime song, ye singers.

   George Ratcliffe Woodward (1848-1934)

110

1. Disposer supreme
   and Judge of the earth,
   thou choosest for thine
   the meek and the poor;
   to frail earthen vessels
   and things of no worth,
   entrusting thy riches
   which ay shall endure.

2. Those vessels are frail,
   though full of thy light,
   and many, once made,
   are broken and gone;
   thence brightly appeareth
   thy truth in its might,
   as through the clouds riven
   the lightnings have shone.

3. Like clouds are they borne
   to do thy great will,
   and swift as the winds
   about the world go:
   the Word with his wisdom
   their spirits doth fill;
   they thunder, they lighten,
   the waters o'erflow.

4. Their sound goeth forth,
   'Christ Jesus the Lord!'
   then Satan doth fear,
   his citadels fall;
   as when the dread trumpets
   went forth at thy word,
   and one long blast shattered
   the Canaanites' wall.

5. O loud be their cry,
   and stirring their sound,
   to rouse us, O Lord,
   from slumber of sin:
   the lights thou hast kindled
   in darkness around,
   O may they awaken
   our spirits within.

6. All honour and praise,
   dominion and might,
   to God, Three in One,
   eternally be,
   who round us hath shed
   his own marvellous light,
   and called us from darkness
   his glory to see.

J. B. de Santeuil (1630-1697)
trans. Isaac Williams (1802-1865) alt.

111

Do not be afraid,
for I have redeemed you.
I have called you by your name;
you are mine.

1. When you walk through the waters,
   I'll be with you.
   You will never sink beneath the waves.

2. When the fire is burning
   all around you,
   you will never be consumed
     by the flames.

3. When the fear of loneliness
   is looming,
   then remember I am at your side.

4. When you dwell in the exile
   of the stranger,
   remember you are precious in my eyes.

5. You are mine, O my child;
   I am your Father,
   and I love you with a perfect love.

Gerard Markland, based on Isaiah 43:1-4

112

1. Drop, drop, slow tears,
   and bathe those beauteous feet,
   which brought from heav'n
   the news and Prince of peace.

2. Cease not, wet eyes,
   his mercies to entreat;
   to cry for vengeance
   sin doth never cease.

3. In your deep floods
   drown all my faults and fears;
   nor let his eye
   see sin, but through my tears.

   Phineas Fletcher (1582-1650)

113

1. Earth has many a noble city;
   Bethl'em, thou dost all excel:
   out of thee the Lord from heaven
   came to rule his Israel.

2. Fairer than the sun at morning
   was the star that told his birth,
   to the world its God announcing,
   seen in fleshly form on earth.

3. Eastern sages at his cradle
   make oblations rich and rare;
   see them give in deep devotion
   gold and frankincense and myrrh.

4. Sacred gifts of mystic meaning:
   incense doth their God disclose,
   gold the King of kings proclaimeth,
   myrrh his sepulchre foreshows.

5. Jesu, whom the Gentiles worshipped
   at thy glad Epiphany,
   unto thee with God the Father
   and the Spirit glory be.

   Aurelius Clemens Prudentius (348-c. 413)
   trans. Edward Caswall (1814-1878) alt.

114

1. Eternal Father, strong to save,
   whose arm doth bind the restless wave,
   who bidd'st the mighty ocean deep
   its own appointed limits keep:
   O hear us when we cry to thee
   for those in peril on the sea.

2. O Saviour, whose almighty word
   the winds and waves submissive heard,
   who walkedst on the foaming deep,
   and calm, amid its rage, didst sleep:
   O hear us when we cry to thee
   for those in peril on the sea.

3. O sacred Spirit, who didst brood
   upon the waters dark and rude,
   and bid their angry tumult cease,
   and give, for wild confusion, peace:
   O hear us when we cry to thee
   for those in peril on the sea.

4. O Trinity of love and pow'r,
   our brethren shield in danger's hour.
   From rock and tempest, fire and foe,
   protect them whereso'er they go,
   and ever let there rise to thee
   glad hymns of praise from land and sea.

   William Whiting (1825-1878)

115

1. Eternal Ruler of the ceaseless round
   of circling planets singing on their way;
   guide of the nations from the night
      profound
   into the glory of the perfect day;
   rule in our hearts, that we may ever be
   guided and strengthened and upheld
      by thee.

2. We are of thee, the children of thy love,
   by virtue of thy well-belovèd Son;
   descend, O Holy Spirit, like a dove,
   into our hearts, that we may be as one:
   as one with thee, to whom we ever tend;
   as one with him, our Brother and our
      Friend.

3. We would be one in hatred of all wrong,
   one in our love of all things sweet and
      fair,
   one with the joy that breaketh into song,
   one with the grief that trembles into
      prayer,
   one in the pow'r that makes thy children
      free
   to follow truth, and thus to follow thee.

4. O clothe us with thy heav'nly armour,
      Lord,
   thy trusty shield, thy sword of love
      divine;
   our inspiration be thy constant word;
   we ask no victories that are not thine:
   give or withhold, let pain or pleasure be;
   enough to know that we are serving
      thee.

   John White Chadwick (1840-1904) alt.

116

1. Fair waved the golden corn
   in Canaan's pleasant land,
   when full of joy, some shining morn,
   went forth the reaper-band.

2. To God so good and great
   their cheerful thanks they pour;
   then carry to his temple-gate
   the choicest of their store.

3. Like Israel, Lord, we give
   our earliest fruits to thee,
   and pray that, long as we shall live,
   we may thy children be.

4. Thine is our youthful prime,
   and life and all its pow'rs;
   be with us in our morning time,
   and bless our evening hours.

5. In wisdom let us grow,
   as years and strength are giv'n,
   that we may serve thy Church below,
   and join thy saints in heav'n.

   John Hampden Gurney (1802-1862)

117

1. Faithful Shepherd, feed me
   in the pastures green;
   faithful Shepherd, lead me
   where thy steps are seen.

2. Hold me fast, and guide me
   in the narrow way;
   so, with thee beside me,
   I shall never stray.

3. Daily bring me nearer
   to the heav'nly shore;
   may my faith grow clearer,
   may I love thee more.

4. Hallow every pleasure,
   ev'ry gift and pain;
   be thyself my treasure,
   though none else I gain.

5. Day by day prepare me
   as thou seest best,
   then let angels bear me
   to thy promised rest.

   Thomas Benson Pollock (1836-1896)

118

1. Faithful vigil ended,
   watching, waiting cease;
   Master, grant thy servant
   his discharge in peace.

2. All the Spirit promised,
   all the Father willed,
   now these eyes behold it
   perfectly fulfilled.

3. This thy great deliv'rance
   sets thy people free;
   Christ, their light, uplifted
   all the nations see.

4. Christ, thy people's glory!
   watching, doubting, cease;
   grant to us thy servants
   our discharge in peace.

   Timothy Dudley-Smith (b.1926)
   based on Luke 2:29-32

119

1. Father God, I wonder how
   I managed to exist
   without the knowledge
   of your parenthood
   and your loving care.
   But now I am your child,
   I am adopted in your family,
   and I can never be alone
   'cause, Father God,
   you're there beside me.

   I will sing your praises,
   I will sing your praises,
   I will sing your praises
   for evermore.

   Ian Smale
   © 1984 Kingsway's Thankyou Music

120

1. Father, hear the prayer we offer:
   not for ease that prayer shall be,
   but for strength that we may ever
   live our lives courageously.

2. Not for ever in green pastures
   do we ask our way to be;
   but the steep and rugged pathway
   may we tread rejoicingly.

3. Not for ever by still waters
   would we idly rest and stay;
   but would smite the living fountains
   from the rocks along our way.

4. Be our strength in hours of weakness,
   in our wand'rings be our guide;
   through endeavour, failure, danger,
   Father, be thou at our side.

   Maria Willis (1824-1908)

121

1. Father, I place into your hands
   the things that I can't do.
   Father, I place into your hands
   the times that I've been through.
   Father, I place into your hands
   the way that I should go,
   for I know I always can trust you.

2. Father, I place into your hands
   my friends and family.
   Father, I place into your hands
   the things that trouble me.
   Father, I place into your hands
   the person I would be,
   for I know I always can trust you.

3. Father, we love to seek your face,
   we love to hear your voice.
   Father, we love to sing your praise,
   and in your name rejoice.
   Father, we love to walk with you
   and in your presence rest,
   for we know we always can trust you.

4. Father, I want to be with you
   and do the things you do.
   Father, I want to speak the words
   that you are speaking too.
   Father, I want to love the ones
   that you will draw to you,
   for I know that I am one with you.

Jenny Hewer (b. 1945)
© 1975 Kingsway's Thankyou Music

122

1. Father, Lord of all creation,
   ground of Being, Life and Love;
   height and depth beyond description
   only life in you can prove:
   you are mortal life's dependence:
   thought, speech, sight are ours by grace;
   yours is ev'ry hour's existence,
   sov'reign Lord of time and space.

2. Jesus Christ, the Man for Others,
   we, your people, make our prayer:
   help us love – as sisters, brothers –
   all whose burdens we can share.
   Where your name binds us together
   you, Lord Christ, will surely be;
   where no selfishness can sever
   there your love the world may see.

3. Holy Spirit, rushing, burning
   wind and flame of Pentecost,
   fire our hearts afresh with yearning
   to regain what we have lost.
   May your love unite our action,
   nevermore to speak alone:
   God, in us abolish faction,
   God, through us your love make known.

Stewart Cross (1928-1989)

123

1. Father most holy,
   merciful and loving,
   Jesu, Redeemer,
   ever to be worshipped,
   life-giving Spirit,
   Comforter most gracious,
   God everlasting.

2. Three in a wondrous
   Unity unbroken,
   One perfect Godhead,
   love that never faileth,
   light of the angels,
   succour of the needy,
   hope of all living.

3. All thy creation
   serveth its Creator,
   thee ev'ry creature
   praiseth without ceasing;
   we too would sing thee
   psalms of true devotion:
   hear, we beseech thee

4. Lord God Almighty,
   unto thee be glory,
   One in three Persons,
   over all exalted.
   Thine, as is meet, be honour,
   praise and blessing
   now and for ever.

Latin (c. 10th century)
trans. Alfred E. Alston (1862-1927)

124

1. Father of heav'n, whose love profound
   a ransom for our souls hath found,
   before thy throne we sinners bend,
   to us thy pard'ning love extend.

2. Almighty Son, incarnate Word,
   our Prophet, Priest, Redeemer, Lord,
   before thy throne we sinners bend,
   to us thy saving grace extend.

3. Eternal Spirit, by whose breath
   the soul is raised from sin and death,
   before thy throne we sinners bend,
   to us thy quick'ning pow'r extend.

4. Thrice Holy! Father, Spirit, Son;
   mysterious Godhead, Three in One,
   before thy throne we sinners bend,
   grace, pardon, life, to us extend.

Edward Cooper (1770-1833)

125

1. Father, we adore you,
   lay our lives before you.
   How we love you!

2. Jesus, we adore you,
   lay our lives before you.
   How we love you!

3. Spirit, we adore you,
   lay our lives before you.
   How we love you!

Terrye Coelho (b.1952)
© 1972 Maranatha! Music/CopyCare Ltd

126

1. Father, we love you,
   we praise you, we adore you.
   Glorify your name in all the earth.
   Glorify your name, glorify your name,
   glorify your name in all the earth.

2. Jesus, we love you,
   we praise you, we adore you.
   Glorify your name in all the earth.
   Glorify your name, glorify your name,
   glorify your name in all the earth.

3. Spirit, we love you,
   we praise you, we adore you.
   Glorify your name in all the earth.
   Glorify your name, glorify your name,
   glorify your name in all the earth.

Donna Adkins (b. 1940)
© 1976 Maranatha! Music/CopyCare Ltd

127

1. Father, who in Jesus found us,
   God, whose love is all around us,
   who to freedom new unbound us,
   keep our hearts with joy aflame.

2. For the sacramental breaking,
   for the honour of partaking,
   for your life our lives remaking,
   young and old, we praise your name.

3. From the service of this table
   lead us to a life more stable,
   for our witness make us able;
   blessings on our work we claim.

4. Through our calling closely knitted,
   daily to your praise committed,
   for a life of service fitted,
   let us now your love proclaim.

Fred Kaan (b. 1929)

128

1. Fight the good fight with all thy might;
   Christ is thy strength and Christ thy
      right;
   lay hold on life, and it shall be
   thy joy and crown eternally.

2. Run the straight race through God's
      good grace,
   lift up thine eyes and seek his face;
   life with its way before us lies;
   Christ is the path and Christ the prize.

3. Cast care aside, lean on thy guide;
   his boundless mercy will provide;
   trust, and thy trusting soul shall prove
   Christ is its life and Christ its love.

4. Faint not nor fear, his arms are near;
   he changeth not and thou art dear;
   only believe, and thou shalt see
   that Christ is all in all to thee.

John Samuel Bewley Monsell (1811-1875) alt.

129

1. Fill thou my life, O Lord my God,
   in ev'ry part with praise,
   that my whole being may proclaim
   thy being and thy ways.

2. Not for the lip of praise alone,
   nor e'en the praising heart,
   I ask, but for a life made up
   of praise in ev'ry part.

3. Praise in the common things of life,
   its goings out and in;
   praise in each duty and each deed,
   however small and mean.

4. Fill ev'ry part of me with praise:
   let all my being speak
   of thee and of thy love, O Lord,
   poor though I be and weak.

5. So shalt thou, Lord, receive from me
   the praise and glory due;
   and so shall I begin on earth
   the song for ever new.

6. So shall each fear, each fret, each care,
   be turnèd into song;
   and ev'ry winding of the way
   the echo shall prolong.

7. So shall no part of day or night
   unblest or common be;
   but all my life, in ev'ry step,
   be fellowship with thee.

Horatius Bonar (1808-1889) alt.

130

1. Fill your hearts with joy and gladness,
   sing and praise your God and mine!
   Great the Lord in love and wisdom,
   might and majesty divine!
   He who framed the starry heavens
   knows and names them as they shine.
   Fill your hearts with joy and gladness,
   sing and praise your God and mine!

2. Praise the Lord, his people,
        praise him!
   Wounded souls his comfort know.
   Those who fear him find his mercies,
   peace for pain and joy for woe;
   humble hearts are high exalted,
   human pride and pow'r laid low.
   Praise the Lord, his people,
        praise him!
   Wounded souls his comfort know.

3. Praise the Lord for times and seasons,
   cloud and sunshine, wind and rain;
   spring to melt the snows of winter
   till the waters flow again;
   grass upon the mountain pastures,
   golden valleys thick with grain.
   Praise the Lord for times and seasons,
   cloud and sunshine, wind and rain.

4. Fill your hearts with joy and gladness,
   peace and plenty crown your days!
   Love his laws, declare his judgements,
   walk in all his words and ways;
   he the Lord and we his children,
   praise the Lord, all people, praise!
   Fill your hearts with joy and gladness,
   peace and plenty crown your days!

   Timothy Dudley-Smith (b. 1926)

131

1. Filled with the Spirit's pow'r,
   with one accord
   the infant Church
   confessed its risen Lord.
   O Holy Spirit,
   in the Church today
   no less your pow'r
   of fellowship display.

2. Now with the mind of Christ
   set us on fire,
   that unity
   may be our great desire.
   Give joy and peace;
   give faith to hear your call,
   and readiness
   in each to work for all.

3. Widen our love, good Spirit,
   to embrace
   in your strong care
   the people of each race.
   Like wind and fire
   with life among us move,
   till we are known as Christ's,
   and Christians prove.

   John Raphael Peacey (1896-1971)

132

1. Finished the strife of battle now,
   gloriously crowned the victor's brow;
   sing with gladness, banish sadness:
   Alleluia, alleluia!

2. After the death that him befell,
   Jesus Christ has harrowed hell;
   songs of praising we are raising:
   Alleluia, alleluia!

Continued overleaf

3. On the third morning he arose,
   shining with vict'ry o'er his foes;
   earth is singing, heav'n is ringing:
   Alleluia, alleluia!

4. Lord, by your wounds on you we call,
   you, by your death, have freed us all;
   may our living be thanksgiving:
   Alleluia, alleluia!

trans. John Mason Neale (1818-1866) alt.

133

1. Firmly I believe and truly
   God is Three and God is One;
   and I next acknowledge duly
   manhood taken by the Son.

2. And I trust and hope most fully
   in the Saviour crucified;
   and each thought and deed unruly
   do to death as he has died.

3. Simply to his grace and wholly
   light and life and strength belong,
   and I love supremely, solely,
   him the holy, him the strong.

4. And I hold in veneration,
   for the love of him alone,
   holy Church as his creation,
   and her teachings as his own.

5. Adoration ay be given,
   with and through th'angelic host,
   to the God of earth and heaven,
   Father, Son and Holy Ghost.

*When the tune 'Alton' is used the following
last line is added:*
   Amen. Father, Son and Holy Ghost.

John Henry Newman (1801-1890) alt.

134

1. For all the saints
   who from their labours rest,
   who thee by faith
   before the world confessed,
   thy name, O Jesus,
   be for ever blest.
   Alleluia, alleluia!

2. Thou wast their rock,
   their fortress and their might;
   thou, Lord, their captain
   in the well-fought fight;
   thou in the darkness drear
   their one true light.
   Alleluia, alleluia!

3. O may thy soldiers,
   faithful, true and bold,
   fight as the saints
   who nobly fought of old,
   and win, with them,
   the victor's crown of gold.
   Alleluia, alleluia!

4. O blest communion!
   fellowship divine!
   We feebly struggle,
   they in glory shine;
   yet all are one in thee,
   for all are thine.
   Alleluia, alleluia!

5. And when the strife is fierce,
   the warfare long,
   steals on the ear
   the distant triumph-song,
   and hearts are brave again,
   and arms are strong.
   Alleluia, alleluia!

6. The golden evening
   brightens in the west;
   soon, soon to faithful
   warriors cometh rest:
   sweet is the calm
   of paradise the blest.
   Alleluia, alleluia!

7. But lo! there breaks
   a yet more glorious day;
   the saints triumphant
   rise in bright array:
   the King of glory
   passes on his way.
   Alleluia, alleluia!

8. From earth's wide bounds,
   from ocean's farthest coast,
   through gates of pearl
   streams in the countless host,
   singing to Father,
   Son and Holy Ghost.
   Alleluia, alleluia!

   William Walsham How (1823-1897)

135

For I'm building a people of power
and I'm making a people of praise,
that will move through this land
by my Spirit,
and will glorify my precious name.
Build your Church, Lord,
make us strong, Lord,
join our hearts, Lord, through your Son.
Make us one, Lord, in your body,
in the kingdom of your Son.

Dave Richards (b. 1947) based on Ephesians 2:21,22
© 1977 Kingsway's Thankyou Music

136

1. For Mary, mother of our Lord,
   God's holy name be praised,
   who first the Son of God adored,
   as on her child she gazed.

2. The angel Gabriel brought the word
   she should Christ's mother be;
   Our Lady, handmaid of the Lord,
   made answer willingly.

3. The heav'nly call she thus obeyed,
   and so God's will was done;
   the second Eve love's answer made
   which our redemption won.

4. She gave her body for God's shrine,
   her heart to piercing pain,
   and knew the cost of love divine
   when Jesus Christ was slain.

5. Dear Mary, from your lowliness
   and home in Galilee,
   there comes a joy and holiness
   to ev'ry family.

6. Hail, Mary, you are full of grace,
   above all women blest;
   and blest your Son, whom your embrace
   in birth and death confessed.

   John Raphael Peacey (1896-1971)

137

1. For the beauty of the earth,
   for the beauty of the skies,
   for the love which from our birth
   over and around us lies:

   Lord of all, to thee we raise
   this our sacrifice of praise.

2. For the beauty of each hour
   of the day and of the night,
   hill and vale and tree and flow'r,
   sun and moon and stars of light:

3. For the joy of human love,
   brother, sister, parent, child,
   friends on earth, and friends above,
   pleasures pure and undefiled:

4. For each perfect gift of thine,
   to our race so freely giv'n,
   graces human and divine,
   flow'rs of earth and buds of heav'n:

5. For thy Church which evermore
   lifteth holy hands above,
   off'ring up on ev'ry shore
   her pure sacrifice of love:

   Folliot Sandford Pierpoint (1835-1917)

138

1. For the fruits of his creation,
   thanks be to God;
   for his gifts to ev'ry nation,
   thanks be to God;
   for the ploughing, sowing, reaping,
   silent growth while we are sleeping,
   future needs in earth's safe-keeping,
   thanks be to God.

2. In the just reward of labour,
   God's will is done;
   in the help we give our neighbour,
   God's will is done;
   in our world-wide task of caring
   for the hungry and despairing,
   in the harvests we are sharing,
   God's will is done.

3. For the harvests of his Spirit,
   thanks be to God;
   for the good we all inherit,
   thanks be to God;
   for the wonders that astound us,
   for the truths that still confound us,
   most of all, that love has found us,
   thanks be to God.

   Fred Pratt Green (b. 1903)

139

1. For the healing of the nations,
   Lord, we pray with one accord;
   for a just and equal sharing
   of the things that earth affords.
   To a life of love in action
   help us rise and pledge our word.

2. Lead us, Father, into freedom,
   from despair your world release;
   that, redeemed from war and hatred,
   all may come and go in peace.
   Show us how through care and
     goodness
   fear will die and hope increase.

3. All that kills abundant living,
   let it from the earth be banned;
   pride of status, race or schooling,
   dogmas that obscure your plan.
   In our common quest for justice
   may we hallow life's brief span.

4. You, creator-God, have written
   your great name on humankind;
   for our growing in your likeness,
   bring the life of Christ to mind;
   that by our response and service
   earth its destiny may find.

   Fred Kaan (b. 1929)

140

1. For thy mercy and thy grace,
   faithful through another year,
   hear our song of thankfulness;
   Jesus, our Redeemer, hear.

2. In our weakness and distress,
   Rock of Strength, be thou our stay;
   in the pathless wilderness
   be our true and living Way.

3. Keep us faithful, keep us pure,
   keep us evermore thine own,
   Help, O help us to endure,
   fit us for thy promised crown.

4. So within thy palace gate
   we shall praise on golden strings
   thee, the only potentate,
   Lord of lords and King of kings.

   Henry Downton (1818-1885)

141

1. 'Forgive our sins as we forgive',
   you taught us, Lord, to pray;
   but you alone can grant us grace
   to live the words we say.

2. How can your pardon reach and bless
   the unforgiving heart
   that broods on wrongs, and will not let
   old bitterness depart?

3. In blazing light your Cross reveals
   the truth we dimly knew:
   what trivial debts are owed to us,
   how great our debt to you!

4. Lord, cleanse the depths within our
      souls,
   and bid resentment cease.
   Then, bound to all in bonds of love,
   our lives will spread your peace.

   Rosamond E. Herklots (1905-1987) alt.

142

1. Forth in the peace of Christ we go;
   Christ to the world with joy we bring;
   Christ in our minds, Christ on our lips,
   Christ in our hearts, the world's true
      King.

2. King of our hearts, Christ makes us
      kings;
   kingship with him his servants gain;
   with Christ, the Servant-Lord of all,
   Christ's world we serve to share Christ's
      reign.

3. Priests of the world, Christ sends us
      forth
   this world of time to consecrate,
   our world of sin by grace to heal,
   Christ's world in Christ to re-create.

4. Prophets of Christ, we hear his Word:
   he claims our minds to search his ways;
   he claims our lips to speak his truth;
   he claims our hearts to sing his praise.

5. We are his Church, he makes us one:
   here is one hearth for all to find;
   here is one flock, one Shepherd-King;
   here is one faith, one heart, one mind.

   James Quinn (b. 1919)

143

1. Forth in thy name, O Lord, I go,
my daily labour to pursue;
thee, only thee, resolved to know,
in all I think or speak or do.

2. The task thy wisdom hath assigned
O let me cheerfully fulfil;
in all my works thy presence find,
and prove thy good and perfect will.

3. Thee may I set at my right hand,
whose eyes my inmost substance see,
and labour on at thy command,
and offer all my works to thee.

4. Give me to bear thy easy yoke,
and ev'ry moment watch and pray,
and still to things eternal look,
and hasten to thy glorious day.

5. For thee delightfully employ
whate'er thy bounteous grace hath giv'n,
and run my course with even joy,
and closely walk with thee to heav'n.

Charles Wesley (1707-1788) alt.

144

1. Forty days and forty nights
in Judah's desert Jesus stayed;
all alone he fought temptation,
all alone he fasted, prayed.
When the heat of passion rules me,
when I feel alone, betrayed,
Lord, you meet me in the desert,
strong in faith and unafraid.

2. In the garden, his disciples
slept the darkest hours away,
but our Lord did not condemn them
when they would not watch or pray.
Make me constant in your service,
keeping watch both night and day.
Give me grace that I may never
such a love as yours betray.

3. When the rooster crowed at daybreak,
Peter's fear and panic grew.
He denied three times the charge
that Jesus was a man he knew.
When my love for you is challenged,
when the faithful ones are few,
give me courage and conviction
to proclaim my Lord anew.

4. Soldiers came, the Galilean
was arrested, bound and tried,
and upon a wooden cross
the Son of God was crucified.
In the darkest hour of torture,
Jesus raised his head and cried,
'Why hast thou forsaken me?',
and faithful to the end, he died.

5. With a sword they pierced his side –
himself, they jeered, he could not save;
Joseph then prepared the body
with sweet spices for the grave.
This the precious, broken body
which for me my Saviour gave;
such a love as his I long for,
such a faith as his I crave.

Jean Holloway (b. 1939)

145

1. Forty days and forty nights
   thou wast fasting in the wild;
   forty days and forty nights
   tempted, and yet undefiled.

2. Sunbeams scorching all the day,
   chilly dew-drops nightly shed,
   prowling beasts about thy way,
   stones thy pillow, earth thy bed.

3. Shall not we thy sorrows share,
   and from earthly joys abstain,
   fasting with unceasing prayer,
   glad with thee to suffer pain?

4. And if Satan, vexing sore,
   flesh or spirit should assail,
   thou, his vanquisher before,
   grant we may not faint nor fail.

5. So shall we have peace divine;
   holier gladness ours shall be;
   round us too shall angels shine,
   such as ministered to thee.

6. Keep, O keep us, Saviour dear,
   ever constant by thy side,
   that with thee we may appear
   at th'eternal Eastertide.

George Hunt Smyttan (1822-1870) and
Francis Pott (1832-1909)

146

1. From all that dwell below the skies
   let the Creator's praise arise:
   let the Redeemer's name be sung
   through ev'ry land by ev'ry tongue.

2. Eternal are thy mercies, Lord;
   eternal truth attends thy word:
   thy praise shall sound from shore to
   shore,
   till suns shall rise and set no more.

Isaac Watts (1674-1748) based on Psalm 117

147

1. From glory to glory advancing,
   we praise thee, O Lord;
   thy name with the Father and Spirit
   be ever adored.
   From strength unto strength we go
   forward
   on Sion's highway,
   to appear before God
   in the city of infinite day.

2. Thanksgiving and glory and worship
   and blessing and love,
   one heart and one song have the saints
   upon earth and above.
   Evermore, O Lord, to thy servants
   thy presence be nigh;
   ever fit us by service on earth
   for thy service on high.

Liturgy of St. James
trans. Charles Humphreys (1840-1921)

148

1. From heav'n you came, helpless babe,
   entered our world, your glory veiled;
   not to be served but to serve,
   and give your life that we might live.

   This is our God, the Servant King,
   he calls us now to follow him,
   to bring our lives as a daily offering
   of worship to the Servant King.

2. There in the garden of tears,
   my heavy load he chose to bear;
   his heart with sorrow was torn,
   'Yet not my will but yours,' he said.

3. Come see his hands and his feet,
   the scars that speak of sacrifice,
   hands that flung stars into space
   to cruel nails surrendered.

4. So let us learn how to serve,
   and in our lives enthrone him;
   each other's needs to prefer,
   for it is Christ we're serving.

   Graham Kendrick (b. 1950)
   © 1983 Kingsway's Thankyou Music

149

1. From many grains,
   once scattered far and wide,
   each one alone, to grow
   as best it may,
   now safely gathered in and unified,
   one single loaf
   we offer here today.
   So may your Church,
   in ev'ry time and place,
   be in this meal
   united by your grace.

2. From many grapes,
   once living on the vine,
   now crushed and broken
   under human feet,
   we offer here this single cup of wine:
   the sign of love,
   unbroken and complete.
   So may we stand
   among the crucified,
   and live the risen life
   of him who died.

3. From many places gathered,
   we are here,
   each with a gift
   that we alone can bring.
   O Spirit of the living God, draw near,
   make whole by grace
   our broken offering.
   O crush the pride
   that bids us stand alone;
   let flow the love
   that makes our spirits one.

   Michael Forster (b. 1946)

150

1. From the sun's rising
   unto the sun's setting,
   Jesus our Lord
   shall be great in the earth;
   and all earth's kingdoms
   shall be his dominion,
   all of creation
   shall sing of his worth.

Let ev'ry heart, ev'ry voice,
ev'ry tongue join with spirits ablaze;
one in his love, we will circle the world
with the song of his praise.
O let all his people rejoice,
and let all the earth hear his voice!

2. To ev'ry tongue,
   tribe and nation he sends us,
   to make disciples,
   to teach and baptise;
   for all authority
   to him is given;
   now as his witnesses
   we shall arise.

3. Come let us join
   with the Church from all nations,
   cross ev'ry border,
   throw wide ev'ry door;
   workers with him
   as he gathers his harvest,
   till earth's far corners
   our Saviour adore.

Graham Kendrick (b. 1950)
© 1988 Make Way Music Ltd

151

1. From the very depths of darkness
   springs a bright and living light,
   out of falsehood and deceit
   a greater truth is brought to sight,
   in the halls of death, defiant,
   life is dancing with delight!
   The Lord is risen indeed!

Christ is risen! Hallelujah!
Christ is risen! Hallelujah!
Christ is risen! Hallelujah!
The Lord is risen indeed!

2. In the light of resurrection,
   Jesus calls us all by name,
   'Do not cling to what is past,
   for things can never be the same;
   to the trembling and the fearful,
   we've a gospel to proclaim:
   The Lord is risen indeed!'

3. So proclaim it in the high rise,
   in the hostel let it ring,
   make it known in Cardboard City,
   let the homeless rise and sing:
   'He is Lord of life abundant,
   and he changes everything,
   the Lord is risen indeed!'

4. In the heartlands of oppression,
   sound the cry of liberty,
   where the poor are crucified,
   behold the Lord of Calvary!
   From the fear of death and dying,
   Christ has set his people free!
   The Lord is risen indeed!

5. Tell the despots and dictators
   of a love that can't be known
   in a guarded palace-tomb,
   condemned to live and die alone:
   'Take the risk of love and freedom;
   Christ has rolled away the stone!
   The Lord is risen indeed!'

6. When our spirits are entombed
   in mortal prejudice and pride,
   when the gates of hell itself
   are firmly bolted from inside,
   at the bidding of his Spirit,
   we may fling them open wide!
   The Lord is risen indeed!

Michael Forster (b. 1946)

152

Gather around, for the table is spread,
welcome the food and rest!
Wide is our circle, with Christ at the
   head,
he is the honoured guest.
Learn of his love, grow in his grace,
pray for the peace he gives;
here at this meal, here in this place,
know that his spirit lives!
Once he was known
in the breaking of bread,
shared with a chosen few;
multitudes gathered
and by him were fed,
so will he feed us too.

Jean Holloway (b. 1939)

153

1. Give me joy in my heart,
   keep me praising,
   give me joy in my heart, I pray.
   Give me joy in my heart,
   keep me praising,
   keep me praising till the end of day.

   Sing hosanna! Sing hosanna!
   Sing hosanna to the King of kings!
   Sing hosanna! Sing hosanna!
   Sing hosanna to the King!

2. Give me peace in my heart,
   keep me resting,
   give me peace in my heart, I pray.
   Give me peace in my heart,
   keep me resting,
   keep me resting till the end of day.

3. Give me love in my heart,
   keep me serving,
   give me love in my heart, I pray.
   Give me love in my heart,
   keep me serving,
   keep me serving till the end of day.

4. Give me oil in my lamp,
   keep me burning,
   give me oil in my lamp, I pray.
   Give me oil in my lamp,
   keep me burning,
   keep me burning till the end of day.

Traditional

154

Give thanks with a grateful heart,
give thanks to the Holy One;
give thanks because he's given
Jsus Christ, his Son.
Give thanks with a grateful heart,
give thanks to the Holy One;
give thanks because he's given
Jesus Christ, his Son

And now let the weak say 'I am strong',
let the poor say 'I am rich',
because of what the Lord has done for us;
and now let the weak say 'I am strong',
let the poor say 'I am rich',
because of what the Lord has done for us.

Henry Smith
© 1978 Integrity's Hosanna! Music/
Kingsway's Thankyou Music

155

1. Give to our God immortal praise;
   mercy and truth are all his ways:
   wonders of grace to God belong,
   repeat his mercies in your song.

2. Give to the Lord of lords renown,
   the King of kings with glory crown:
   his mercies ever shall endure
   when earthly pow'rs are known no
        more.

3. He sent his Son with pow'r to save
   from guilt and darkness and the grave:
   wonders of grace to God belong,
   repeat his mercies in your song.

4. Through earthly life he guides our feet,
   and leads us to his heav'nly seat:
   his mercies ever shall endure
   when earthly pow'rs are known no
        more.

   Isaac Watts (1674-1748) based on Psalm 136 alt.

156

1. Give us the wings of faith to rise
   within the veil, and see
   the saints above, how great their joys,
   how bright their glories be.

2. Once they were mourning here below,
   their couch was wet with tears;
   they wrestled hard, as we do now,
   with sins and doubts and fears.

3. We ask them whence their vict'ry
        came:
   they, with united breath,
   ascribe the conquest to the Lamb,
   their triumph to his death.

4. They marked the footsteps that he
        trod,
   his zeal inspired their breast,
   and, foll'wing their incarnate God,
   they reached the promised rest.

5. Our glorious Leader claims our praise
   for his own pattern giv'n;
   while the great cloud of witnesses
   show the same path to heav'n.

   Isaac Watts (1674-1748) alt.

157

Gloria, gloria in excelsis Deo!
Gloria, gloria, alleluia, alleluia!

   From Scripture

158

1. Glorious things of thee are spoken,
   Zion, city of our God;
   he whose word cannot be broken
   formed thee for his own abode.
   On the Rock of Ages founded,
   what can shake thy sure repose?
   With salvation's walls surrounded,
   thou may'st smile at all thy foes.

2. See, the streams of living waters,
   springing from eternal love,
   well supply thy sons and daughters,
   and all fear of want remove.
   Who can faint while such a river
   ever flows their thirst to assuage?
   Grace which, like the Lord, the giver,
   never fails from age to age.

   Continued overleaf

3. Round each habitation hov'ring,
   see the cloud and fire appear
   for a glory and a cov'ring,
   showing that the Lord is near.
   Thus they march, the pillar leading,
   light by night and shade by day;
   daily on the manna feeding
   which he gives them when they pray.

4. Saviour, if of Zion's city
   I through grace a member am,
   let the world deride or pity,
   I will glory in thy name.
   Fading is the worldling's pleasure,
   boasted pomp and empty show;
   solid joys and lasting treasure
   none but Zion's children know.

   John Newton (1725-1807)
   based on Isaiah 33:20-21, alt.

3. Blest, through endless ages,
   be the precious stream
   which, from endless torments,
   did the world redeem.

4. Abel's blood for vengeance
   pleaded to the skies,
   but the blood of Jesus
   for our pardon cries.

5. Oft as it is sprinkled
   on our guilty hearts,
   Satan in confusion
   terror-struck departs.

6. Oft as earth exulting
   wafts its praise on high,
   angel-hosts rejoicing
   make their glad reply.

7. Lift ye then your voices;
   swell the mighty flood;
   louder still and louder
   praise the precious blood.

   18th century Italian
   trans. Edward Caswall (1814-1878)

159

1. Glory be to Jesus,
   who, in bitter pains,
   poured for me the life-blood
   from his sacred veins.

2. Grace and life eternal
   in that blood I find:
   blest be his compassion,
   infinitely kind.

160

1. Glory, love, and praise, and honour
   for our food, now bestowed,
   render we the Donor.
   Bounteous God, we now confess thee;
   God, who thus blessest us,
   meet it is to bless thee.

2. Thankful for our ev'ry blessing,
let us sing Christ the Spring,
never, never ceasing.
Source of all our gifts and graces
Christ we own; Christ alone
calls for all our praises.

3. He dispels our sin and sadness,
life imparts, cheers our hearts,
fills with food and gladness.
Who himself for all hath given,
us he feeds, us he leads
to a feast in heaven.

Charles Wesley (1707-1788) alt.

161

1. Glory to God, glory to God,
glory to the Father.
Glory to God, glory to God,
glory to the Father.
To him be glory for ever.
To him be glory for ever.
Alleluia, amen.
Alleluia, amen,
alleluia, amen,
alleluia, amen.

2. Glory to God, glory to God,
Son of the Father.
Glory to God, glory to God,
Son of the Father.
To him be glory for ever.
To him be glory for ever.
Alleluia, amen.
Alleluia, amen,
alleluia, amen,
alleluia, amen.

3. Glory to God, glory to God,
glory to the Spirit.
Glory to God, glory to God,
glory to the Spirit.
To him be glory for ever.
To him be glory for ever.
Alleluia, amen.
Alleluia, amen,
alleluia, amen,
alleluia, amen.

Traditional Peruvian,
collected by John Ballantine (b. 1945)

162

1. Glory to thee, my God, this night
for all the blessings of the light;
keep me, O keep me, King of kings,
beneath thine own almighty wings.

2. Forgive me, Lord, for thy dear Son,
the ill that I this day have done,
that with the world, myself and thee,
I, ere I sleep, at peace may be.

3. Teach me to live, that I may dread
the grave as little as my bed;
teach me to die, that so I may
rise glorious at the aweful day.

4. O may my soul on thee repose,
and with sweet sleep mine eyelids
close;
sleep that may me more vig'rous make
to serve my God when I awake.

5. Praise God, from whom all blessings
flow;
praise him, all creatures here below;
praise him above, ye heav'nly host;
praise Father, Son and Holy Ghost.

Thomas Ken (1637-1711)

163

1. Glory to thee, O God,
   for all thy saints in light,
   who nobly strove and conquered
   in the well fought fight.
   Their praises sing,
   who life outpoured
   by fire and sword for Christ their King.

2. Thanks be to thee, O Lord,
   for saints thy Spirit stirred
   in humble paths to live thy life and
   speak thy word.
   Unnumbered they,
   whose candles shine
   to lead our footsteps after thine.

3. Lord God of truth and love,
   'thy kingdom come', we pray;
   give us thy grace to know thy truth and
   walk thy way:
   that here on earth
   thy will be done,
   till saints in earth and heav'n are one.

   Howard Charles Adie Gaunt (1902-1983)

164

1. Go forth and tell!
   O Church of God, awake!
   God's saving news
   to all the nations take:
   proclaim Christ Jesus,
   Saviour, Lord and King,
   that all the world
   his worthy praise may sing.

2. Go forth and tell!
   God's love embraces all;
   he will in grace
   respond to all who call;
   how shall they call
   if they have never heard
   the gracious invitation
   of his word?

3. Go forth and tell!
   where still the darkness lies;
   in wealth or want,
   the sinner surely dies:
   give us, O Lord,
   concern of heart and mind,
   a love like yours
   which cares for humankind.

4. Go forth and tell!
   the doors are open wide:
   share God's good gifts –
   let no-one be denied;
   live out your life
   as Christ your Lord shall choose,
   your ransomed pow'rs
   for his sole glory use.

5. Go forth and tell!
   O Church of God, arise!
   Go in the strength
   which Christ your Lord supplies;
   go till all nations
   his great name adore
   and serve him, Lord and King,
   for evermore.

   James Edward Seddon (1915-1983)

165

Go, tell it on the mountain,
over the hills and ev'rywhere.
Go, tell it on the mountain
that Jesus Christ is born.

1. While shepherds kept their watching
   o'er wand'ring flocks by night,
   behold, from out of heaven,
   there shone a holy light.

2. And lo, when they had seen it,
   they all bowed down and prayed;
   they travelled on together
   to where the babe was laid.

3. When I was a seeker,
   I sought both night and day:
   I asked my Lord to help me
   and he showed me the way.

4. He made me a watchman
   upon the city wall,
   and, if I am a Christian,
   I am the least of all.

   Traditional

166

God be in my head,
and in my understanding;
God be in mine eyes,
and in my looking;
God be in my mouth,
and in my speaking;
God be in my heart,
and in my thinking;
God be at mine end,
and at my departing.

'Book of Hours' (1514)

167

1. God forgave my sin in Jesus' name.
   I've been born again in Jesus' name.
   And in Jesus' name I come to you
   to share his love as he told me to.

He said: 'Freely, freely
you have received;
freely, freely give.
Go in my name,
and because you believe,
others will know that I live.'

2. All pow'r is giv'n in Jesus' name,
   in earth and heav'n in Jesus' name.
   And in Jesus' name I come to you
   to share his pow'r as he told me to.

3. God gives us life in Jesus' name,
   he lives in us in Jesus' name.
   And in Jesus' name I come to you
   to share his peace as he told me to.

   Carol Owens
   © 1972 Bud John Songs/Alliance Media Ltd/CopyCare Ltd

168

God is good, we sing and shout it,
God is good, we celebrate.
God is good, no more we doubt it,
God is good, we know it's true.
(*Last Time* Hey!)

And when I think of his love for me,
my heart fills with praise
and I feel like dancing.
For in his heart there is room for me
and I run with arms opened wide.

Graham Kendrick (b. 1950)
© 1985 Kingsway's Thankyou Music

169

1. God is love: his the care,
   tending each, ev'rywhere.
   God is love, all is there!
   Jesus came to show him,
   that mankind might know him!

   Sing aloud, loud, loud!
   Sing aloud, loud, loud!
   God is good! God is truth!
   God is beauty! Praise him!

2. None can see God above;
   we can share life and love;
   thus may we Godward move,
   seek him in creation,
   holding ev'ry nation.

3. Jesus lived on the earth,
   life and hope brought to birth
   and affirmed human worth,
   for he came to save us
   by the truth he gave us.

4. To our Lord praise we sing,
   light and life, friend and king,
   coming down, love to bring,
   pattern for our duty,
   showing God in beauty.

   Percy Dearmer (1867-1936) alt.

170

1. God is love: let heav'n adore him;
   God is love: let earth rejoice;
   let creation sing before him,
   and exalt him with one voice.
   He who laid the earth's foundation,
   he who spread the heav'ns above,
   he who breathes through all creation,
   he is love, eternal Love.

2. God is love: and he enfoldeth
   all the world in one embrace;
   with unfailing grasp he holdeth
   ev'ry child of ev'ry race.
   And when human hearts are breaking
   under sorrow's iron rod,
   then they find that self-same aching
   deep within the heart of God.

3. God is love: and though with blindness
   sin afflicts the human soul,
   God's eternal loving-kindness
   guides and heals and makes us whole.
   Sin and death and hell shall never
   o'er us final triumph gain;
   God is love, so love for ever
   o'er the universe must reign.

   Timothy Rees (1874-1939) alt.

171

1. God is our strength from days of old,
   the hope of ev'ry nation;
   whose pow'r conceived the universe
   and set the earth's foundation.
   Though hidden from our sight
   in uncreated light,
   his presence yet is known,
   his wondrous purpose shown
   resplendent in creation!

2. That Word of Life, before all things
   in primal darkness spoken,
   became for us the Word made flesh
   for our redemption broken.
   His glory set aside,
   for us he lived and died,
   obedient to the death,
   renewed in life and breath,
   to endless glory woken!

3. That Breath of God, who brooded first
   upon the new creation,
   who lit with light the Virgin's womb
   to bear the world's salvation;
   that Dove whose shadow graced
   th'anointed Saviour's face,
   now challenges us all
   to recognise the call
   to hope and liberation.

4. O great Creator, Spirit, Word,
   the well-spring of creation,
   our Alpha and our Omega,
   our hope and our salvation;
   to Father, Spirit, Son,
   the Three for ever One,
   and One for ever Three,
   mysterious Trinity,
   be praise and adoration.

Michael Forster (b. 1946)

172

1. God is working his purpose out
   as year succeeds to year.
   God is working his purpose out,
   and the day is drawing near.
   Nearer and nearer draws the time,
   the time that shall surely be,
   when the earth shall be filled
   with the glory of God
   as the waters cover the sea.

2. From the east to the utmost west
   wherever foot has trod,
   through the mouths of his messengers
   echoes forth the voice of God:
   'Listen to me, ye continents,
   ye islands, give ear to me,
   that the earth shall be filled
   with the glory of God
   as the waters cover the sea.'

3. How can we do the work of God,
   how prosper and increase
   harmony in the human race
   and the reign of perfect peace?
   What can we do to urge the time,
   the time that shall surely be,
   when the earth shall be filled
   with the glory of God
   as the waters cover the sea?

4. March we forth in the strength of God,
   his banner is unfurled;
   let the light of the gospel shine
   in the darkness of the world:
   strengthen the weary, heal the sick
   and set ev'ry captive free,
   that the earth shall be filled
   with the glory of God
   as the waters cover the sea.

5. All our efforts are nothing worth
   unless God bless the deed;
   vain our hopes for the harvest tide
   till he brings to life the seed.
   Yet ever nearer draws the time,
   the time that shall surely be,
   when the earth shall be filled
   with the glory of God
   as the waters cover the sea.

Arthur Campbell Ainger (1841-1919)
adapted by Michael Forster (b. 1946)

173

1. God moves in a mysterious way
his wonders to perform;
he plants his footsteps in the sea,
and rides upon the storm.

2. Deep in unfathomable mines
of never-failing skill,
he treasures up his bright designs,
and works his sov'reign will.

3. Ye fearful saints, fresh courage take;
the clouds ye so much dread
are big with mercy, and shall break
in blessings on your head.

4. Judge not the Lord by feeble sense,
but trust him for his grace;
behind a frowning providence
he hides a shining face.

5. His purposes will ripen fast,
unfolding ev'ry hour;
the bud may have a bitter taste,
but sweet will be the flow'r.

6. Blind unbelief is sure to err,
and scan his work in vain;
God is his own interpreter,
and he will make it plain.

William Cowper (1731-1800)

174

1. God of grace and God of glory,
on thy people pour thy pow'r;
now fulfil thy Church's story;
bring her bud to glorious flow'r.
Grant us wisdom, grant us courage,
for the facing of this hour.

2. Lo, the hosts of evil round us
scorn thy Christ, assail his ways;
from the fears that long have bound us
free our hearts to faith and praise.
Grant us wisdom, grant us courage,
for the living of these days.

3. Cure thy children's warring madness,
bend our pride to thy control;
shame our wanton selfish gladness,
rich in goods and poor in soul.
Grant us wisdom, grant us courage,
lest we miss thy kingdom's goal.

4. Set our feet on lofty places,
gird our lives that they may be
armoured with all Christlike graces
as we set your people free.
Grant us wisdom, grant us courage,
lest we fail the world or thee.

Harry Emerson Fosdick (1878-1969) alt.

175

1. God of mercy, God of grace,
show the brightness of thy face;
shine upon us, Saviour, shine,
fill thy Church with light divine;
and thy saving health extend
unto earth's remotest end.

2. Let the people praise thee, Lord;
be by all that live adored;
let the nations shout and sing
glory to their Saviour King;
at thy feet their tribute pay,
and thy holy will obey.

3. Let the people praise thee, Lord;
earth shall then her fruits afford;
God to us his blessing give,
we to God devoted live;
all below, and all above,
one in joy and light and love.

Henry Francis Lyte (1793-1847) based on Psalm 67, alt.

176

1. God rest you merry, gentlemen,
   let nothing you dismay,
   for Jesus Christ our Saviour
   was born on Christmas day,
   to save us all from Satan's pow'r
   when we were gone astray:

   O tidings of comfort and joy,
   comfort and joy,
   O tidings of comfort and joy.

2. In Bethlehem, in Jewry,
   this blessèd babe was born,
   and laid within a manger,
   upon this blessèd morn;
   the which his mother Mary
   did nothing take in scorn.

3. From God, our heav'nly Father,
   a blessèd angel came,
   and unto certain shepherds
   brought tidings of the same,
   how that in Bethlehem was born
   the Son of God by name.

4. 'Fear not,' then said the angel,
   'let nothing you affright,
   this day is born a Saviour,
   of virtue, pow'r and might;
   by him the world is overcome
   and Satan put to flight.'

5. The shepherds at those tidings
   rejoicèd much in mind,
   and left their flocks a-feeding,
   in tempest, storm and wind,
   and went to Bethlehem straightway
   this blessèd babe to find.

6. But when to Bethlehem they came,
   whereat this infant lay,
   they found him in a manger,
   where oxen feed on hay;
   his mother Mary kneeling,
   unto the Lord did pray.

7. Now to the Lord sing praises,
   all you within this place,
   and with true love and fellowship
   each other now embrace;
   this holy tide of Christmas
   all others doth deface.

   Traditional English alt.

177

1. God save our gracious Queen,
   long live our noble Queen,
   God save the Queen.
   Send her victorious,
   happy and glorious,
   long to reign over us:
   God save the Queen.

2. Thy choicest gifts in store
   on her be pleased to pour,
   long may she reign:
   may she defend our laws,
   and ever give us cause
   to sing with heart and voice
   God save the Queen!

3. Not on this land alone,
   but be God's mercies known
   on ev'ry shore.
   Lord, make the nations see
   that all humanity
   should form one family
   the wide world o'er.

   vs. 1 & 2: unknown (17th or 18th century);
   v.3: William E. Hickson (1803-1870) alt.

178

1. God that madest earth and heaven,
   darkness and light;
   who the day for toil hast given,
   for rest the night;
   may thine angel-guards defend us,
   slumber sweet thy mercy send us,
   holy dreams and hopes attend us,
   this livelong night.

2. Guard us waking, guard us sleeping,
   and, when we die,
   may we in thy mighty keeping
   all peaceful lie:
   when the last dread call shall wake us,
   do not thou our God forsake us,
   but to reign in glory take us
   with thee on high.

v. 1: Reginald Heber (1783-1826);
v. 2: Richard Whately (1787-1863)

179

1. God, whose farm is all creation,
   take the gratitude we give;
   take the finest of our harvest,
   crops we grow that all may live.

2. Take our ploughing, seeding, reaping,
   hopes and fears of sun and rain,
   all our thinking, planning, waiting,
   ripened in this fruit and grain.

3. All our labour, all our watching,
   all our calendar of care,
   in these crops of your creation,
   take, O God: they are our prayer.

John Arlott (1914-1991) alt.

180

1. God's Spirit is in in my heart.
   He has called me and set me apart.
   This is what I have to do,
   what I have to do.

   He sent me to give
   the Good News to the poor,
   tell pris'ners that
   they are pris'ners no more,
   tell blind people that they can see,
   and set the downtrodden free,
   and go tell ev'ryone the news
   that the kingdom of God has come,
   and go tell ev'ryone the news
   that God's kingdom has come.

2. Just as the Father sent me,
   so I'm sending you out to be
   my witnesses throughout the world,
   the whole of the world.

3. Don't carry a load in your pack,
   you don't need two shirts on your back.
   A workman can earn his own keep,
   can earn his own keep.

4. Don't worry what you have to say,
   don't worry because on that day
   God's Spirit will speak in your heart,
   will speak in your heart.

Hubert J. Richards. (b. 1921)

181

1. Good Christians all, rejoice and sing.
   Now is the triumph of our King.
   To all the world glad news we bring:
   Alleluia!

2. The Lord of Life is ris'n for ay:
   bring flow'rs of song to strew his way;
   let all mankind rejoice and say:
   Alleluia!

3. Praise we in songs of victory
   that Love, that Life, which cannot die
   and sing with hearts uplifted high:
   Alleluia!

4. Thy name we bless, O risen Lord,
   and sing today with one accord
   the life laid down, the life restored:
   Alleluia!

Cyril Argentine Alington (1872-1955) alt.

182

1. Good Christians all, rejoice
   with heart and soul and voice!
   Give ye heed to what we say:
   News! News!
   Jesus Christ is born today;
   ox and ass before him bow,
   and he is in the manger now:
   Christ is born today,
   Christ is born today!

2. Good Christians all, rejoice
   with heart and soul and voice!
   Now ye hear of endless bliss:
   Joy! Joy!
   Jesus Christ was born for this.
   He hath opened heaven's door,
   and we are blest for evermore:
   Christ was born for this,
   Christ was born for this.

3. Good Christians all, rejoice
   with heart and soul and voice!
   Now ye need not fear the grave:
   Peace! Peace!
   Jesus Christ was born to save;
   calls you one, and calls you all,
   to gain his everlasting hall:
   Christ was born to save,
   Christ was born to save.

John Mason Neale (1818-1866) alt.

183

1. Good King Wenceslas looked out
   on the feast of Stephen,
   when the snow lay round about,
   deep, and crisp, and even:
   brightly shone the moon that night,
   though the frost was cruel,
   when a poor man came in sight,
   gath'ring winter fuel.

2. 'Hither, page, and stand by me,
   if thou know'st it, telling,
   yonder peasant, who is he,
   where and what his dwelling?'
   'Sire, he lives a good league hence,
   underneath the mountain,
   right against the forest fence,
   by Saint Agnes' fountain.'

3. 'Bring me flesh, and bring me wine,
   bring me pine logs hither:
   thou and I will see him dine,
   when we bring them thither.'
   Page and monarch, forth they went,
   forth they went together;
   through the rude wind's wild lament,
   and the bitter weather.

Continued overleaf

4. 'Sire, the night is darker now,
   and the wind blows stronger;
   fails my heart, I know not how;
   I can go no longer.'
   'Mark my footsteps good, my page;
   tread thou in them boldly:
   thou shalt find the winter's rage
   freeze thy blood less coldly.'

5. In his master's steps he trod,
   where the snow lay dinted;
   heat was in the very sod
   which the Saint had printed.
   Therefore, Christians all, be sure,
   wealth or rank possessing,
   ye who now will bless the poor,
   shall yourselves find blessing.

   John Mason Neale (1818-1866) alt.

184

1. Gracious Spirit, Holy Ghost,
   taught by thee, we covet most
   of thy gifts at Pentecost,
   holy, heav'nly love.

2. Love is kind, and suffers long,
   love is meek, and thinks no wrong,
   love than death itself more strong;
   therefore give us love.

3. Prophecy will fade away,
   melting in the light of day;
   love will ever with us stay;
   therefore give us love.

4. Faith will vanish into sight;
   hope be emptied in delight;
   love in heav'n will shine more bright;
   therefore give us love.

5. Fatih and hope and love we see
   joining hand in hand agree;
   but the greatest of the three,
   and the best, is love.

6. From the overshadowing
   of thy gold and silver wing
   shed on us, who to thee sing,
   holy, heav'nly love.

   Christopher Wordsworth (1807-1885)
   based on 1 Corinthians 13; Psalm 68:13

185

Great is the Lord
and most worthy of praise,
the city of our God, the holy place,
the joy of the whole earth.
Great is the Lord
in whom we have the victory,
he aids us against the enemy,
we bow down on our knees.
And, Lord,
we want to lift your name on high,
and, Lord, we want to thank you
for the works you've done in our lives,
and, Lord,
we trust in your unfailing love,
for you alone are God eternal,
throughout earth and heaven above.

Steve McEwan
©1985 Body Songs/CopyCare Ltd

186

1. Great is thy faithfulness,
   O God my Father,
   there is no shadow
   of turning with thee;
   thou changest not,
   thy compassions, they fail not;
   as thou hast been
   thou for ever wilt be.

   Great is thy faithfulness!
   Great is thy faithfulness!
   Morning by morning
   new mercies I see;
   all I have needed
   thy hand hath provided,
   great is thy faithfulness,
   Lord, unto me!

2. Summer and winter,
   and springtime and harvest,
   sun, moon and stars
   in their courses above,
   join with all nature
   in manifold witness
   to thy great faithfulness,
   mercy and love.

3. Pardon for sin
   and a peace that endureth,
   thine own dear presence
   to cheer and to guide;
   strength for today
   and bright hope for tomorrow,
   blessings all mine,
   with ten thousand beside!

   Thomas Obadiah Chisholm (1866-1960)
   © 1951 Hope Publishing Co.

187

1. Great Son of God,
   you once on Cal'vry's cross
   fought the long fight
   for truth and freedom's sake,
   endured the scourge,
   the crown of thorns,
   the nails that fixed
   your youthful body to a stake.
   For six long hours
   you suffered searing pain
   to set your captive
   people free again.

2. 'Give us a sign from heav'n,'
   the people cried.
   'If you are Christ,
   leap down, alive and free.
   Who could accept as Saviour
   one who died
   like some poor miscreant
   skewered to a tree?'
   Lord Christ, our Saviour,
   you would not descend
   until your glorious work
   achieved its end.

3. 'My God, my God,
   where have you gone?' you called,
   alone and helpless,
   willing still to share
   through all the gath'ring
   gloom of Calvary,
   the depth of dying sinners'
   deep despair.
   But then triumphant,
   ready now to die,
   'The work is finished!'
   was your glorious cry.

   Edwin Le Grice (1911-1992)

188

1. Guide me, O thou great Redeemer,
pilgrim through this barren land;
I am weak, but thou art mighty;
hold me with thy pow'rful hand:
bread of heaven, bread of heaven,
feed me now and evermore,
feed me now and evermore.

2. Open now the crystal fountain,
whence the healing stream doth flow;
let the fiery cloudy pillar
lead me all my journey through:
strong deliv'rer, strong deliv'rer,
be thou still my strength and shield,
be thou still my strength and shield.

3. When I tread the verge of Jordan,
bid my anxious fears subside;
death of death, and hell's destruction,
land me safe on Canaan's side:
songs of praises, songs of praises,
I will ever give to thee,
I will ever give to thee.

William Williams (1717-1791)
trans. Peter Williams (1727-1796) and others

189

1. Hail, gladdening Light,
of his pure glory poured
from the immortal Father,
heav'nly, blest,
holiest of holies,
Jesus Christ our Lord.

2. Now we are come
to the sun's hour of rest,
the lights of evening
round us shine,
we hymn the Father,
Son and Holy Spirit divine.

3. Worthiest art thou at all times
to be sung with undefilèd tongue,
Son of our God,
giver of life, alone:
therefore in all the world thy glories,
Lord, they own.

Greek (3rd century or earlier)
trans. John Keble (1792-1866)

190

1. Hail, O Star that pointest
t'wards the port of heaven,
thou to whom as maiden
God for Son was given.

2. When the salutation
Gabriel had spoken,
peace was shed upon us,
Eva's bonds were broken.

3. Bound by Satan's fetters,
health and vision needing,
God will aid and light us
at thy gentle pleading.

4. Jesu's tender mother,
make the supplication
unto him who chose thee
at his incarnation.

5. That, O matchless maiden,
passing meek and lowly,
thy dear son may make us
blameless, chaste and holy.

6. So, as now we journey,
aid our weak endeavour
till we gaze on Jesus,
and rejoice for ever.

7. Father, Son and Spirit,
   Three in One confessing,
   give we equal glory,
   equal praise and blessing.

   Latin (c. 9th century)
   trans. Athelstan Riley (1858-1945)

191

1. Hail the day that sees him rise,
   alleluia!
   to his throne above the skies;
   alleluia!
   Christ the Lamb for sinners giv'n,
   alleluia!
   enters now the highest heav'n!
   alleluia!

2. There for him high triumph waits;
   lift your heads, eternal gates!
   He hath conquered death and sin;
   take the King of Glory in!

3. Circled round with angel-pow'rs,
   their triumphant Lord and ours;
   wide unfold the radiant scene,
   take the King of Glory in!

4. Lo, the heav'n its Lord receives,
   yet he loves the earth he leaves;
   though returning to his throne,
   calls the human race his own.

5. See, he lifts his hands above;
   see, he shows the prints of love;
   hark, his gracious lips bestow,
   blessings on his Church below.

6. Still for us he intercedes,
   his prevailing death he pleads;
   near himself prepares our place,
   he the first-fruits of our race.

7. Lord, though parted from our sight,
   far above the starry height,
   grant our hearts may thither rise,
   seeking thee above the skies.

8. Ever upward let us move,
   wafted on the wings of love;
   looking when our Lord shall come,
   longing, sighing after home.

   Charles Wesley (1707- 1788), Thomas Cotterill
   (1779-1823) and others, alt.

192

1. Hail, thou once despisèd Jesus,
   hail, thou Galilean King!
   Thou didst suffer to release us;
   thou didst free salvation bring.
   Hail, thou universal Saviour,
   bearer of our sin and shame;
   by thy merits we find favour;
   life is given through thy name.

2. Paschal Lamb, by God appointed,
   all our sins on thee were laid;
   by almighty love anointed,
   thou hast full atonement made.
   All thy people are forgiven
   through the virtue of thy blood;
   opened is the gate of heaven,
   we are reconciled to God.

3. Jesus, hail! enthroned in glory,
   there for ever to abide;
   all the heav'nly hosts adore thee,
   seated at thy Father's side:
   there for sinners thou art pleading,
   there thou dost our place prepare;
   ever for us interceding,
   till in glory we appear.

Continued overleaf

4. Worship, honour, pow'r and blessing,
   thou art worthy to receive;
   loudest praises, without ceasing,
   it is right for us to give:
   help, ye bright angelic spirits!
   bring your sweetest, noblest lays;
   help to sing our Saviour's merits,
   help to chant Immanuel's praise.

   John Bakewell (1721-1819) alt.

193

1. Hail to the Lord's anointed,
   Great David's greater son!
   Hail, in the time appointed,
   his reign on earth begun!
   He comes to break oppression,
   to set the captive free;
   to take away transgression,
   and rule in equity.

2. He comes with succour speedy
   to those who suffer wrong;
   to help the poor and needy,
   and bid the weak be strong;
   to give them songs for sighing,
   their darkness turn to light,
   whose souls, condemned and dying,
   were precious in his sight.

3. He shall come down like showers
   upon the fruitful earth,
   and love, joy, hope, like flowers,
   spring in his path to birth:
   before him on the mountains
   shall peace the herald go;
   and righteousness in fountains
   from hill to valley flow.

4. Kings shall fall down before him,
   and gold and incense bring;
   all nations shall adore him,
   his praise all people sing;
   to him shall prayer unceasing
   and daily vows ascend;
   his kingdom still increasing,
   a kingdom without end.

5. O'er ev'ry foe victorious,
   he on his throne shall rest,
   from age to age more glorious,
   all-blessing and all-blest;
   the tide of time shall never
   his covenant remove;
   his name shall stand for ever;
   that name to us is love.

   James Montgomery (1771-1854) based on Psalm 72

194

Hallelujah, my Father,
for giving us your Son;
sending him into the world
to be given up for all,
knowing we would bruise him
and smite him from the earth!
Hallelujah, my Father,
in his death is my birth.
Hallelujah, my Father,
in his life is my life.

Tim Cullen, alt.
© 1975 Celebration/Kingsway's Thankyou Music

195

1. Happy are they, they that love God,
   whose hearts have Christ confessed,
   who by his cross have found their life,
   and 'neath his yoke their rest.

2. Glad is the praise, sweet are the songs,
when they together sing;
and strong the prayers that bow the ear
of heav'n's eternal King.

3. Christ to their homes giveth his peace,
and makes their loves his own:
but ah, what tares the evil one
hath in his garden sown!

4. Sad were our lot, evil this earth,
did not its sorrows prove
the path whereby the sheep may find
the fold of Jesus' love.

5. Then shall they know, they that love
him,
how hope is wrought through pain;
their fellowship, through death itself,
unbroken will remain.

*Robert Bridges (1844-1930) based on 'O quam juvat',
Charles Coffin (1676-1749) alt.*

196

1. Hark! a herald voice is calling:
'Christ is nigh!' it seems to say;
'Cast away the dreams of darkness,
O ye children of the day!'

2. Startled at the solemn warning,
let the earth-bound soul arise;
Christ, her sun, all sloth dispelling,
shines upon the morning skies.

3. Lo, the Lamb, so long expected,
comes with pardon down from heav'n;
let us haste, with tears of sorrow,
one and all to be forgiv'n.

4. So when next he comes with glory,
wrapping all the earth in fear,
may he then, as our defender,
on the clouds of heav'n appear.

5. Honour, glory, virtue, merit,
to the Father and the Son,
with the co-eternal Spirit,
while unending ages run.

6th century trans. Edward Caswall (1814-1878)

197

1. Hark, my soul, it is the Lord;
'tis thy Saviour, hear his word;
Jesus speaks, and speaks to thee,
'Say, poor sinner, lov'st thou me?

2. 'I delivered thee when bound,
and, when wounded, healed thy
wound;
sought thee wand'ring, set thee right,
turned thy darkness into light.

3. 'Can a woman's tender care
cease towards the child she bare?
yes, she may forgetful be,
yet will I remember thee.

4. 'Mine is an unchanging love,
higher than the heights above,
deeper than the depths beneath,
free and faithful, strong as death.

5. 'Thou shalt see my glory soon,
when the work of grace is done;
partner of my throne shalt be:
say, poor sinner, lov'st thou me?'

6. Lord, it is my chief complaint
that my love is weak and faint;
yet I love thee, and adore;
O for grace to love thee more!

William Cowper (1731-1800) based on John 21:16

198

1. Hark the glad sound! the Saviour
      comes,
   the Saviour promised long:
   let ev'ry heart prepare a throne,
   and ev'ry voice a song.

2. He comes, the pris'ners to release
   in Satan's bondage held;
   the gates of brass before him burst,
   the iron fetters yield.

3. He comes, the broken heart to bind,
   the bleeding soul to cure,
   and with the treasures of his grace
   to bless the humble poor.

4. Our glad hosannas, Prince of Peace,
   thy welcome shall proclaim;
   and heav'n's eternal arches ring
   with thy belovèd name.

Philip Doddridge (1702-1751) based on Luke 4:18-19

199

1. Hark, the herald-angels sing
   glory to the new-born King;
   peace on earth and mercy mild,
   God and sinners reconciled:
   joyful, all ye nations rise,
   join the triumph of the skies,
   with th'angelic host proclaim,
   'Christ is born in Bethlehem.'

   Hark, the herald-angels sing
   glory to the new-born King.

2. Christ, by highest heav'n adored,
   Christ, the everlasting Lord,
   late in time behold him come,
   offspring of a virgin's womb!
   Veiled in flesh the Godhead see,
   hail, th'incarnate Deity!
   Pleased as man with us to dwell,
   Jesus, our Emmanuel.

3. Hail, the heav'n-born Prince of Peace!
   Hail, the Sun of Righteousness!
   Light and life to all he brings,
   ris'n with healing in his wings;
   mild he lays his glory by,
   born that we no more may die,
   born to raise us from the earth,
   born to give us second birth.

*Charles Wesley (1707-1788), George Whitefield
(1714-1770), Martin Madan (1726-1790)
and others, alt.*

200

1. Hark! the sound of holy voices,
   chanting at the crystal sea:
   Alleluia, alleluia,
   alleluia, Lord, to thee;
   multitude, which none can number,
   like the stars in glory stands,
   clothed in white apparel,
   holding palms of vict'ry in their hands.

2. Patriarch and holy prophet,
   who prepared the way of Christ,
   king, apostle, saint, confessor,
   martyr and evangelist,
   saintly maiden, godly matron,
   widows who have watched to prayer,
   joined in holy concert, singing
   to the Lord of all, are there.

3. They have come from tribulation,
   and have washed their robes in blood,
   washed them in the blood of Jesus;
   tried they were, and firm they stood;
   gladly, Lord, with thee they suffered;
   gladly, Lord, with thee they died,
   and by death to life immortal
   they were born and glorified.

4. Now they reign in heav'nly glory,
   now they walk in golden light,
   now they drink, as from a river,
   holy bliss and infinite;
   love and peace they taste for ever,
   and all truth and knowledge see
   in the beatific vision
   of the blessèd Trinity.

5. God of God, the one-begotten,
   Light of Light, Emmanuel,
   in whose body joined together
   all the saints for ever dwell;
   pour upon us of thy fullness,
   that we may for evermore
   Father, Son and Holy Spirit
   truly worship and adore.

   Christopher Wordsworth (1807-1885) alt.

201

1. Have faith in God, my heart,
   trust and be unafraid;
   God will fulfil in ev'ry part
   each promise he has made.

2. Have faith in God, my mind,
   though oft thy light burns low;
   God's mercy holds a wiser plan
   than thou canst fully know.

3. Have faith in God, my soul,
   his Cross for ever stands;
   and neither life nor death can pluck
   his children from his hands.

4. Lord Jesus, make me whole;
   grant me no resting-place,
   until I rest, heart, mind and soul,
   the captive of thy grace.

   Bryan Austin Rees (1911-1983)

202

1. Have you heard the raindrops
   drumming on the rooftops?
   Have you heard the raindrops
   dripping on the ground?
   Have you heard the raindrops
   splashing in the streams
   and running to the rivers all around?

   There's water, water of life
   Jesus gives us the water of life;
   there's water, water of life,
   Jesus gives us the water of life.

2. There's a busy worker
   digging in the desert,
   digging with a spade
   that flashes in the sun;
   soon there will be water
   rising in the well-shaft,
   spilling from the bucket as it comes.

3. Nobody can live
   who hasn't any water,
   when the land is dry
   then nothing much grows;
   Jesus gives us life
   if we drink the living water,
   sing it so that ev'rybody knows.

   Christian Strover

203

He is exalted,
the King is exalted on high;
I will praise him.
He is exalted,
for ever exalted
and I will praise his name!
He is the Lord;
for ever his truth shall reign.
Heaven and earth rejoice
in his holy name.
He is exalted,
the King is exalted on high.

Twila Paris
© 1985 Straightway Music/Alliance Media Ltd/CopyCare Ltd

204

1. He is Lord, he is Lord.
   He is risen from the dead
   and he is Lord.
   Ev'ry knee shall bow,
   ev'ry tongue confess
   that Jesus Christ is Lord.

2. He is King, he is King.
   He is risen from the dead
   and he is King.
   Ev'ry knee shall bow,
   ev'ry tongue confess
   that Jesus Christ is King.

3. He is love, he is love.
   He is risen from the dead
   and he is love.
   Ev'ry knee shall bow,
   ev'ry tongue confess
   that Jesus Christ is love.

Unknown

205

1. He who would valiant be
   'gainst all disaster,
   let him in constancy
   follow the Master.
   There's no discouragement
   shall make him once relent
   his first avowed intent
   to be a pilgrim.

2. Who so beset him round
   with dismal stories,
   do but themselves confound –
   his strength the more is.
   No foes shall stay his might,
   though he with giants fight:
   he will make good his right
   to be a pilgrim.

3. Since, Lord, thou dost defend
   us with thy Spirit,
   we know we at the end
   shall life inherit.
   Then fancies flee away!
   I'll fear not what men say,
   I'll labour night and day
   to be a pilgrim.

Percy Dearmer (1867-1936)
after John Bunyan (1628-1688)

206

1. He's got the whole world in his hand.
   He's got the whole world in his hand.
   He's got the whole world in his hand.
   He's got the whole world in his hand.

2. He's got you and me, brother, in his
   hand. (3)
   He's got the whole world in his hand.

3. He's got you and me, sister, in his
   hand. (3)
   He's got the whole world in his hand.

4. He's got the little tiny baby in his
   hand. (3)
   He's got the whole world in his hand.

5. He's got ev'rybody here in his hand. (3)
   He's got the whole world in his hand.

Traditional

207

1. Heav'n shall not wait
   for the poor to lose their patience,
   the scorned to smile,
   the despised to find a friend:
   Jesus is Lord,
   he has championed the unwanted;
   in him injustice
   confronts its timely end.

2. Heav'n shall not wait
   for the rich to share their fortunes,
   the proud to fall,
   the élite to tend the least:
   Jesus is Lord;
   he has shown the masters' privilege –
   to kneel and wash
   servants' feet before they feast.

3. Heav'n shall not wait
   for the dawn of great ideas,
   thoughts of compassion
   divorced from cries of pain:
   Jesus is Lord;
   he has married word and action;
   his cross and company
   make his purpose plain.

4. Heav'n shall not wait
   for our legalised obedience,
   defined by statute,
   to strict conventions bound:
   Jesus is Lord;
   he has hallmarked true allegiance –
   goodness appears
   where his grace is sought and found.

5. Heav'n shall not wait
   for triumphant hallelujahs,
   when earth has passed
   and we reach another shore:
   Jesus is Lord
   in our present imperfection;
   his pow'r and love
   are for now and then for evermore.

John L. Bell (b. 1949) and Graham Maule (b. 1958)

208

1. Help us to help each other, Lord,
   each other's cross to bear;
   let each a helping hand afford,
   and feel each other's care.

2. Up into thee, our living head,
   let us in all things grow,
   and by thy sacrifice be led
   the fruits of love to show.

3. Drawn by the magnet of thy love
   let all our hearts agree;
   and ever t'wards each other move,
   and ever move t'wards thee.

4. This is the bond of perfectness,
   thy spotless charity.
   O let us still we pray, possess
   the mind that was in thee.

After Charles Wesley (1707-1788) alt.

209

1. Hills of the north, rejoice,
   echoing songs arise,
   hail with united voice
   him who made earth and skies:
   he comes in righteousness and love,
   he brings salvation from above.

2. Isles of the southern seas
   sing to the list'ning earth,
   carry on ev'ry breeze
   hope of a world's new birth:
   in Christ shall all be made anew,
   his word is sure, his promise true.

3. Lands of the east, arise,
   he is your brightest morn,
   greet him with joyous eyes,
   praise shall his path adorn:
   the God whom you have longed to
     know
   in Christ draws near, and calls you now.

4. Shores of the utmost west,
   lands of the setting sun,
   welcome the heav'nly guest
   in whom the dawn has come:
   he brings a never-ending light
   who triumphed o'er our darkest night.

5. Shout, as you journey on,
   songs be in ev'ry mouth,
   lo, from the north they come,
   from east and west and south:
   in Jesus all shall find their rest,
   in him the longing earth be blest.

Charles Edward Oakley (1832-1865), adapted

210

1. Holy, holy, holy, holy.
   Holy, holy, holy Lord
   God almighty;
   and we lift our hearts before you
   as a token of our love,
   holy, holy, holy, holy.

2. Gracious Father, gracious Father,
   we are glad to be your children,
   gracious Father;
   and we lift our heads before you
   as a token of our love,
   gracious Father, gracious Father.

3. Risen Jesus, risen Jesus,
   we are glad you have redeemed us,
   risen Jesus;
   and we lift our hands before you
   as a token of our love,
   risen Jesus, risen Jesus.

4. Holy Spirit, Holy Spirit,
   come and fill our hearts anew,
   Holy Spirit;
   and we lift our voice before you
   as a token of our love,
   Holy Spirit, Holy Spirit.

5. Hallelujah, hallelujah,
   hallelujah, hallelujah,
   hallelujah;
   and we lift our hearts before you
   as a token of our love,
   hallelujah, hallelujah.

Jimmy Owens
© Bud John Songs/Alliance Media Ltd/Copycare Ltd

211

1. Holy, holy, holy is the Lord,
   holy is the Lord God almighty.
   Holy, holy, holy is the Lord,
   holy is the Lord God almighty:
   who was, and is, and is to come;
   holy, holy, holy is the Lord.

2. Jesus, Jesus, Jesus is the Lord,
   Jesus is the Lord God almighty:
   Jesus, Jesus, Jesus is the Lord,
   Jesus is the Lord God almighty:
   who was, and is, and is to come;
   Jesus, Jesus, Jesus is the Lord.

3. Worthy, worthy, worthy is the Lord,
   worthy is the Lord God almighty:
   worthy, worthy, worthy is the Lord,
   worthy is the Lord God almighty:
   who was, and is, and is to come;
   worthy, worthy, worthy is the Lord.

4. Glory, glory, glory to the Lord,
   glory to the Lord God almighty:
   glory, glory, glory to the Lord,
   glory to the Lord God almighty:
   who was, and is, and is to come;
   glory, glory, glory to the Lord.

Unknown

212

1. Holy, holy, holy!
   Lord God almighty!
   Early in the morning
   our song shall rise to thee;
   holy, holy, holy!
   merciful and mighty!
   God in three persons,
   blessèd Trinity!

2. Holy, holy, holy!
   all the saints adore thee,
   casting down their golden crowns
   around the glassy sea;
   cherubim and seraphim
   falling down before thee,
   which wert, and art,
   and evermore shalt be.

3. Holy, holy, holy!
   though the darkness hide thee,
   though the eye made blind by sin
   thy glory may not see,
   only thou art holy,
   there is none beside thee,
   perfect in pow'r,
   in love, and purity.

4. Holy, holy, holy!
   Lord God almighty!
   All thy works shall praise thy name,
   in earth, and sky, and sea;
   holy, holy, holy!
   merciful and mighty!
   God in three persons,
   blessèd Trinity!

Reginald Heber (1783-1826) alt.

213

1. Holy Jesu, by thy passion,
   by the woes which none can share,
   borne in more than kingly fashion,
   by thy love beyond compare:

   Crucified, I turn to thee,
   Son of Mary, plead for me.

2. By the treachery and trial,
   by the blows and sore distress,
   by desertion and denial,
   by thine awful loneliness:

Continued overleaf

3. By thy look so sweet and lowly,
   while they smote thee on the face,
   by thy patience, calm and holy,
   in the midst of keen disgrace:

   Crucified, I turn to thee,
   Son of Mary, plead for me.

4. By the hour of condemnation,
   by the blood which trickled down,
   when, for us and our salvation,
   thou didst wear the robe and crown:

5. By the path of sorrows dreary,
   by the cross, thy dreadful load,
   by the pain, when, faint and weary,
   thou didst sink upon the road:

6. By the Spirit which could render
   love for hate and good for ill,
   by the mercy, sweet and tender,
   poured upon thy murd'rers still:

   William John Sparrow-Simpson (1859-1952)

214

1. Holy Spirit, come, confirm us
   in the truth that Christ makes known;
   we have faith and understanding
   through your promised light alone.

2. Holy Spirit, come, console us,
   come as Advocate to plead;
   loving Spirit from the Father,
   grant in Christ the help we need.

3. Holy Spirit, come, renew us,
   come yourself to make us live;
   holy through your loving presence,
   holy through the gifts you give.

4. Holy Spirit, come, possess us,
   you the love of Three in One,
   Holy Spirit of the Father,
   Holy Spirit of the Son.

   Brian Foley (b. 1919)

215

1. Hosanna, hosanna,
   hosanna in the highest!
   Hosanna, hosanna,
   hosanna in the highest!
   Lord, we lift up your name
   with hearts full of praise;
   be exalted, O Lord, our God!
   Hosanna in the highest!

2. Glory, glory,
   glory to the King of kings!
   Glory, glory,
   glory to the King of kings!
   Lord, we lift up your name
   with hearts full of praise;
   be exalted, O Lord, our God!
   Glory to the King of kings!

   Carl Tuttle, based on Matthew 21:9
   © 1985 Mercy Vineyard Music/Kingsway's Thankyou Music

216

1. How firm a foundation,
   ye saints of the Lord,
   is laid for your faith
   in his excellent word;
   what more can he say
   than to you he hath said,
   you who unto Jesus
   for refuge have fled?

2. Fear not, he is with thee,
   O be not dismayed;
   for he is thy God,
   and will still give thee aid:
   he'll strengthen thee, help thee,
   and cause thee to stand,
   upheld by his righteous,
   omnipotent hand.

3. In ev'ry condition,
   in sickness, in health,
   in poverty's vale,
   or abounding in wealth;
   at home and abroad,
   on the land, on the sea,
   as thy days may demand
   shall thy strength ever be.

4. When through the deep waters
   he calls thee to go,
   the rivers of grief
   shall not thee overflow;
   for he will be with thee
   in trouble to bless,
   and sanctify to thee
   thy deepest distress.

5. When through fiery trials
   thy pathway shall lie,
   his grace all-sufficient
   shall be thy supply;
   the flame shall not hurt thee,
   his only design
   thy dross to consume
   and thy gold to refine.

6. The soul that on Jesus
   has leaned for repose
   he will not, he cannot,
   desert to its foes;
   that soul, though all hell
   should endeavour to shake,
   he never will leave,
   he will never forsake.

Richard Keen (c. 1787)

217

1. How good is the God we adore!
   Our faithful, unchangeable friend:
   his love is as great as his pow'r
   and knows neither measure nor end.

2. For Christ is the first and the last;
   his Spirit will guide us safe home;
   we'll praise him for all that is past
   and trust him for all that's to come.

Joseph Hart (1712-1768)

218

1. How lovely, Lord, how lovely
   is your abiding place;
   my soul is longing, fainting
   to feast upon your grace.
   The sparrow finds a shelter,
   a place to build her nest;
   and so your temple calls us
   within its walls to rest.

2. In your blest courts to worship,
   O God, a single day
   is better than a thousand
   if I from you should stray.
   I'd rather keep the entrance
   and claim you as my Lord,
   than revel in the riches
   the ways of sin afford.

3. A sun and shield for ever
   are you, O God most high;
   you shower us with blessings,
   no good will you deny.
   The saints, your grace receiving,
   from strength to strength shall go,
   and from their life shall rivers
   of blessing overflow.

Arlo D. Duba, based on Psalm 84

219

1. How lovely on the mountains
   are the feet of him
   who brings good news, good news,
   announcing peace,
   proclaiming news of happiness:
   our God reigns, our God reigns.

2. You watchmen, lift your voices
   joyfully as one,
   shout for your King, your King!
   See eye to eye,
   the Lord restoring Sion:
   our God reigns, our God reigns.

3. Waste places of Jerusalem,
   break forth with joy!
   We are redeemed, redeemed.
   The Lord has saved
   and comforted his people:
   our God reigns, our God reigns.

4. Ends of the earth,
   see the salvation of our God!
   Jesus is Lord, is Lord!
   Before the nations,
   he has bared his holy arm:
   our God reigns, our God reigns.

Based on Isaiah 52, v.1: Leonard E. Smith Jnr. (b. 1942)
vs. 2-4: unknown
© 1974 Kingsway's Thankyou Music

220

1. How sweet the name of Jesus sounds
   in a believer's ear!
   It soothes our sorrows, heals our
     wounds,
   and drives away our fear.

2. It makes the wounded spirit whole,
   and calms the troubled breast;
   'tis manna to the hungry soul,
   and to the weary rest.

3. Dear name! the rock on which I build,
   my shield and hiding-place,
   my never-failing treas'ry filled
   with boundless stores of grace.

4. Jesus! my shepherd, brother, friend,
   my prophet, priest, and king,
   my Lord, my life, my way, my end,
   accept the praise I bring.

5. Weak is the effort of my heart,
   and cold my warmest thought;
   but when I see thee as thou art,
   I'll praise thee as I ought.

6. Till then I would thy love proclaim
   with ev'ry fleeting breath;
   and may the music of thy name
   refresh my soul in death.

John Newton (1725-1807) alt.

221

I am a new creation,
no more in condemnation,
here in the grace of God I stand.
My heart is overflowing,
my love just keeps on growing,
here in the grace of God I stand.
And I will praise you, Lord,
yes, I will praise you, Lord,
and I will sing of all that you have done.
A joy that knows no limit,
a lightness in my spirit,
here in the grace of God I stand.

Dave Bilbrough
© 1983 Kingsway's Thankyou Music

222

1. I am the bread of life.
   You who come to me shall not hunger;
   and who believe in me shall not thirst.
   No-one can come to me
   unless the Father beckons.

   And I will raise you up,
   and I will raise you up,
   and I will raise you up on the last day.

2. The bread that I will give
   is my flesh for the life of the world,
   and if you eat of this bread,
   you shall live for ever,
   you shall live for ever.

3. Unless you eat
   of the flesh of the Son of Man,
   and drink of his blood,
   and drink of his blood,
   you shall not have life within you.

4. I am the resurrection,
   I am the life.
   If you believe in me,
   even though you die,
   you shall live for ever.

5. Yes, Lord, I believe
   that you are the Christ,
   the Son of God,
   who has come
   into the world.

   Suzanne Toolan (b. 1927)

223

1. I am trusting thee, Lord Jesus,
   trusting only thee;
   trusting thee for full salvation,
   great and free.

2. I am trusting thee for pardon,
   at thy feet I bow;
   for thy grace and tender mercy,
   trusting now.

3. I am trusting thee for cleansing
   in the crimson flood;
   trusting thee to make me holy
   by thy blood.

4. I am trusting thee to guide me;
   thou alone shalt lead,
   ev'ry day and hour supplying
   all my need.

5. I am trusting thee for power,
   thine can never fail;
   words which thou thyself shalt give me
   must prevail.

6. I am trusting thee, Lord Jesus;
   never let me fall;
   I am trusting thee for ever,
   and for all.

   Frances Ridley Havergal (1836-1879)

224

1. I believe in Jesus;
   I believe he is the Son of God.
   I believe he died and rose again.
   I believe he paid for us all.
   And I believe he's here now
   standing in our midst;
   here with the power to heal now,
   and the grace to forgive.

   Continued overleaf

2. I believe in you, Lord;
   I believe you are the Son of God.
   I believe you died and rose again.
   I believe you paid for us all.
   And I believe you're here now
   standing in our midst;
   here with the power to heal now,
   and the grace to forgive.

Marc Nelson
© 1987 Mercy Vineyard Music/Kingsway's Thankyou Music

225

1. I bind unto myself today
   the strong name of the Trinity,
   by invocation of the same,
   Three in One and One in Three.

2. I bind this day to me for ever,
   by pow'r of faith, Christ's incarnation,
   his baptism in the Jordan river,
   his death on cross for my salvation;
   his bursting from the spicèd tomb,
   his riding up the heav'nly way,
   his coming at the day of doom,
   I bind unto myself today.

3. I bind unto myself the pow'r
   of the great love of cherubim;
   the sweet 'Well done!' in judgement
       hour;
   the service of the seraphim,
   confessors' faith, apostles' word,
   the patriarchs' prayers, the prophets'
       scrolls,
   all good deeds done unto the Lord,
   and purity of faithful souls.

PART TWO

4. Christ be with me, Christ within me,
   Christ behind me, Christ before me.
   Christ beside me, Christ to win me,
   Christ to comfort and restore me.
   Christ beneath me, Christ above me,
   Christ in quiet, Christ in danger,
   Christ in hearts of all that love me,
   Christ in mouth of friend and stranger.

DOXOLOGY

5. I bind unto myself the name,
   the strong name of the Trinity,
   by invocation of the same,
   the Three in One and One in Three,
   of whom all nature hath creation,
   eternal Father, Spirit, Word.
   Praise to the Lord of my salvation:
   salvation is of Christ the Lord.
   Amen.

ascribed to St. Patrick (373-463),
trans. Cecil Frances Alexander (1818-1895) alt.

226

1. I cannot tell
   how he whom angels worship
   should stoop to love
   the peoples of the earth,
   or why as shepherd
   he should seek the wand'rer
   with his mysterious promise
   of new birth.
   But this I know,
   that he was born of Mary,
   when Bethl'em's manger
   was his only home,
   and that he lived at
   Nazareth and laboured,
   and so the Saviour,
   Saviour of the world, is come.

2. I cannot tell
   how silently he suffered,
   as with his peace
   he graced this place of tears,
   or how his heart
   upon the cross was broken,
   the crown of pain
   to three and thirty years.
   But this I know,
   he heals the broken-hearted,
   and stays our sin,
   and calms our lurking fear,
   and lifts the burden
   from the heavy laden,
   for yet the Saviour,
   Saviour of the world, is here.

3. I cannot tell
   how he will win the nations,
   how he will claim
   his earthly heritage,
   how satisfy
   the needs and aspirations
   of east and west,
   of sinner and of sage.
   But this I know,
   all flesh shall see his glory,
   and he shall reap
   the harvest he has sown,
   and some glad day
   his sun shall shine in splendour
   when he the Saviour,
   Saviour of the world, is known.

4. I cannot tell
   how all the lands shall worship,
   when, at his bidding,
   ev'ry storm is stilled,
   or who can say
   how great the jubilation
   when ev'ry heart
   with perfect love is filled.

But this I know,
the skies will thrill with rapture,
and myriad, myriad
human voices sing,
and earth to heav'n,
and heav'n to earth, will answer:
'At last the Saviour,
Saviour of the world, is King!'

William Young Fullerton (1857-1932) alt.

227

1. I come with joy, a child of God,
   forgiven, loved and free,
   the life of Jesus to recall,
   in love laid down for me.

2. I come with Christians far and near
   to find, as all are fed,
   the new community of love
   in Christ's communion bread.

3. As Christ breaks bread, and bids us
      share,
   each proud division ends.
   The love that made us, makes us one,
   and strangers now are friends.

4. The Spirit of the risen Christ,
   unseen, but ever near,
   is in such friendship better known,
   alive among us here.

5. Together met, together bound
   by all that God has done,
   we'll go with joy, to give the world
   the love that makes us one.

Brian A. Wren (b. 1936)

228

1. I danced in the morning
   when the world was begun,
   and I danced in the moon
   and the stars and the sun,
   and I came down from heaven
   and I danced on the earth;
   at Bethlehem I had my birth.

   Dance, then, wherever you may be;
   I am the Lord of the Dance, said he,
   and I'll lead you all,
   wherever you may be,
   and I'll lead you all
   in the dance, said he.

2. I danced for the scribe
   and the pharisee,
   but they would not dance
   and they wouldn't follow me;
   I danced for the fishermen,
   for James and John;
   they came with me
   and the dance went on:

3. I danced on the Sabbath
   and I cured the lame:
   the holy people
   said it was a shame.
   They whipped and they stripped
   and they hung me high,
   and they left me there
   on a cross to die:

4. I danced on a Friday
   when the sky turned black;
   it's hard to dance
   with the devil on your back.
   They buried my body
   and they thought I'd gone;
   but I am the dance
   and I still go on:

5. They cut me down
   and I leapt up high;
   I am the life
   that'll never, never die;
   I'll live in you
   if you'll live in me:
   I am the Lord
   of the Dance, said he:

   Sydney Carter (b. 1915)

229

1. 'I do not know the man,'
   the fearful Peter said.
   No sharper nail could pierce the hand
   by which the world is fed,
   by which the world is fed!

2. The great disciple failed;
   his weakness we may own,
   and stand with him where judgement
     meets
   with grace, at Calv'ry's throne,
   with grace, at Calv'ry's throne.

3. Christ stands among us still,
   in those the world denies,
   and in the faces of the poor,
   we see his grieving eyes,
   we see his grieving eyes.

4. We cannot cleanse our hands
   of that most shameful spot,
   since of our brother we have said,
   'His keeper, I am not!'
   'His keeper, I am not!'

5. And yet, what love is this?
   Forgiveness all divine!
   Christ says of our poor faithless souls,
   'I know them, they are mine.'
   'I know them, they are mine.'

   Michael Forster (b. 1946)

230

1. I give you all the honour
   and praise that's due your name,
   for you are the King of Glory,
   the Creator of all things.

   And I worship you,
   I give my life to you,
   I fall down on my knees.
   Yes, I worship you,
   I give my life to you,
   I fall down on my knees.

2. As your Spirit moves upon me now,
   you meet my deepest need,
   and I lift my hands up to your throne,
   your mercy I've received.

3. You have broken chains that bound
     me,
   you've set this captive free;
   I will lift my voice to praise your name
   for all eternity.

   Carl Tuttle
   © *1982 Mercy Vineyard Music/Kingsway's Thankyou Music*

231

1. I heard the voice of Jesus say,
   'Come unto me and rest;
   lay down, thou weary one, lay down
   thy head upon my breast.'
   I came to Jesus as I was,
   so weary, worn and sad;
   I found in him a resting-place,
   and he has made me glad.

2. I heard the voice of Jesus say,
   'Behold, I freely give
   the living water, thirsty one;
   stoop down and drink and live.'
   I came to Jesus, and I drank
   of that life-giving stream;
   my thirst was quenched, my soul
     revived,
   and now I live in him.

3. I heard the voice of Jesus say,
   'I am this dark world's light;
   look unto me, thy morn shall rise,
   and all thy day be bright.'
   I looked to Jesus, and I found
   in him my star, my sun;
   and in that light of life I'll walk
   till trav'lling days are done.

   Horatius Bonar (1808-1889)

232

1. I know that my Redeemer lives!
   What joy the blest assurance gives!
   He lives, he lives, who once was dead;
   he lives, my everlasting Head!

2. He lives, to bless me with his love;
   he lives, to plead for me above;
   he lives, my hungry soul to feed;
   he lives, to help in time of need.

3. He lives, and grants me daily breath;
   he lives – for me he conquered death;
   he lives, my mansion to prepare;
   he lives, to lead me safely there.

4. He lives, all glory to his name;
   he lives, my Saviour, still the same;
   what joy the blest assurance gives!
   I know that my Redeemer lives!

   Samuel Medley (1738-1799) alt.

233

I love you, Lord,
and I lift my voice to worship you;
O my soul, rejoice.
Take joy, my King, in what you hear,
may it be a sweet, sweet sound
in your ear.

Laurie Klein
© 1978 Marantha! Music/CopyCare Ltd

234

1. I need thee ev'ry hour,
   most gracious Lord;
   no tender voice like thine
   can peace afford.

   I need thee, O I need thee!
   ev'ry hour I need thee;
   O bless me now,
   my Saviour! I come to thee.

2. I need thee ev'ry hour;
   stay thou near by;
   temptations lose their pow'r
   when thou art nigh.

3. I need thee ev'ry hour,
   in joy or pain;
   come quickly and abide,
   or life is vain.

4. I need thee ev'ry hour;
   teach me thy will,
   and thy rich promises
   in me fulfil.

5. I need thee ev'ry hour,
   most Holy One;
   O make me thine indeed,
   thou blessèd Son!

Annie Sherwood Hawks (1835-1918)

235

1. I, the Lord of sea and sky,
   I have heard my people cry.
   All who dwell in dark and sin
   my hand will save.
   I who made the stars of night,
   I will make their darkness bright.
   Who will bear my light to them?
   Whom shall I send?

   Here I am, Lord. Is it I, Lord?
   I have heard you calling in the night.
   I will go, Lord, if you lead me.
   I will hold your people in my heart.

2. I, the Lord of snow and rain,
   I have borne my people's pain.
   I have wept for love of them.
   They turn away.
   I will break their hearts of stone,
   give them hearts for love alone.
   I will speak my word to them.
   Whom shall I send?

3. I, the Lord of wind and flame,
   I will tend the poor and lame.
   I will set a feast for them.
   My hand will save.
   Finest bread I will provide
   till their hearts be satisfied.
   I will give my life to them.
   Whom shall I send?

Dan Schutte, based on Isaiah 6
© 1981 Daniel L. Schutte & New Dawn Music

236

I will enter his gates
with thanksgiving in my heart,
I will enter his courts with praise.
I will say this is the day
that the Lord has made.
I will rejoice
for he has made me glad.
He has made me glad.
He has made me glad.
I will rejoice
for he has made me glad.
He has made me glad.
He has made me glad.
I will rejoice
for he has made me glad.

Leona von Brethorst, based on Scripture
© 1976 Maranatha! Music/CopyCare Ltd

237

1. I will sing the wondrous story
   of the Christ who died for me,
   how he left the realms of glory
   for the cross on Calvary.
   Yes, I'll sing the wondrous story
   of the Christ who died for me –
   sing it with his saints in glory,
   gathered by the crystal sea.

2. I was lost but Jesus found me,
   found the sheep that went astray,
   raised me up and gently led me
   back into the narrow way.
   Days of darkness still may meet me,
   sorrow's path I oft may tread;
   but his presence still is with me,
   by his guiding hand I'm led.

3. He will keep me till the river
   rolls its waters at my feet:
   then he'll bear me safely over,
   made by grace for glory meet.
   Yes, I'll sing the wondrous story
   of the Christ who died for me –
   sing it with his saints in glory,
   gathered by the crystal sea.

Francis Harold Rawley (1854-1952)
© HarperCollins Religious/CopyCare Ltd

238

1. I wonder as I wander
   out under the sky,
   how Jesus the Saviour
   did come for to die
   for poor ord'n'ry people
   like you and like I.
   I wonder as I wander
   out under the sky.

2. When Mary birthed Jesus,
   'twas in a cow's stall
   with wise men and farmers
   and shepherds and all.
   But high from God's heaven
   a star's light did fall,
   and the promise of ages
   it did then recall.

3. If Jesus had wanted
   for any wee thing,
   a star in the sky,
   or a bird on the wing,
   or all of God's angels
   in heav'n for to sing,
   he surely could have it,
   'cause he was the King.

Traditional North American

239

I'm accepted, I'm forgiven,
I am fathered by the true
and living God.
I'm accepted, no condemnation,
I am loved by the true
and living God.
There's no guilt or fear as I draw near
to the Saviour
and Creator of the world.
There is joy and peace as I release
my worship to you, O Lord.

Rob Hayward
© 1985 Kingsway's Thankyou Music

240

1. I'm not ashamed to own my Lord,
   or to defend his cause;
   maintain the honour of his word,
   the glory of his cross.

2. Jesus, my God, I know his name;
   his name is all my trust;
   nor will he put my soul to shame,
   nor let my hope be lost.

3. Firm as his throne his promise stands;
   and he can well secure
   what I've committed to his hands,
   till the decisive hour.

4. Then will he own my worthless name
   before his Father's face;
   and in the new Jerusalem
   appoint my soul a place.

Isaac Watts (1674-1748)

241

1. If I were a butterfly,
   I'd thank you, Lord,
   for giving me wings,
   and if I were a robin in a tree,
   I'd thank you, Lord, that I could sing,
   and if I were a fish in the sea,
   I'd wiggle my tail
   and I'd giggle with glee,
   but I just thank you,
   Father, for making me me.

   For you gave me a heart
   and you gave me a smile,
   you gave me Jesus
   and you made me your child,
   and I just thank you,
   Father, for making me me.

2. If I were an elephant,
   I'd thank you, Lord,
   by raising my trunk,
   and if I were a kangaroo,
   you know I'd hop right up to you,
   and if I were an octopus,
   I'd thank you, Lord,
   for my fine looks,
   but I just thank you, Father,
   for making me me.

3. If I were a wiggly worm,
   I'd thank you, Lord,
   that I could squirm,
   and if I were a billy goat,
   I'd thank you, Lord,
      for my strong throat,
   and if I were a fuzzy wuzzy bear,
   I'd thank you, Lord,
   for my fuzzy wuzzy hair,
   but I just thank you, Father,
   for making me me.

Brian Howard
© 1974 Celebration/Kingsway's Thankyou Music

4. Great Father of glory,
   pure Father of light,
   thine angels adore thee,
   all veiling their sight;
   all laud we would render,
   O help us to see
   'tis only the splendour
   of light hideth thee.

Walter Chalmers Smith (1824-1908)
based on 1 Timothy 1:17

242

1. Immortal, invisible,
   God only wise,
   in light inaccessible
   hid from our eyes,
   most blessèd, most glorious,
   the Ancient of Days,
   almighty, victorious,
   thy great name we praise.

2. Unresting, unhasting,
   and silent as light,
   nor wanting, nor wasting,
   thou rulest in might;
   thy justice like mountains
   high soaring above
   thy clouds which are fountains
   of goodness and love.

3. To all life thou givest,
   to both great and small;
   in all life thou livest,
   the true life of all;
   we blossom and flourish
   as leaves on the tree,
   and wither and perish;
   but naught changeth thee.

243

1. Immortal love, for ever full,
   for ever flowing free,
   for ever shared, for ever whole,
   a never-ebbing sea.

2. Our outward lips confess the name
   all other names above;
   love only knoweth whence it came
   and comprehendeth love.

3. O warm, sweet, tender, even yet
   a present help is he;
   and faith has still its Olivet,
   and love its Galilee.

4. The healing of his seamless dress
   is by our beds of pain;
   we touch him in life's throng and press,
   and we are whole again.

5. Through him the first fond prayers
      are said
   our lips of childhood frame;
   the last low whispers of our dead
   are burdened with his name.

Continued overleaf

6. Alone, O love ineffable,
   thy saving name is giv'n;
   to turn aside from thee is hell,
   to walk with thee is heav'n.

   John Greenleaf Whittier (1807-1892)

244

1. In Christ there is no east or west,
   in him no south or north,
   but one great fellowship of love
   throughout the whole wide earth.

2. In him shall true hearts ev'rywhere
   their high communion find;
   his service is the golden cord,
   close binding humankind.

3. Join hands, united in the faith,
   whate'er your race may be;
   who serve my Father as their own
   are surely kin to me.

4. In Christ now meet both east and west,
   in him meet south and north;
   all Christlike souls are one in him,
   throughout the whole wide earth.

   John Oxenham (1852-1941) alt.

245

1. In full and glad surrender,
   I give myself to thee,
   thine utterly and only
   and evermore to be.

2. O Son of God, who lov'st me,
   I will be thine alone;
   and all I have and am, Lord,
   shall henceforth be thine own!

3. Reign over me, Lord Jesus,
   O make my heart thy throne;
   it shall be thine, dear Saviour,
   it shall be thine alone.

4. O come and reign, Lord Jesus,
   rule over ev'rything!
   And keep me always loyal
   and true to thee, my King.

   Frances Ridley Havergal (1836-1879)

246

1. In heav'nly love abiding,
   no change my heart shall fear;
   and safe is such confiding,
   for nothing changes here.
   The storm may roar without me,
   my heart may low be laid,
   but God is round about me,
   and can I be dismayed?

2. Wherever he may guide me,
   no want shall turn me back;
   my Shepherd is beside me,
   and nothing can I lack.
   His wisdom ever waketh,
   his sight is never dim,
   he knows the way he taketh,
   and I will walk with him.

3. Green pastures are before me,
   which yet I have not seen;
   bright skies will soon be o'er me,
   where the dark clouds have been.
   My hope I cannot measure,
   my path to life is free,
   my Saviour has my treasure,
   and he will walk with me.

   Anna Laetitia Waring (1820-1910) based on Psalm 23

247

1. In our day of thanksgiving
   one psalm let us offer
   for the saints who before us
   have found their reward;
   when the shadow of death
   fell upon them, we sorrowed,
   but now we rejoice
   that they rest in the Lord.

2. In the morning of life,
   and at noon, and at even,
   he called them away
   from our worship below;
   but not till his love,
   at the font and the altar,
   supplied them with grace
   for the way they should go.

3. These stones that have echoed
   their praises are holy,
   and dear is the ground
   where their feet have once trod;
   yet here they confessed
   they were strangers and pilgrims,
   and still they were seeking
   the city of God.

4. Sing praise, then, for all who
   here sought and here found him,
   whose journey is ended,
   whose perils are past:
   they believed in the light;
   and its glory is round them,
   where the clouds of earth's sorrow
   are lifted at last.

   William Henry Draper (1855-1993) alt.

248

1. In the bleak mid-winter
   frosty wind made moan,
   earth stood hard as iron,
   water like a stone;
   snow had fallen, snow on snow,
   snow on snow,
   in the bleak mid-winter, long ago.

2. Our God, heav'n cannot hold him
   nor earth sustain;
   heav'n and earth shall flee away
   when he comes to reign.
   In the bleak mid-winter
   a stable place sufficed
   the Lord God almighty, Jesus Christ.

3. Enough for him, whom cherubim
   worship night and day,
   a breastful of milk,
   and a mangerful of hay:
   enough for him, whom angels
   fall down before,
   the ox and ass and camel which adore.

4. Angels and archangels
   may have gathered there,
   cherubim and seraphim
   thronged the air;
   but only his mother
   in her maiden bliss
   worshipped the beloved with a kiss.

5. What can I give him,
   poor as I am?
   If I were a shepherd
   I would bring a lamb;
   If I were a wise man
   I would do my part,
   yet what I can I give him:
   give my heart.

   Christina Georgina Rossetti (1830-1894)

249

1. In the Cross of Christ I glory,
tow'ring o'er the wrecks of time;
all the light of sacred story
gathers round its head sublime.

2. When the woes of life o'ertake me,
hopes deceive, and fears annoy,
never shall the Cross forsake me;
Lo! it glows with peace and joy.

3. When the sun of bliss is beaming
light and love upon my way,
from the Cross the radiance streaming
adds more lustre to the day.

4. Bane and blessing, pain and pleasure,
by the Cross are sanctified;
peace is there that knows no measure,
joys that through all time abide.

John Bowring (1792-1872) based on Galatians 6:14

250

In the Lord I'll be ever thankful,
in the Lord I will rejoice!
Look to God, do not be afraid;
lift up your voices: the Lord is near,
lift up your voices: the Lord is near.

Taizé Community

251

1. Infant holy, infant lowly,
for his bed a cattle stall;
oxen lowing, little knowing
Christ the babe is Lord of all.
Swift are winging angels singing,
nowells ringing, tidings bringing,
Christ the babe is Lord of all,
Christ the babe is Lord of all.

2. Flocks were sleeping, shepherds keeping
vigil till the morning new;
saw the glory, heard the story,
tidings of a gospel true.
Thus rejoicing, free from sorrow,
praises voicing, greet the morrow,
Christ the babe was born for you,
Christ the babe was born for you.

From the Polish
trans. Edith Margaret Gellibrand Reed (1885-1933)

252

1. Inspired by love and anger,
disturbed by endless pain,
aware of God's own bias,
we ask him once again:
'How long must some folk suffer?
How long can few folk mind?
How long dare vain self-int'rest
turn prayer and pity blind?'

2. From those for ever victims
of heartless human greed,
their cruel plight composes
a litany of need:
'Where are the fruits of justice?
Where are the signs of peace?
When is the day when pris'ners
and dreams find their release?'

3. From those for ever shackled
to what their wealth can buy,
the fear of lost advantage
provokes the bitter cry:
'Don't query our position!
Don't criticise our wealth!
Don't mention those exploited
by politics and stealth!'

4. To God, who through the prophets
   proclaimed a diff'rent age,
   we offer earth's indiff'rence,
   its agony and rage:
   'When will the wronged be righted?
   When will the kingdom come?
   When will the world be gen'rous
   to all instead of some?'

5. God asks: 'Who will go for me?
   Who will extend my reach?
   And who, when few will listen,
   will prophesy and preach?
   And who, when few bid welcome,
   will offer all they know?
   And who, when few dare follow,
   will walk the road I show?'

6. Amused in someone's kitchen,
   asleep in someone's boat,
   attuned to what the ancients
   exposed, proclaimed and wrote,
   a Saviour without safety,
   a tradesman without tools
   has come to tip the balance
   with fishermen and fools.

   John L. Bell (b. 1949) and Graham Maule (b. 1958)

253

1. It came upon the midnight clear,
   that glorious song of old,
   from angels bending near the earth
   to touch their harps of gold:
   'Peace on the earth, goodwill to all,
   from heav'n's all-gracious King!'
   The world in solemn stillness lay
   to hear the angels sing.

2. Still through the cloven skies they
      come,
   with peaceful wings unfurled;
   and still their heav'nly music floats
   o'er all the weary world:
   above its sad and lowly plains
   they bend on hov'ring wing;
   and ever o'er its Babel-sounds
   the blessèd angels sing.

3. Yet with the woes of sin and strife
   the world has suffered long;
   beneath the angel-strain have rolled
   two thousand years of wrong;
   and warring humankind hears not
   the love-song which they bring:
   O hush the noise of mortal strife,
   and hear the angels sing!

4. And ye, beneath life's crushing load,
   whose forms are bending low,
   who toil along the climbing way
   with painful steps and slow:
   look now! for glad and golden hours
   come swiftly on the wing;
   O rest beside the weary road,
   and hear the angels sing.

5. For lo, the days are hast'ning on,
   by prophets seen of old,
   when with the ever-circling years
   comes round the age of gold;
   when peace shall over all the earth
   its ancient splendours fling,
   and all the world give back the song
   which now the angels sing.

   Edmund Hamilton Sears (1810-1876) alt.

254

1. It fell upon a summer day,
   when Jesus walked in Galilee,
   the mothers from a village
   brought their children to his knee.

2. He took them in his arms, and laid
   his hands on each remembered head;
   'Allow these little ones to come
   to me,' he gently said.

3. 'Forbid them not: unless ye bear
   the childlike heart your hearts within,
   unto my kingdom ye may come,
   but may not enter in.'

4. My Lord, I fain would enter there;
   O let me follow thee, and share
   thy meek and lowly heart, and be
   freed from all worldly care.

5. O happy thus to live and move,
   and sweet this world, where I shall find
   God's beauty everywhere, his love,
   his good in humankind.

6. Then, Father, grant this childlike heart,
   that I may come to Christ, and feel
   his hands on me in blessing laid,
   love-giving, strong to heal.

   Stopford Augustus Brooke (1832-1916) alt.

255

1. It is a thing most wonderful,
   almost too wonderful to be,
   that God's own Son should come from
     heav'n,
   and die to save a child like me.

2. And yet I know that it is true:
   he chose a poor and humble lot,
   and wept and toiled, and mourned and
     died,
   for love of those who loved him not.

3. I cannot tell how he could love
   a child so weak and full of sin;
   his love must be most wonderful,
   if he could die my love to win.

4. I sometimes think about the cross,
   and shut my eyes, and try to see
   the cruel nails and crown of thorns,
   and Jesus crucified for me.

5. But even could I see him die,
   I could but see a little part
   of that great love which, like a fire,
   is always burning in his heart.

6. It is most wonderful to know
   his love for me so free and sure;
   but 'tis more wonderful to see
   my love for him so faint and poor.

7. And yet I want to love thee, Lord;
   O light the flame within my heart,
   and I will love thee more and more,
   until I see thee as thou art.

   William Walsham How (1823-1897)

256

It's me, it's me, it's me, O Lord,
standing in the need of prayer.
It's me, it's me, it's me, O Lord,
standing in the need of prayer.

1. Not my brother or my sister,
   but it's me, O Lord,
   standing in the need of prayer.
   Not my brother or my sister,
   but it's me, O Lord,
   standing in the need of prayer.

2. Not my mother or my father,
   but it's me, O Lord,
   standing in the need of prayer.
   Not my mother or my father,
   but it's me, O Lord,
   standing in the need of prayer.

3. Not the stranger or my neighbour,
   but it's me, O Lord,
   standing in the need of prayer.
   Not the stranger or my neighbour,
   but it's me, O Lord,
   standing in the need of prayer.

Spiritual

5. 'Stir then the waters, Lord, stir up the
      wind;
   stir the hope that needs to be stretched;
   stir up the love that needs to be
      ground;
   stir the faith that needs to be fetched.'

6. James and Andrew, Peter and John,
   and the women close by his side,
   hear how the Lord calls each by their
      name,
   asking all to turn like the tide.

John L. Bell (b. 1949) and Graham Maule (b. 1958)

257

1. 'James and Andrew, Peter and John,
   men of temper, talent and tide,
   your nets are empty, empty and bare.
   Cast them now on the opposite side.'

2. 'Jesus, you're only a carpenter's son:
   joints and joists are part of your trade,
   but ours the skill to harvest the deep.
   Why presume to come to our aid?'

3. 'Friends of mine and brothers through
      love,
   I mean more than fishing for food.
   I call your skill to service my will,
   call your lives to harvest the good.'

4. 'Cast your nets where you think is
      right;
   spend your lives where you think is
      need;
   but if you long for that which is best,
   let it be on my word you feed.'

258

1. Jerusalem, my happy home,
   name ever dear to me,
   when shall my labours have an end?
   thy joys when shall I see?

2. Apostles, martyrs, prophets, there
   around my Saviour stand;
   and all I love in Christ below
   will join the glorious band.

3. Jerusalem, my happy home,
   when shall I come to thee?
   when shall my labours have an end?
   thy joys when shall I see?

4. O Christ, do thou my soul prepare
   for that bright home of love;
   that I may see thee and adore
   with all thy saints above.

Based on verses by F. B. P.,
an unknown author (c. 1600)

259

1. Jerusalem the golden,
   with milk and honey blest,
   beneath thy contemplation
   sink heart and voice oppressed.
   I know not, ah, I know not
   what joys await us there,
   what radiancy of glory,
   what bliss beyond compare.

2. They stand, those halls of Sion,
   all jubilant with song,
   and bright with many angels,
   and all the martyr throng;
   the prince is ever in them,
   the daylight is serene;
   the pastures of the blessèd
   are decked in glorious sheen.

3. There is the throne of David;
   and there, from care released,
   the shout of them that triumph,
   the song of them that feast;
   and they, who with their leader
   have fully run the race,
   are robed in white for ever
   before their Saviour's face.

4. O sweet and blessèd country,
   shall I e'er see thy face?
   O sweet and blessèd country,
   shall I e'er win thy grace?
   Exult, O dust and ashes!
   The Lord shall be thy part:
   his only, his for ever,
   thou shalt be, and thou art!

*from 'De Contemptu Mundi' by St. Bernard of Cluny
(12th century) trans. John Mason Neale
(1818-1866) alt.*

260

1. Jesu, grant me this, I pray,
   ever in thy heart to stay;
   let me evermore abide
   hidden in thy wounded side.

2. If the world or Satan lay
   tempting snares about my way,
   I am safe when I abide
   in thy heart and wounded side.

3. If the flesh, more dang'rous still,
   tempt my soul to deeds of ill,
   naught I fear when I abide
   in thy heart and wounded side.

4. Death will come one day to me;
   Jesu, cast me not from thee:
   dying let me still abide
   in thy heart and wounded side.

*Latin (17th century)
trans. Henry Williams Baker (1821-1877)*

261

1. Jesu, lover of my soul,
   let me to thy bosom fly,
   while the gath'ring waters roll,
   while the tempest still is high:
   hide me, O my Saviour, hide,
   till the storm of life is past;
   safe into the haven guide,
   O receive my soul at last.

2. Other refuge have I none,
hangs my helpless soul on thee;
leave, ah, leave me not alone,
still support and comfort me.
All my trust on thee is stayed,
all my help from thee I bring;
cover my defenceless head
with the shadow of thy wing.

3. Plenteous grace with thee is found,
grace to cleanse from ev'ry sin;
let the healing streams abound,
make and keep me pure within.
Thou of life the fountain art,
freely let me take of thee,
spring thou up within my heart,
rise to all eternity.

Charles Wesley (1707-1788) alt.

262

1. Jesu, priceless treasure,
source of purest pleasure,
truest friend to me;
ah, how long I've panted,
and my heart hath fainted,
thirsting, Lord, for thee!
Thine I am, O spotless Lamb,
I will let no other hide thee,
naught I ask beside thee.

2. Hence, all fears and sadness,
for the Lord of gladness,
Jesus, enters in;
they who love the Father,
though the storms may gather,
still have peace within;
yea, whate'er I here must bear,
still in thee lies purest pleasure,
Jesu, priceless treasure.

Johann Franck (1618-1677) alt.

263

1. Jesu, Son of Mary,
fount of life alone,
here we hail thee present
on thine altar-throne.

2. Humbly we adore thee,
Lord of endless might,
in the mystic symbols
veiled from earthly sight.

3. Think, O Lord, in mercy
on the souls of those
who, in faith gone from us,
now in death repose.

4. Here 'mid stress and conflict
toils can never cease;
there, the warfare ended,
bid them rest in peace.

5. Often were they wounded
in the deadly strife;
heal them, good Physician,
with the balm of life.

6. Ev'ry taint of evil,
frailty and decay,
good and gracious Saviour,
cleanse and purge away.

7. Rest eternal grant them,
after weary fight;
shed on them the radiance
of thy heav'nly light.

8. Lead them onward, upward,
to the holy place,
where thy saints made perfect
gaze upon thy face.

From the Swahili
trans. Edmund S. Palmer (1856-1931)

264

1. Jesu, the very thought of thee
   with sweetness fills the breast;
   but sweeter far thy face to see,
   and in thy presence rest.

2. No voice can sing, no heart can frame,
   nor can the mem'ry find,
   a sweeter sound than Jesu's name,
   the Saviour of mankind.

3. O hope of ev'ry contrite heart,
   O joy of all the meek,
   to those who ask how kind thou art,
   how good to those who seek!

4. But what to those who find? Ah, this
   nor tongue nor pen can show;
   the love of Jesus, what it is
   his true disciples know.

5. Jesu, our only joy be thou,
   as thou our prize wilt be;
   in thee be all our glory now,
   and through eternity.

St. Bernard of Clairvaux (1091-1153)
trans. Edward Caswall (1814-1878) alt.

265

1. Jesu, thou joy of loving hearts,
   thou fount of life, thou perfect grace;
   from the best bliss that earth imparts
   we turn unfilled to seek thy face.

2. Thy truth unchanged hath ever stood;
   thou savest those that on thee call;
   to them that seek thee thou art good,
   to them that find thee, all in all.

3. We taste thee, O thou living bread,
   and long to feast upon thee still;
   we drink of thee, the fountain-head,
   and thirst our souls from thee to fill.

4. Our restless spirits yearn for thee,
   where'er our changeful lot is cast,
   glad when thy gracious smile we see,
   blest when our faith is holding fast.

5. O Jesu, ever with us stay;
   make all our moments calm and bright;
   chase the dark night of sin away;
   shed o'er the world thy holy light.

'Jesu, dulcis memoria' (12th century)
trans. Ray Palmer (1808-1887) alt.

266

1. Jesus calls us: o'er the tumult
   of our life's wild, restless sea;
   day by day his sweet voice soundeth,
   saying, 'Christian, follow me.'

2. As of old Saint Andrew heard it
   by the Galilean lake,
   turned from home and toil and kindred,
   leaving all for his dear sake.

3. Jesus calls us from the worship
   of the vain world's golden store,
   from each idol that would keep us,
   saying, 'Christian, love me more.'

4. In our joys and in our sorrows,
   days of toil and hours of ease,
   still he calls, in cares and pleasures,
   that we love him more than these.

5. Jesus call us: by thy mercies,
   Saviour, make us hear thy call,
   give our hearts to thine obedience,
   serve and love thee best of all.

   Cecil Frances Alexander (1818-1895)

267

1. Jesus Christ is ris'n today, *alleluia!*
   our triumphant holy day, *alleluia!*
   who did once, upon the cross, *alleluia!*
   suffer to redeem our loss, *alleluia!*

2. Hymns of praise then let us sing,
   unto Christ, our heav'nly King,
   who endured the cross and grave,
   sinners to redeem and save.

3. But the pains that he endured,
   our salvation have procured;
   now above the sky he's King,
   where the angels ever sing.

   from 'Lyra Davidica' (1708)

268

1. Jesus Christ is waiting,
   waiting in the streets;
   no-one is his neighbour,
   all alone he eats.
   Listen, Lord Jesus,
   I am lonely too;
   make me, friend or stranger,
   fit to wait on you.

2. Jesus Christ is raging,
   raging in the streets
   where injustice spirals
   and all hope retreats.
   Listen, Lord Jesus,
   I am angry too;
   in the kingdom's causes
   let me rage with you.

3. Jesus Christ is healing,
   healing in the streets;
   curing those who suffer,
   touching those he greets.
   Listen, Lord Jesus,
   I have pity too;
   let my care be active,
   healing just like you.

4. Jesus Christ is dancing,
   dancing in the streets,
   where each sign of hatred
   his strong love defeats.
   Listen, Lord Jesus,
   I feel triumph too;
   on suspicion's graveyard,
   let me dance with you.

5. Jesus Christ is calling,
   calling in the streets,
   'Come and walk faith's tightrope,
   I will guide your feet.'
   Listen, Lord Jesus,
   let my fears be few;
   walk one step before me,
   I will follow you.

   John L. Bell (b. 1949) and Graham Maule (b. 1958)

269

1. Jesus, good above all other,
   gentle child of gentle mother,
   in a stable born our brother,
   give us grace to persevere.

2. Jesus, cradled in a manger,
   for us facing ev'ry danger,
   living as a homeless stranger,
   make we thee our King most dear.

3. Jesus, for thy people dying,
   risen Master, death defying,
   Lord in heav'n thy grace supplying,
   keep us to thy presence near.

4. Jesus, who our sorrows bearest,
   all our thoughts and hopes thou sharest,
   thou to us the truth declarest;
   help us all thy truth to hear.

5. Lord, in all our doings guide us;
   pride and hate shall ne'er divide us;
   we'll go on with thee beside us,
   and with joy we'll persevere.

Percy Dearmer (1867-1936)
after John Mason Neale (1818-1866) alt.

270

1. Jesus is Lord!
   Creation's voice proclaims it,
   for by his pow'r each tree and flow'r
   was planned and made.
   Jesus is Lord!
   The universe declares it;
   sun, moon and stars in heaven cry:
   Jesus is Lord!

Jesus is Lord!
Jesus is Lord!
Praise him with hallelujahs,
for Jesus is Lord.

2. Jesus is Lord!
   Yet from his throne eternal
   in flesh he came to die in pain
   on Calv'ry's tree.
   Jesus is Lord!
   From him all life proceeding,
   yet gave his life a ransom
   thus setting us free.

3. Jesus is Lord!
   O'er sin the mighty conqu'ror,
   from death he rose and all his foes
   shall own his name.
   Jesus is Lord!
   God sends his Holy Spirit
   to show by works of power
   that Jesus is Lord.

David J. Mansell
© *1982 Springtide/Word Music (UK)/CopyCare Ltd*

271

Jesus, Jesus,
holy and anointed one, Jesus.
Jesus, Jesus,
risen and exalted one, Jesus.
Your name is like honey on my lips,
your Spirit like water to my soul.
Your word is a lamp unto my feet.
Jesus, I love you, I love you.
Jesus, Jesus,
holy and anointed one, Jesus.
Jesus, Jesus,
risen and exalted one, Jesus.

John Barnett
© *1988 Mercy Vineyard Music/Kingsway's Thankyou Music*

272

1. Jesus lives! thy terrors now
   can no more, O death, appal us;
   Jesus lives! by this we know
   thou, O grave, canst not enthral us.
   Alleluia.

2. Jesus lives! henceforth is death
   but the gate of life immortal:
   this shall calm our trembling breath,
   when we pass its gloomy portal.
   Alleluia.

3. Jesus lives! for us he died;
   then, alone to Jesus living,
   pure in heart may we abide,
   glory to our Saviour giving.
   Alleluia.

4. Jesus lives! our hearts know well
   naught from us his love shall sever;
   life nor death nor pow'rs of hell
   tear us from his keeping ever.
   Alleluia.

5. Jesus lives! to him the throne
   over all the world is given:
   may we go where he is gone,
   rest and reign with him in heaven.
   Alleluia.

Christian Fürchtegott Gellert (1715-1769)
trans. Frances Elizabeth Cox (1812-1897) alt.

273

Jesus, name above all names,
beautiful Saviour, glorious Lord,
Emmanuel, God with us,
blessèd Redeemer, living Word.

Naida Hearn (b. 1944)
© 1974 Scripture in Song/CopyCare Ltd

274

1. Jesus, Prince and Saviour,
   Lord of life who died;
   Christ, the friend of sinners,
   mocked and crucified;
   for a world's salvation,
   he his body gave,
   lay at last death's victim,
   lifeless in the grave.

   Lord of life triumphant,
   risen now to reign!
   King of endless ages,
   Jesus lives again!

2. In his pow'r and Godhead
   ev'ry vict'ry won;
   pain and passion ended,
   all his purpose done.
   Christ the Lord is risen!
   sighs and sorrows past,
   death's dark night is over,
   morning comes at last!

3. Resurrection morning!
   sinners' bondage freed;
   Christ the Lord is risen –
   he is ris'n indeed!
   Jesus, Prince and Saviour,
   Lord of Life who died,
   Christ the King of Glory
   now is glorified!

Timothy Dudley-Smith (b. 1926)

275

1. Jesus put this song into our hearts,
   Jesus put this song into our hearts;
   it's a song of joy
   no-one can take away.
   Jesus put this song into our hearts.

2. Jesus taught us how to live in harmony,
   Jesus taught us how to live in harmony;
   diff'rent faces, diff'rent races,
   he made us one.
   Jesus taught us how to live in harmony.

3. Jesus taught us how to be a family,
   Jesus taught us how to be a family,
   loving one another
   with the love that he gives.
   Jesus taught us how to be a family.

4. Jesus turned our sorrow into dancing,
   Jesus turned our sorrow into dancing;
   changed our tears of sadness
   into rivers of joy.
   Jesus turned our sorrow into a dance.

Each verse should be sung faster

Graham Kendrick (b. 1950)
© 1986 Kingsway's Thankyou Music

276

Jesus, remember me
when you come into your kingdom.
Jesus, remember me
when you come into your kingdom.

Based on Scripture

277

1. Jesus shall reign where'er the sun
   does his successive journeys run;
   his kingdom stretch from shore to shore,
   till moons shall wax and wane no more.

2. People and realms of ev'ry tongue
   dwell on his love with sweetest song,
   and infant voices shall proclaim
   their early blessings on his name.

3. Blessings abound where'er he reigns:
   the pris'ners leap to lose their chains;
   the weary find eternal rest,
   and all the humble poor are blest.

4. To him shall endless prayer be made,
   and praises throng to crown his head;
   his name like incense shall arise
   with ev'ry morning sacrifice.

5. Let ev'ry creature rise and bring
   peculiar honours to our King;
   angels descend with songs again,
   and earth repeat the loud amen.

Isaac Watts (1674-1748)

278

Jesus shall take the highest honour,
Jesus shall take the highest praise;
let all earth join heav'n in exalting
the name which is
above all other names.
Let's bow the knee
in humble adoration,
for at his name ev'ry knee must bow;
let ev'ry tongue confess he is Christ,
God's only Son.

Sov'reign Lord, we give you glory now,
for all honour and blessing
and power belongs to you,
belongs to you.
All honour and blessing
and power belongs to you,
belongs to you,
Lord Jesus Christ,
Son of the living God.

Chris Bowater
© *1988 Sovereign Lifestyle Music*

279

1. Jesus, stand among us
   at the meeting of our lives,
   be our sweet agreement
   at the meeting of our eyes.

   O Jesus, we love you,
   so we gather here,
   join our hearts in unity
   and take away our fear.

2. So to you we're gath'ring
   out of each and ev'ry land,
   Christ the love between us
   at the joining of our hands.

   Optional verse for Communion

3. Jesus stand among us
   at the breaking of the bread;
   join us as one body
   as we worship you, our Head.

Graham Kendrick (b. 1950)
© *1977 Kingsway's Thankyou Music*

280

1. Jesus, stand among us
   in thy risen pow'r;
   let this time of worship
   be a hallowed hour.

2. Breathe the Holy Spirit
   into ev'ry heart;
   bid the fears and sorrows
   from each soul depart.

3. Thus with quickened footsteps
   we'll pursue our way,
   watching for the dawning
   of eternal day.

William Pennefather (1816-1873)

281

Jesus took a piece of bread,
he shared a cup of wine.
'Eat and drink with me,' he said,
'because you're friends of mine!'

1. We eat and drink with Jesus
   because we are his friends,
   remembering his promise
   of life that never ends.

2. We share with one another
   the bread and wine he gives,
   and celebrate together
   the special life he lives.

3. We rise up from the table,
   and go where Jesus sends,
   to tell the world the gospel
   of love that never ends.

Michael Forster (b. 1946)

282

1. Jesus, where'er thy people meet,
   there they behold thy mercy seat;
   where'er they seek thee thou art found,
   and ev'ry place is hallowed ground.

2. For thou, within no walls confined,
   inhabitest the humble mind;
   such ever bring thee when they come,
   and, going, take thee to their home.

3. Dear Shepherd of thy chosen few,
   thy former mercies here renew;
   here to our waiting hearts proclaim
   the sweetness of thy saving name.

4. Here may we prove the pow'r of prayer
   to strengthen faith and sweeten care,
   to teach our faint desires to rise,
   and bring all heav'n before our eyes.

5. Lord, we are few, but thou art near;
   nor short thine arm, nor deaf thine ear;
   O rend the heav'ns, come quickly down,
   and make a thousand hearts thine own.

William Cowper (1731-1800)

283

1. Joy to the world! The Lord is come;
   let earth receive her King;
   let ev'ry heart prepare him room
   and heav'n and nature sing,
   and heav'n and nature sing,
   and heav'n, and heav'n and nature sing!

2. Joy to the earth! The Saviour reigns;
   let us our songs employ;
   while fields and floods, rocks, hills and
     plains
   repeat the sounding joy,
   repeat the sounding joy,
   repeat, repeat the sounding joy.

3. He rules the world with truth and grace,
   and makes the nations prove
   the glories of his righteousness,
   and wonders of his love,
   and wonders of his love,
   and wonders, and wonders of his love.

Isaac Watts (1674-1748) alt.

284

Jubilate, ev'rybody,
serve the Lord in all your ways,
and come before his presence singing;
enter now his courts with praise.
For the Lord our God is gracious,
and his mercy everlasting.
Jubilate, jubilate, jubilate Deo!

Fred Dunn (1907-1979)
© 1977 Kingsway's Thankyou Music

285

1. Judge eternal, throned in splendour,
   Lord of lords and King of kings,
   with thy living fire of judgement
   purge this realm of bitter things:
   solace all its wide dominion
   with the healing of thy wings.

2. Still the weary folk are pining
   for the hour that brings release:
   and the city's crowded clangour
   cries aloud for sin to cease;
   and the homesteads and the
     woodlands
   plead in silence for their peace.

3. Crown, O God, thine own endeavour;
   cleave our darkness with thy sword;
   feed thy people's hungry spirits
   with the richness of thy word:
   cleanse the body of this nation
   through the glory of the Lord.

   Henry Scott Holland (1847-1918) alt.

286

1. Just a closer walk with thee,
   grant it, Jesus, if you please;
   daily walking close to thee,
   let it be, dear Lord, let it be.

2. Through the day of toil that's near,
   if I fall, dear Lord, who cares?
   Who with me my burden shares?
   None but thee, dear Lord, none but
     thee.

3. When my feeble life is o'er,
   time for me will be no more.
   Guide me gently, safely on
   to the shore, dear Lord, to the shore.

   Traditional

287

1. Just as I am, without one plea
   but that thy blood was shed for me,
   and that thou bidst me come to thee,
   O Lamb of God, I come.

2. Just as I am, though tossed about
   with many a conflict, many a doubt,
   fightings and fears within, without,
   O Lamb of God, I come.

3. Just as I am, poor, wretched, blind;
   sight, riches, healing of the mind,
   yea, all I need, in thee to find,
   O Lamb of God, I come.

4. Just as I am, thou wilt receive,
   wilt welcome, pardon, cleanse, relieve:
   because thy promise I believe,
   O Lamb of God, I come.

5. Just as I am, thy love unknown
   has broken ev'ry barrier down,
   now to be thine, yea, thine alone,
   O Lamb of God, I come.

6. Just as I am, of that free love
   the breadth, length, depth and height
     to prove,
   here for a season, then above,
   O Lamb of God, I come.

*When the tune 'Maunder' is used this
Refrain is added to each verse:*

*Just as I am, just as I am,
just as I am, I come.*

   Charlotte Elliott (1789-1871)

288

1. King of glory, King of peace,
   I will love thee;
   and, that love may never cease,
   I will move thee.
   Thou has granted my request,
   thou hast heard me;
   thou didst note my working breast,
   thou hast spared me.

2. Wherefore with my utmost art,
   I will sing thee,
   and the cream of all my heart
   I will bring thee.
   Though my sins against me cried,
   thou didst clear me,
   and alone, when they replied,
   thou didst hear me.

3. Sev'n whole days, not one in sev'n,
   I will praise thee;
   in my heart, though not in heav'n,
   I can raise thee.
   Small it is, in this poor sort
   to enrol thee:
   e'en eternity's too short
   to extol thee.

George Herbert (1593-1633)

289

1. Kum ba yah, my Lord, kum ba yah,
   kum ba yah, my Lord, kum ba yah,
   kum ba yah, my Lord, kum ba yah,
   O Lord, kum ba yah.

2. Someone's crying, Lord, kum ba yah,
   someone's crying, Lord, kum ba yah,
   someone's crying, Lord, kum ba yah,
   O Lord, kum ba yah.

3. Someone's singing, Lord, kum ba yah,
   someone's singing, Lord, kum ba yah,
   someone's singing, Lord, kum ba yah,
   O Lord, kum ba yah.

4. Someone's praying, Lord, kum ba yah,
   someone's praying, Lord, kum ba yah,
   someone's praying, Lord, kum ba yah,
   O Lord, kum ba yah.

Spiritual

290

Kyrie, Kyrie, eleison.

From the Roman Missal

291

Latin text

Laudate Dominum,
laudate Dominum,
omnes gentes, alleluia!
Laudate Dominum,
laudate Dominum,
omnes gentes, alleluia!

English text

Sing, praise and bless the Lord.
Sing, praise and bless the Lord,
peoples! nations! Alleluia!
Sing, praise and bless the Lord.
Sing, praise and bless the Lord,
peoples! nations! Alleluia!

Taizé Community (Psalm 117)

292

1. Lead, kindly Light,
   amid th'encircling gloom,
   lead thou me on;
   the night is dark,
   and I am far from home;
   lead thou me on.
   Keep thou my feet;
   I do not ask to see
   the distant scene;
   one step enough for me.

2. I was not ever thus,
   nor prayed that thou
   shouldst lead me on;
   I loved to choose
   and see my path; but now
   lead thou me on.
   I loved the garish day,
   and, spite of fears,
   pride ruled my will:
   remember not past years.

3. So long thy pow'r
   hath blest me, sure it still
   will lead me on,
   o'er moor and fen,
   o'er crag and torrent, till
   the night is gone;
   and with the morn
   those angel faces smile,
   which I have loved long since,
   and lost awhile.

John Henry Newman (1801-1890)

293

1. Lead us, heav'nly Father, lead us
   o'er the world's tempestuous sea;
   guard us, guide us, keep us, feed us,
   for we have no help but thee;
   yet possessing ev'ry blessing
   if our God our Father be.

2. Saviour, breathe forgiveness o'er us:
   all our weakness thou dost know;
   thou didst tread this earth before us,
   thou didst feel its keenest woe;
   lone and dreary, faint and weary,
   through the desert thou didst go.

3. Spirit of our God, descending,
   fill our hearts with heav'nly joy,
   love with ev'ry passion blending,
   pleasure that can never cloy:
   thus provided, pardoned, guided,
   nothing can our peace destroy.

James Edmeston (1791-1867)

294

1. Led like a lamb to the slaughter,
   in silence and shame,
   there on your back you carried a world
   of violence and pain.
   Bleeding, dying, bleeding, dying.

   You're alive, you're alive,
   you have risen!
   Alleluia! And the pow'r
   and the glory is given,
   alleluia! Jesus to you.

2. At break of dawn, poor Mary,
   still weeping she came,
   when through her grief she heard your
      voice
   now speaking her name.
   Mary, Master, Mary, Master.

3. At the right hand of the Father
   now seated on high
   you have begun your eternal reign
   of justice and joy.
   Glory, glory, glory, glory.

Graham Kendrick (b. 1950)
© 1983 Kingsway's Thankyou Music

295

1. Let all mortal flesh keep silence
   and with fear and trembling stand;
   ponder nothing earthly-minded,
   for with blessing in his hand
   Christ our God on earth descendeth,
   our full homage to demand.

2. King of kings, yet born of Mary,
   as of old on earth he stood,
   Lord of lords, in human vesture,
   in the body and the blood.
   He will give to all the faithful
   his own self for heav'nly food.

3. Rank on rank the host of heaven
   spreads its vanguard on the way,
   as the Light of light descendeth
   from the realms of endless day,
   that the pow'rs of hell may vanish
   as the darkness clears away.

4. At his feet the six-winged seraph;
   cherubim, with sleepless eye,
   veil their faces to the Presence,
   as with ceaseless voice they cry,
   Alleluia, Alleluia,
   Alleluia, Lord most high.

Liturgy of St. James trans. Gerard Moultrie (1829-1885)

296

1. Let all the world in ev'ry corner sing,
   my God and King!
   The heav'ns are not too high,
   his praise may thither fly;
   the earth is not too low,
   his praises there may grow.
   Let all the world in ev'ry corner sing,
   my God and King!

2. Let all the world in ev'ry corner sing,
   my God and King!
   The Church with psalms must shout,
   no door can keep them out;
   but, above all, the heart
   must bear the longest part.
   Let all the world in ev'ry corner sing,
   my God and King!

George Herbert (1593-1633)

297

1. Let saints on earth in concert sing
   with those whose work is done;
   for all the servants of our King
   in heav'n and earth are one.

2. One family, we dwell in him,
   one Church, above, beneath;
   though now divided by the stream,
   the narrow stream of death.

3. The people of the living God,
   to his command we bow:
   part of the host have crossed the flood,
   and part are crossing now.

4. E'en now to their eternal home
   there pass some spirits blest;
   while others to the margin come,
   waiting their call to rest.

5. Jesu, be thou our constant guide;
   then, when the word is giv'n,
   bid Jordan's narrow stream divide,
   and bring us safe to heav'n.

Charles Wesley (1707-1788) and others, alt.

298

1. Let there be love shared among us,
   let there be love in our eyes.
   May now your love sweep this nation;
   cause us, O Lord, to arise.
   Give us a fresh understanding,
   brotherly love that is real.
   Let there be love shared among us,
   Let there be love.

2. Let there be peace shared among us,
   let there be peace in our eyes.
   May now your peace sweep this nation;
   cause us, O Lord, to arise.
   Give us a fresh understanding,
   sisterly love that is real.
   Let there be peace shared among us,
   let there be peace.

3. Let there be hope shared among us,
   let there be hope in our eyes.
   May now your hope sweep this nation;
   cause us, O Lord, to arise.
   Give us a fresh understanding,
   brotherly love that is real.
   Let there be hope shared among us,
   let there be hope.

4. Let there be joy shared among us,
   let there be joy in our eyes.
   May now your joy sweep this nation;
   cause us, O Lord, to arise.
   Give us a fresh understanding,
   sisterly love that is real.
   Let there be joy shared among us,
   let there be joy.

5. Let there be love shared among us,
   let there be love in our eyes.
   May now your love sweep this nation;
   cause us, O Lord, to arise.
   Give us a fresh understanding,
   brotherly love that is real.
   Let there be love shared among us,
   let there be love.

Dave Bilbrough
© 1979 Kingway's Thankyou Music

299

1. Let us break bread together
   on our knees,
   let us break bread together
   on our knees.
   When I fall on my knees
   with my face to the rising sun,
   O Lord, have mercy on me.

2. Let us share wine together
   on our knees,
   let us share wine together
   on our knees.
   When I fall on my knees
   with my face to the rising sun,
   O Lord, have mercy on me.

3. Let us praise God together
   on our knees,
   let us praise God together
   on our knees.
   When I fall on my knees
   with my face to the rising sun,
   O Lord, have mercy on me.

Unknown

300

1. Let us praise God together, let us praise;
   let us praise God together all our days.
   He is faithful in all his ways,
   he is worthy of all our praise,
   his name be exalted on high.

2. Let us seek God together, let us pray;
   let us seek his forgiveness as we pray.
   He will cleanse us from all sin,
   he will help us the fight to win,
   his name be exalted on high.

3. Let us serve God together, him obey;
   let our lives show his goodness
      through each day.
   Christ the Lord is the world's true light,
   let us serve him with all our might,
   his name be exalted on high.

James Edward Seddon (1915-1983)

301

1. Let us talents and tongues employ,
   reaching out with a shout of joy:
   bread is broken, the wine is poured,
   Christ is spoken and seen and heard.

   Jesus lives again,
   earth can breathe again,
   pass the word around:
   loaves abound!

2. Christ is able to make us one,
   at his table he sets the tone,
   teaching people to live to bless,
   love in word and in deed express.

3. Jesus calls us in, sends us out
   bearing fruit in a world of doubt,
   gives us love to tell, bread to share:
   God-Immanuel everywhere!

Fred Kaan (b. 1929)

302

1. Let us, with a gladsome mind,
   praise the Lord, for he is kind;

   for his mercies ay endure,
   ever faithful, ever sure.

2. Let us blaze his name abroad,
   for of gods he is the God;

3. He, with all-commanding might,
   filled the new-made world with light;

4. He the golden-tressèd sun
   caused all day his course to run;

5. And the moon to shine at night,
   'mid her starry sisters bright;

6. All things living he doth feed,
   his full hand supplies their need;

7. Let us, with a gladsome mind,
   praise the Lord, for he is kind;

John Milton (1608-1674) based on Psalm 136

303

Lift high the Cross,
the love of Christ proclaim
till all the world
adore his sacred name!

1. Come, Christians, follow
   where our Saviour trod,
   o'er death victorious,
   Christ the Son of God.

2. Led on their way
   by this triumphant sign,
   the hosts of God
   in joyful praise combine:

3. Each new disciple
   of the Crucified
   is called to bear
   the seal of him who died:

4. Saved by the Cross
   whereon their Lord was slain,
   now Adam's children
   their lost home regain:

5. From north and south,
   from east and west they raise
   in growing harmony
   their song of praise:

6. O Lord, once lifted
   on the glorious tree,
   as thou hast promised,
   draw us unto thee:

7. Let ev'ry race
   and ev'ry language tell
   of him who saves
   from fear of death and hell:

8. From farthest regions,
   let them homage bring,
   and on his Cross
   adore their Saviour King:

9. Set up thy throne,
   that earth's despair may cease
   beneath the shadow
   of its healing peace:

10. For thy blest Cross
    which doth for all atone,
    creation's praises
    rise before thy throne:

11. So let the world
    proclaim with one accord
    the praises of
    our everliving Lord.

George William Kitchin (1827-1912)
and Michael Robert Newbolt (1874-1956) alt.

304

1. 'Lift up your hearts!'
   We lift them, Lord, to thee;
   here at thy feet
   none other may we see:
   'Lift up your hearts!'
   E'en so, with one accord,
   we lift them up,
   we lift them to the Lord.

2. Above the swamps
   of subterfuge and shame,
   the deeds, the thoughts,
   that honour may not name,
   the halting tongue
   that dares not tell the whole,
   O Lord of truth,
   lift ev'ry human soul.

3. Lift ev'ry gift
   that thou thyself hast giv'n:
   low lies the best
   till lifted up to heav'n;
   low lie the bounding heart,
   the teeming brain,
   till, sent from God,
   they mount to God again.

4. Then, as the trumpet-call,
   in after years,
   'Lift up your hearts!'
   rings pealing in our ears,
   still shall those hearts respond,
   with full accord,
   'We lift them up,
   we lift them to the Lord.'

Henry Montagu Butler (1833-1918) alt.

305

1. Light's abode, celestial Salem,
   vision whence true peace doth spring,
   brighter than the heart can fancy,
   mansion of the highest King;
   O how glorious are the praises
   which of thee the prophets sing!

2. There for ever and for ever
   alleluia is outpoured;
   for unending, for unbroken
   is the feast-day of the Lord;
   all is pure and all is holy
   that within thy walls is stored.

3. There no cloud or passing vapour
   dims the brightness of the air;
   endless noon-day, glorious noon-day,
   from the Sun of suns is there;
   there no night brings rest from labour,
   for unknown are toil and care.

4. O how glorious and resplendent,
   fragile body, shalt thou be,
   when endued with so much beauty,
   full of health and strong and free,
   full of vigour, full of pleasure
   that shall last eternally.

5. Now with gladness, now with courage,
   bear the burden on thee laid,
   that hereafter these thy labours
   may with endless gifts be paid;
   and in everlasting glory
   thou with brightness be arrayed.

6. Laud and honour to the Father,
   laud and honour to the Son,
   laud and honour to the Spirit,
   ever Three and ever One,
   consubstantial, co-eternal,
   while unending ages run.

Ascribed to Thomas à Kempis (c. 1379-1471)
trans. John Mason Neale (1818-1866)

306

1. Little Jesus, sweetly sleep, do not stir;
   we will lend a coat of fur;
   we will rock you, rock you, rock you,
   we will rock you, rock you, rock you,
   see the fur to keep you warm,
   snugly round your tiny form.

2. Mary's little baby sleep, sweetly sleep,
   sleep in comfort, slumber deep;
   we will rock you, rock you, rock you,
   we will rock you, rock you, rock you;
   we will serve you all we can,
   darling, darling little man.

Traditional Czech carol
trans. Percy Dearmer (1867-1936)

307

1. Lo, he comes with clouds descending,
   once for mortal sinners slain;
   thousand thousand saints attending
   swell the triumph of his train.
   Alleluia! Alleluia!
   Alleluia!
   Christ appears on earth to reign.

2. Ev'ry eye shall now behold him
   robed in dreadful majesty;
   we who set at naught and sold him,
   pierced and nailed him to the tree,
   deeply wailing, deeply wailing,
   deeply wailing,
   shall the true Messiah see.

3. Those dear tokens of his passion
   still his dazzling body bears,
   cause of endless exultation
   to his ransomed worshippers:
   with what rapture, with what rapture,
   with what rapture
   gaze we on those glorious scars!

4. Yea, amen, let all adore thee,
high on thine eternal throne;
Saviour, take the pow'r and glory,
claim the kingdom for thine own.
Alleluia! Alleluia!
Alleluia!
Thou shalt reign, and thou alone.

Charles Wesley (1707-1788), John Cennick
(1718-1755) and Martin Madan (1726-1790) alt.

308

1. Lord Christ, who on thy heart didst
bear
the burden of our shame and sin,
and now on high dost stoop to share
the fight without, the fear within;

2. Thy patience cannot know defeat,
thy pity will not be denied,
thy loving-kindness still is great,
thy tender mercies still abide.

3. O brother Man, for this we pray,
thou brother Man and sov'reign Lord,
that we thy brethren, day by day,
may follow thee and keep thy word;

4. That we may care, as thou hast cared,
for sick and lame, for deaf and blind,
and freely share, as thou hast shared,
in all the woes of humankind;

5. That ours may be the holy task
to help and bless, to heal and save;
this is the happiness we ask,
and this the service that we crave.
Amen.

Arnold Thomas (1848-1924) alt.

309

1. Lord, enthroned in heav'nly splendour,
first begotten from the dead,
thou alone, our strong defender,
liftest up thy people's head.
Alleluia, alleluia,
Jesu, true and living bread.

2. Here our humblest homage pay we,
here in loving rev'rence bow;
here for faith's discernment pray we,
lest we fail to know thee now.
Alleluia, alleluia,
thou art here, we ask not how.

3. Though the lowliest form doth veil
thee
as of old in Bethlehem,
here as there thine angels hail thee,
Branch and Flow'r of Jesse's Stem.
Alleluia, alleluia,
we in worship join with them.

4. Paschal Lamb, thine off'ring, finished
once for all when thou wast slain,
in its fulness undiminished
shall for evermore remain.
Alleluia, alleluia,
cleansing souls from ev'ry stain.

5. Life-imparting heav'nly manna,
stricken rock with streaming side,
heav'n and earth with loud hosanna
worship thee, the Lamb who died.
Alleluia, alleluia,
ris'n, ascended, glorified!

George Hugh Bourne (1840-1925)

310

1. Lord for the years
   your love has kept and guided,
   urged and inspired us,
   cheered us on our way,
   sought us and saved us,
   pardoned and provided:
   Lord of the years,
   we bring our thanks today.

2. Lord, for that word,
   the word of life which fires us,
   speaks to our hearts
   and sets our souls ablaze,
   teaches and trains,
   rebukes us and inspires us:
   Lord of the word,
   receive your people's praise.

3. Lord, for our land
   in this our generation,
   spirits oppressed by pleasure,
   wealth and care:
   for young and old,
   for commonwealth and nation,
   Lord of our land,
   be pleased to hear our prayer.

4. Lord, for our world;
   when we disown and doubt you,
   loveless in strength,
   and comfortless in pain,
   hungry and helpless,
   lost indeed without you:
   Lord of the world,
   we pray that Christ may reign.

5. Lord for ourselves;
   in living pow'r remake us –
   self on the cross
   and Christ upon the throne,
   past put behind us,
   for the future take us:
   Lord of our lives,
   to live for Christ alone.

Timothy Dudley-Smith (b. 1926)

311

1. Lord Jesus Christ,
   you have come to us,
   you are one with us,
   Mary's Son;
   cleansing our souls from all their sin,
   pouring your love and goodness in,
   Jesus, our love for you we sing,
   living Lord.

2. Lord Jesus Christ,
   now and ev'ry day
   teach us how to pray,
   Son of God.
   You have commanded us to do
   this in remembrance, Lord, of you.
   Into our lives your pow'r breaks
       through,
   living Lord.

3. Lord Jesus Christ,
   you have come to us,
   born as one of us,
   Mary's Son.
   Led out to die on Calvary,
   risen from death to set us free,
   living Lord Jesus, help us see
   you are Lord.

4. Lord Jesus Christ,
   I would come to you,
   live my life for you,
   Son of God.
   All your commands I know are true,
   your many gifts will make me new,
   into my life your pow'r breaks
      through,
   living Lord.

   Patrick Appleford (b. 1925)

312

1. Lord Jesus, think on me,
   and purge away my sin;
   from earth-born passions set me free,
   and make me pure within.

2. Lord Jesus, think on me,
   with care and woe opprest;
   let me thy loving servant be
   and taste thy promised rest.

3. Lord Jesus, think on me
   amid the battle's strife;
   in all my pain and misery
   be thou my health and life.

4. Lord Jesus, think on me,
   nor let me go astray;
   through darkness and perplexity
   point thou the heav'nly way.

5. Lord Jesus, think on me,
   when flows the tempest high:
   when on doth rush the enemy,
   O Saviour, be thou nigh.

6. Lord Jesus, think on me,
   that, when the flood is past,
   I may th'eternal brightness see,
   and share thy joy at last.

   Bishop Synesius (375-430)
   trans. Allen William Chatfield (1808-1896)

313

1. Lord of all hopefulness,
   Lord of all joy,
   whose trust, ever childlike,
   no cares could destroy,
   be there at our waking,
   and give us, we pray,
   your bliss in our hearts,
   Lord, at the break of the day.

2. Lord of all eagerness,
   Lord of all faith,
   whose strong hands were skilled
   at the plane and the lathe,
   be there at our labours,
   and give us, we pray,
   your strength in our hearts, Lord,
   at the noon of the day.

3. Lord of all kindliness,
   Lord of all grace,
   your hands swift to welcome,
   your arms to embrace,
   be there at our homing,
   and give us, we pray,
   your love in our hearts, Lord,
   at the eve of the day.

4. Lord of all gentleness,
   Lord of all calm,
   whose voice is contentment,
   whose presence is balm,
   be there at our sleeping,
   and give us, we pray,
   your peace in our hearts, Lord,
   at the end of the day.

   Jan Struther (1901-1953)

314

1. Lord of beauty, thine the splendour
   shown in earth and sky and sea,
   burning sun and moonlight tender,
   hill and river, flow'r and tree:
   lest we fail our praise to render
   touch our eyes that they may see.

2. Lord of wisdom, whom obeying
   mighty waters ebb and flow,
   while unhasting, undelaying,
   planets on their courses go:
   in thy laws thyself displaying,
   teach our minds thyself to know.

3. Lord of life, alone sustaining
   all below and all above,
   Lord of love, by whose ordaining
   sun and stars sublimely move:
   in our earthly spirits reigning,
   lift our hearts that we may love.

4. Lord of beauty, bid us own thee,
   Lord of truth, our footsteps guide,
   till as Love our hearts enthrone thee,
   and, with vision purified,
   Lord of all, when all have known thee,
   thou in all art glorified.

   Cyril Argentine Alington (1872-1955)

315

1. Lord of our life,
   and God of our salvation,
   star of our night,
   and hope of ev'ry nation,
   hear and receive
   thy Church's supplication,
   Lord God almighty.

2. Lord, thou canst help
   when earthly armour faileth,
   Lord, thou canst save
   when deadly sin assaileth;
   Christ, o'er thy rock
   nor death nor hell prevaileth;
   grant us thy peace, Lord.

3. Peace in our hearts,
   our evil thoughts assuaging;
   peace in thy Church,
   where people are engaging;
   peace, when the world
   its busy war is waging:
   calm all our raging.

4. Grant us thy grace
   through trial and temptation,
   grant us thy truth,
   thy promise of salvation,
   grant us thy peace
   in ev'ry heart and nation,
   and in thy heaven.

   *Philip Pusey (1799-1855) based on the German of
   Matthäus Apelles von Löwenstern (1594-1648) alt.*

316

1. Lord, teach us how to pray aright
   with rev'rence and with fear;
   though fallen sinners in thy sight,
   we may, we must, draw near.

2. Our spirits fail through lack of prayer:
   O grant us pow'r to pray;
   and, when to meet thee we prepare,
   Lord, meet us by the way.

3. God of all grace, we bring to thee
   a broken, contrite heart;
   give what thine eye delights to see,
   truth in the inward part;

4. Faith in the only sacrifice
   that can for sin atone,
   to cast our hopes, to fix our eyes,
   on Christ, on Christ alone;

5. Patience to watch and wait and weep,
   though mercy long delay;
   courage our fainting souls to keep,
   and trust in thee alway.

6. Give these, and then thy will be done;
   thus, strengthened with all might,
   we, through thy Spirit and thy Son,
   shall pray, and pray aright.

James Montgomery (1771-1854) alt.

317

1. Lord, the light of your love is shining,
   in the midst of the darkness, shining;
   Jesus, Light of the World,
       shine upon us,
   set us free by the truth
   you now bring us,
   shine on me, shine on me.

   Shine, Jesus, shine,
   fill this land with the Father's glory;
   blaze, Spirit, blaze,
   set our hearts on fire.
   Flow, river, flow,
   flood the nations with grace and
       mercy;
   send forth your Word, Lord,
   and let there be light.

2. Lord, I come to your
       awesome presence,
   from the shadows into your radiance;
   by the blood I may enter
       your brightness,
   search me, try me, consume
   all my darkness.
   Shine on me, shine on me.

3. As we gaze on your kingly brightness
   so our faces display your likeness,
   ever changing from glory to glory,
   mirrored here may our lives
   tell your story.
   Shine on me, shine on me.

Graham Kendrick (b. 1950)
© 1987 Make Way Music Ltd

318

1. Lord, thy word abideth,
   and our footsteps guideth;
   who its truth believeth
   light and joy receiveth.

2. When our foes are near us,
   then thy word doth cheer us,
   word of consolation,
   message of salvation.

3. When the storms are o'er us,
   and dark clouds before us,
   then its light directeth
   and our way protecteth.

4. Who can tell the pleasure,
   who recount the treasure,
   by thy word imparted
   to the simple-hearted?

5. Word of mercy, giving
   succour to the living;
   word of life, supplying
   comfort to the dying.

6. O that we, discerning
   its most holy learning,
   Lord, may love and fear thee,
   evermore be near thee.

Henry Williams Baker (1821-1877)

319

1. Lord, we come to ask your healing,
   teach us of love;
   all unspoken shame revealing,
   teach us of love.
   Take our selfish thoughts and actions,
   petty feuds, divisive factions,
   hear us now to you appealing,
   teach us of love.

2. Soothe away our pain and sorrow,
   hold us in love;
   grace we cannot buy or borrow,
   hold us in love.
   Though we see but dark and danger,
   though we spurn both friend and
       stranger,
   though we often dread tomorrow,
   hold us in love.

3. When the bread is raised and broken,
   fill us with love;
   words of consecration spoken,
   fill us with love.
   As our grateful prayers continue,
   make the faith that we have in you
   more than just an empty token,
   fill us with love.

4. Help us live for one another,
   bind us in love;
   stranger, neighbour, father, mother –
   bind us in love.
   All are equal at your table,
   through your Spirit make us able
   to embrace as sister, brother,
   bind us in love.

   Jean Holloway (b. 1939)

320

1. Love came down at Christmas,
   Love all lovely, Love divine;
   Love was born at Christmas,
   star and angels gave the sign.

2. Worship we the Godhead,
   Love incarnate, Love divine;
   worship we our Jesus:
   but wherewith for sacred sign?

3. Love shall be our token,
   love be yours and love be mine,
   love to God and all men,
   love for plea and gift and sign.

   Christina Georgina Rossetti (1830-1894)

321

1. Love divine, all loves excelling,
   joy of heav'n, to earth come down,
   fix in us thy humble dwelling,
   all thy faithful mercies crown.

2. Jesu, thou art all compassion,
   pure unbounded love thou art;
   visit us with thy salvation,
   enter ev'ry trembling heart.

3. Breathe, O breathe thy loving Spirit
   into ev'ry troubled breast;
   let us all in thee inherit,
   let us find thy promised rest.

4. Take away the love of sinning,
   Alpha and Omega be;
   end of faith, as its beginning,
   set our hearts at liberty.

5. Come, almighty to deliver,
   let us all thy grace receive;
   suddenly return, and never,
   never more thy temples leave.

6. Thee we would be always blessing,
   serve thee as thy hosts above;
   pray, and praise thee without ceasing,
   glory in thy perfect love.

7. Finish then thy new creation,
   pure and spotless let us be;
   let us see thy great salvation
   perfectly restored in thee.

8. Changed from glory into glory,
   till in heav'n we take our place,
   till we cast our crowns before thee,
   lost in wonder, love, and praise.

   Charles Wesley (1707-1788) alt.

322

1. Love is his word, love is his way,
   feasting with all, fasting alone,
   living and dying, rising again,
   love, only love, is his way.

   *Richer than gold is the love of my
      Lord:
   better than splendour and wealth.*

2. Love is his way, love is his mark,
   sharing his last Passover feast,
   Christ at the table, host to the twelve,
   love, only love, is his mark.

3. Love is his mark, love is his sign,
   bread for our strength, wine for our
      joy,
   'This is my body, this is my blood.'
   Love, only love, is his sign.

4. Love is his sign, love is his news,
   'Do this,' he said, 'lest you forget
   all my deep sorrow, all my dear blood.'
   Love, only love, is his news.

5. Love is his news, love is his name,
   we are his own, chosen and called,
   family, brethren, cousins and kin.
   Love, only love, is his name.

6. Love is his name, love is his law,
   hear his command, all who are his,
   'Love one another, I have loved you.'
   Love, only love, is his law.

7. Love is his law, love is his word:
   love of the Lord, Father and Word,
   love of the Spirit, God ever one,
   love, only love, is his word.

   Luke Connaughton (1917-1979) alt.

323

1. Love of the Father,
   love of God the Son,
   from whom all came,
   in whom was all begun;
   who formest heav'nly
   beauty out of strife,
   creation's whole desire
   and breath of life.

2. Thou the all-holy,
   thou supreme in might,
   thou dost give peace,
   thy presence maketh right;
   thou with thy favour
   all things dost enfold,
   with thine all-kindness
   free from harm wilt hold.

   Continued overleaf

3. Hope of all comfort,
   splendour of all aid,
   that dost not fail
   nor leave the heart afraid:
   to all that cry thou dost
   all help accord,
   the angels' armour,
   and the saints' reward.

4. Purest and highest,
   wisest and most just,
   there is no truth save
   only in thy trust;
   thou dost the mind
   from earthly dreams recall,
   and bring, through Christ,
   to him for whom are all.

5. Eternal glory,
   let the world adore,
   who art and shalt be
   worshipped evermore:
   us whom thou madest,
   comfort with thy might,
   and lead us to enjoy
   thy heav'nly light.

   Robert Bridges (1844-1930)
   based on 'Amor Patris et Filii' (12th century) alt.

324

1. Love's redeeming work is done;
   fought the fight, the battle won:
   lo, our Sun's eclipse is o'er,
   lo, he sets in blood no more.

2. Vain the stone, the watch, the seal;
   Christ has burst the gates of hell;
   death in vain forbids his rise;
   Christ has opened paradise.

3. Lives again our glorious King;
   where, O death, is now thy sting?
   Dying once, he all doth save;
   where thy victory, O grave?

4. Soar we now where Christ has led,
   foll'wing our exalted Head;
   made like him, like him we rise;
   ours the cross, the grave, the skies.

5. Hail the Lord of earth and heav'n!
   praise to thee by both be giv'n;
   thee we greet triumphant now;
   hail, the Resurrection thou!

   Charles Wesley (1707-1788)

325

1. Loving Shepherd of thy sheep,
   keep thy lamb, in safety keep;
   nothing can thy pow'r withstand,
   none can pluck me from thy hand.

2. Loving Shepherd, thou didst give
   thine own life that we might live;
   and the hands outstretched to bless
   bear the cruel nails' impress.

3. I would praise thee ev'ry day,
   gladly all thy will obey,
   like thy blessèd ones above
   happy in thy precious love.

4. Loving Shepherd, ever near,
   teach thy lamb thy voice to hear;
   suffer not my steps to stray
   from the straight and narrow way.

5. Where thou leadest I would go,
   walking in thy steps below;
   then, before my Father's throne,
   I shall know as I am known.

   Jane Elizabeth Leeson (1809-1881)

326

1. Low in the grave he lay,
   Jesus, my Saviour;
   waiting the coming day,
   Jesus, my Lord.

   Up from the grave he arose,
   with a mighty triumph o'er his foes;
   he arose a victor
   from the dark domain,
   and he lives for ever
   with his saints to reign.
   He arose! He arose!
   Hallelujah! Christ arose!

2. Vainly they watch his bed,
   Jesus, my Saviour;
   vainly they seal the dead,
   Jesus, my Lord.

3. Death cannot keep its prey,
   Jesus, my Saviour;
   he tore the bars away,
   Jesus, my Lord.

   Robert Lowry (1826-1899)

327

Majesty, worship his majesty;
unto Jesus be glory,
honour and praise.
Majesty, kingdom, authority
flow from his throne unto his own:
his anthem raise.
So exalt, lift up on high
the name of Jesus;

magnify, come glorify
Christ Jesus the King.
Majesty, worship his majesty,
Jesus who died, now glorified,
King of all kings.

Jack W. Hayford (b. 1934)

328

1. Make me a channel of your peace.
   Where there is hatred,
   let me bring your love.
   Where there is injury,
   your pardon, Lord,
   and where there's doubt,
   true faith in you.

   O Master, grant that I may never seek
   so much to be consoled as to console,
   to be understood, as to understand,
   to be loved, as to love with all my soul.

2. Make me a channel of your peace.
   Where there's despair in life,
   let me bring hope.
   Where there is darkness,
   only light,
   and where there's sadness,
   ever joy.

3. Make me a channel of your peace.
   It is in pardoning
   that we are pardoned,
   in giving of ourselves
   that we receive,
   and in dying
   that we're born to eternal life.

   The Refrain is not sung after this verse.

   Sebastian Temple (b. 1928)
   based on the Prayer of St. Francis
   © 1967 OCP Publications

329

1. Make way, make way,
   for Christ the King in splendour arrives;
   fling wide the gates
   and welcome him into your lives.

   Make way, make way,
   for the King of kings;
   make way, make way,
   and let his kingdom in!

2. He comes the broken hearts to heal,
   the pris'ners to free;
   the deaf shall hear, the lame shall dance,
   the blind shall see.

3. And those who mourn with heavy
         hearts,
   who weep and sigh,
   with laughter, joy and royal crown
   he'll beautify.

4. We call you now to worship him
   as Lord of all,
   to have no gods before him,
   their thrones must fall!

   Graham Kendrick (b. 1950)
   © 1986 Make Way Music

330

1. Man of sorrows! What a name
   for the Son of God who came
   ruined sinners to reclaim!
   Alleluia! What a Saviour!

2. Bearing shame and scoffing rude,
   in my place condemned he stood;
   sealed my pardon with his blood;
   Alleluia! What a Saviour!

3. Guilty, vile and helpless we;
   spotless Lamb of God was he:
   full atonement – can it be?
   Alleluia! What a Saviour!

4. Lifted up was he to die:
   'It is finished!' was his cry;
   now in heav'n exalted high;
   Alleluia! What a Saviour!

5. When he comes, our glorious King,
   all his ransomed home to bring,
   then anew this song we'll sing:
   Alleluia! what a Saviour!

   Philipp Bliss (1838-1876) alt.

331

1. Mary, blessed grieving mother,
   waiting by the cross of shame,
   through your patient, prayerful vigil,
   kindle hope's eternal flame;
   crying in the pains of earth,
   singing of redemption's birth.

2. Where the crosses of the nations
   darken still the noon-day skies,
   see the sad madonna weeping
   through a million mothers' eyes.
   Holy Mary, full of grace,
   all our tears with yours embrace.

3. Standing with the suff'ring Saviour,
   still oppressed by hate and fear,
   where the gentle still are murdered
   and protestors disappear:
   mother of the crucified,
   call his people to your side!

4. Holy mother, watching, waiting,
   for the saving of the earth;
   in the loneliness of dying,
   speak of hope and human worth,
   there for all the world to see,
   lifted up at Calvary!

   Michael Forster (b. 1946)

332

1. Mary, blessed teenage mother,
   with what holy joy you sing!
   Humble, yet above all other,
   from your womb shall healing spring.
   Out of wedlock pregnant found,
   full of grace with blessing crowned.

2. Mother of the homeless stranger
   only outcasts recognise,
   point us to the modern manger;
   not a sight for gentle eyes!
   O the joyful news we tell:
   'Even here, Immanuel!'

3. Now, throughout the townships
      ringing,
   hear the black madonna cry,
   songs of hope and freedom singing,
   poor and humble lifted high.
   Here the Spirit finds a womb
   for the breaker of the tomb!

4. Holy mother, for the nations
   bring to birth the child divine:
   Israel's strength and consolation,
   and the hope of Palestine!
   All creation reconciled
   in the crying of a child!

   Michael Forster (b. 1946)

333

1. May the grace of Christ our Saviour,
   and the Father's boundless love,
   with the Holy Spirit's favour,
   rest upon us from above.

2. Thus may we abide in union
   with each other and the Lord,
   and possess, in sweet communion,
   joys which earth cannot afford.

   John Newton (1725-1807)
   based on 2 Corinthians 13:14

334

1. May the mind of Christ my Saviour
   live in me from day to day,
   by his love and pow'r controlling
   all I do and say.

2. May the word of God dwell richly
   in my heart from hour to hour,
   so that I may triumph only
   in his saving pow'r.

3. May the peace of God my Father
   rule my life in ev'rything,
   that I may be calm to comfort
   sick and sorrowing.

4. May the love of Jesus fill me,
   as the waters fill the sea;
   him exalting, self abasing,
   this is victory.

5. May I run the race before me,
   strong and brave to face the foe,
   looking only unto Jesus,
   as I onward go.

   Kate Barclay Wilkinson (1859-1928)

335

1. Meekness and majesty,
   manhood and deity,
   in perfect harmony,
   the man who is God.
   Lord of eternity
   dwells in humanity,
   kneels in humility
   and washes our feet.

   O, what a mystery,
   meekness and majesty,
   bow down and worship,
   for this is your God.
   This is your God.

2. Father's pure radiance,
   perfect in innocence,
   yet learns obedience
   to death on a cross.
   Suff'ring to give us life,
   conqu'ring through sacrifice;
   and as they crucify
   prays: 'Father forgive'.

3. Wisdom unsearchable,
   God the invisible;
   love indestructible
   in frailty appears.
   Lord of infinity,
   stooping so tenderly,
   lifts our humanity
   to the heights of his throne.

Graham Kendrick (b. 1950)
© 1986 Kingsway's Thankyou Music

336

1. Mine eyes have seen the glory
   of the coming of the Lord.
   He is tramping out the vintage
   where the grapes of wrath are stored.
   He has loosed the fateful lightning
   of his terrible swift sword.
   His truth is marching on.

   Glory, glory hallelujah!
   Glory, glory hallelujah!
   Glory, glory hallelujah!
   His truth is marching on.

2. I have seen him in the watchfires
   of a hundred circling camps.
   They have gilded him an altar
   in the evening dews and damps.
   I can read his righteous sentence
   by the dim and flaring lamps.
   His day is marching on.

3. He has sounded forth the trumpet
   that shall never sound retreat.
   He is sifting out all human hearts
   before his judgement seat.
   O, be swift my soul to answer him,
   be jubilant my feet!
   Our God is marching on.

4. In the beauty of the lilies
   Christ was born across the sea,
   with a glory in his bosom
   that transfigures you and me.
   As he died to make us holy,
   let us live that all be free,
   whilst God is marching on.

Julia Ward Howe (1819-1910) alt.

337

1. Morning has broken
   like the first morning;
   blackbird has spoken
   like the first bird.
   Praise for the singing!
   Praise for the morning!
   Praise for them, springing
   fresh from the Word!

2. Sweet the rain's new fall,
   sunlit from heaven,
   like the first dew-fall
   on the first grass.
   Praise for the sweetness
   of the wet garden,
   sprung from completeness
   where his feet pass.

3. Mine is the sunlight!
   Mine is the morning
   born of the one light
   Eden saw play!
   Praise with elation,
   praise ev'ry morning,
   God's re-creation
   of the new day!

   Eleanor Farjeon (1881-1965)

338

1. 'Moses, I know you're the man,'
   the Lord said.
   'You're going to work out my plan,'
   the Lord said.
   'Lead all the Israelites
   out of slavery,
   and I shall make them a
   wandering race
   called the people of God.'

So ev'ry day
we're on our way,
for we're a travelling, wandering race
called the people of God.

2. 'Don't get too set in your ways,'
   the Lord said.
   'Each step is only a phase,'
   the Lord said.
   'I'll go before you and
   I shall be a sign
   to guide my travelling,
   wandering race.
   You're the people of God.'

3. 'No matter what you may do,'
   the Lord said,
   'I shall be faithful and true,'
   the Lord said.
   'My love will strengthen you
   as you go along,
   for you're my travelling,
   wandering race.
   You're the people of God.'

4. 'Look at the birds in the air,'
   the Lord said.
   'They fly unhampered by care,'
   the Lord said.
   'You will move easier
   if you're travelling light,
   for you're a wandering,
   vagabond race.
   You're the people of God.'

5. 'Foxes have places to go,'
   the Lord said,
   'but I've no home here below,'
   the Lord said.
   'So if you want to be with me
   all your days,
   keep up the moving
   and travelling on.
   You're the people of God.'

   Estelle White (b. 1925)

339

1. My faith looks up to thee,
   thou Lamb of Calvary,
   Saviour divine!
   Now hear me while I pray,
   take all my guilt away,
   O let me from this day
   be wholly thine.

2. May thy rich grace impart
   strength to my fainting heart,
   my zeal inspire.
   As thou hast died for me,
   O may my love to thee
   pure, warm and changeless be,
   a living fire.

3. While life's dark maze I tread,
   and griefs around me spread,
   be thou my guide;
   bid darkness turn to day,
   wipe sorrow's tears away,
   nor let me ever stray
   from thee aside.

4. When ends life's transient dream,
   when death's cold sullen stream
   shall o'er me roll,
   blest Saviour, then in love,
   fear and distrust remove;
   O bear me safe above,
   a ransomed soul.

   Ray Palmer (1808-1887)

340

1. My Father, for another night
   of quiet sleep and rest,
   for all the joy of morning light,
   thy holy name be blest.

2. Now with the new-born day I give
   myself anew to thee,
   that as thou willest I may live,
   and what thou willest be.

3. Whate'er I do, things great or small,
   whate'er I speak or frame,
   thy glory may I seek in all,
   do all in Jesus' name.

4. My Father, for his sake, I pray,
   thy child accept and bless;
   and lead me by thy grace today
   in paths of righteousness.

   Henry Williams Baker (1821-1877)

341

1. My God, accept my heart this day,
   and make it always thine,
   that I from thee no more may stray,
   no more from thee decline.

2. Before the cross of him who died,
   behold, I prostrate fall;
   let ev'ry sin be crucified,
   and Christ be all in all.

3. Anoint me with thy heav'nly grace,
   and seal me for thine own;
   that I may see thy glorious face,
   and worship near thy throne.

4. Let ev'ry thought and work and word
   to thee be ever giv'n:
   then life shall be thy service, Lord,
   and death the gate of heav'n.

5. All glory to the Father be,
   all glory to the Son,
   all glory, Holy Ghost, to thee,
   while endless ages run.

   Matthew Bridges (1800-1894)

342

1. My God, and is thy table spread,
and does thy cup with love o'erflow?
Thither be all thy children led,
and let them all thy sweetness know.

2. Hail, sacred feast, which Jesus makes!
Rich banquet of his flesh and blood!
Thrice happy all, who here partake
that sacred stream, that heav'nly food.

3. What wondrous love! What perfect
grace,
for Jesus, our exalted host,
invites us to this special place
who offer least and need the most.

4. O let thy table honoured be,
and furnished well with joyful guests:
and may each soul salvation see,
that here its sacred pledges tastes.

Philip Doddridge (1702-1751) alt.,
v. 3: Michael Forster (b. 1946)

343

1. My God, how wonderful thou art,
thy majesty how bright,
how beautiful thy mercy-seat,
in depths of burning light!

2. How dread are thine eternal years,
O everlasting Lord,
by prostrate spirits day and night
incessantly adored!

3. How wonderful, how beautiful,
the sight of thee must be,
thine endless wisdom, boundless
pow'r,
and awesome purity!

4. O how I fear thee, living God,
with deepest, tend'rest fears,
and worship thee with trembling hope,
and penitential tears!

5. Yet I may love thee too, O Lord,
almighty as thou art,
for thou hast stooped to ask of me
the love of my poor heart.

6. No earthly father loves like thee,
no mother, e'er so mild,
bears and forbears as thou hast done
with me thy sinful child.

7. Father of Jesus, love's reward,
what rapture will it be,
prostrate before thy throne to lie,
and gaze and gaze on thee!

Frederick William Faber (1814-1863)

344

1. My God, I love thee; not because
I hope for heav'n thereby,
nor yet because who love thee not
are lost eternally.

2. Thou, O my Jesus, thou didst me
upon the cross embrace;
for me didst bear the nails and spear,
and manifold disgrace.

3. And griefs and torments numberless,
and sweat of agony;
yea, death itself – and all for me
who was thine enemy.

4. Then why, O blessèd Jesu Christ,
should I not love thee well?
Not for the sake of winning heav'n,
nor of escaping hell.

Continued overleaf

5. Not from the hope of gaining aught,
   not seeking a reward;
   but as thyself hast lovèd me,
   O ever-loving Lord.

6. So would I love thee, dearest Lord,
   and in thy praise will sing;
   solely because thou art my God,
   and my most loving King.

Latin (17th century)
trans. Edward Caswall (1814-1878)

345

1. My Lord, what love is this
   that pays so dearly,
   that I, the guilty one,
   may go free!

   Amazing love,
   O what sacrifice,
   the Son of God giv'n for me.
   My debt he pays and my death he dies,
   that I might live, that I might live.

2. And so they watched him die,
   despised, rejected;
   but oh, the blood he shed
   flowed for me!

3. And now this love of Christ
   shall flow like rivers;
   come wash your guilt away,
   live again!

Graham Kendrick (b. 1950)
© 1989 Make Way Music Ltd

346

1. My song is love unknown,
   my Saviour's love to me,
   love to the loveless shown,
   that they might lovely be.
   O who am I, that for my sake,
   my Lord should take frail flesh and die?

2. He came from his blest throne,
   salvation to bestow;
   but sin made blind, and none
   the longed-for Christ would know.
   But O, my friend, my friend indeed,
   who at my need his life did spend!

3. Sometimes they strew his way,
   and his sweet praises sing;
   resounding all the day
   hosannas to their King;
   then 'Crucify!' is all their breath,
   and for his death they thirst and cry.

4. Why, what hath my Lord done?
   What makes this rage and spite?
   He made the lame to run,
   he gave the blind their sight.
   Sweet injuries! Yet they at these
   themselves displease, and 'gainst him
     rise.

5. They rise, and needs will have
   my dear Lord made away;
   a murderer they save,
   the Prince of Life they slay.
   Yet cheerful he to suff'ring goes,
   that he his foes from thence might free.

6. Here might I stay and sing,
   no story so divine;
   never was love, dear King,
   never was grief like thine.
   This is my friend in whose sweet praise
   I all my days could gladly spend.

   Samuel Crossman (c. 1624-1684) alt.

347

Spanish text

Nada te turbe,
nada te espante.
Quien a Dios tiene
nada le falta.
Nada te turbe,
nada te espante.
Solo Dios basta.

English text

Nothing can trouble,
nothing can frighten.
Those who seek God shall
never go wanting.
Nothing can trouble,
nothing can frighten.
God alone fills us.

   St. Teresa of Avila

348

1. Nearer, my God, to thee,
   nearer to thee!
   E'en though it be a cross
   that raiseth me:
   still all my song would be,
   'Nearer, my God, to thee,
   nearer to thee.'

2. Though, like the wanderer,
   the sun gone down,
   darkness be over me,
   my rest a stone;
   yet in my dreams I'd be
   nearer, my God, to thee,
   nearer to thee!

3. There let the way appear,
   steps unto heav'n;
   all that thou sendest me
   in mercy giv'n:
   angels to beckon me
   nearer, my God, to thee,
   nearer to thee!

4. Then, with my waking thoughts
   bright with thy praise,
   out of my stony griefs
   Bethel I'll raise;
   so by my woes to be
   nearer, my God, to thee,
   nearer to thee!

5. Or if on joyful wing
   cleaving the sky,
   sun, moon and stars forgot,
   upwards I fly,
   still all my song shall be,
   'Nearer, my God, to thee,
   nearer to thee.'

   Sarah Flower Adams (1805-1848)

349

1. New ev'ry morning is the love
   our wak'ning and uprising prove;
   through sleep and darkness safely
     brought,
   restored to life and pow'r and thought.

2. New mercies, each returning day,
   hover around us while we pray;
   new perils past, new sins forgiv'n,
   new thoughts of God, new hopes of
     heav'n.

3. If on our daily course our mind
   be set to hallow all we find,
   new treasures still, of countless price,
   God will provide for sacrifice.

4. Old friends, old scenes, will lovelier be,
   as more of heav'n in each we see;
   some soft'ning gleam of love and prayer
   shall dawn on ev'ry cross and care.

5. The trivial round, the common task,
   will furnish all we need to ask,
   room to deny ourselves, a road
   to bring us daily nearer God.

6. Only, O Lord, in thy dear love
   fit us for perfect rest above;
   and help us, this and ev'ry day,
   to live more nearly as we pray.

John Keble (1792-1866) based on Lamentations 3:23

350

1. New songs of celebration render
   to him who has great wonders done.
   Love sits enthroned in ageless
     splendour:
   come and adore the mighty one.
   He has made known his great salvation
   which all his friends with joy confess:
   he has revealed to ev'ry nation
   his everlasting righteousness.

2. Joyfully, heartily resounding,
   let ev'ry instrument and voice
   peal out the praise of grace abounding,
   calling the whole world to rejoice.
   Trumpets and organs, set in motion
   such sounds as make the heavens ring;
   all things that live in earth and ocean,
   make music for your mighty King.

3. Rivers and seas and torrents roaring,
   honour the Lord with wild acclaim;
   mountains and stones look up adoring
   and find a voice to praise his name.
   Righteous, commanding, ever glorious,
   praises be his that never cease:
   just is our God, whose truth victorious
   establishes the world in peace.

Erik Routley (1917-1982)
© 1974 Hope Publishing Co

351

1. Now is eternal life,
   if ris'n with Christ we stand,
   in him to life reborn,
   and held within his hand;
   no more we fear death's ancient dread,
   in Christ arisen from the dead.

2. The human mind so long
   brooded o'er life's brief span;
   was it, O God, for naught,
   for naught that life began?
   Thou art our hope, our vital breath;
   shall hope undying end in death?

3. And God, the living God,
   stooped down to share our state;
   by death destroying death,
   Christ opened wide life's gate.
   He lives, who died; he reigns on high;
   who lives in him shall never die.

4. Unfathomed love divine,
   reign thou within my heart;
   from thee nor depth nor height,
   nor life nor death can part;
   my life is hid in God with thee,
   now and through all eternity.

5. Thee will I love and serve
   now in time's passing day;
   thy hand shall hold me fast
   when time is done away,
   in God's unknown eternal spheres
   to serve him through eternal years.

George Wallace Briggs (1875-1959) alt.

352

1. Now let us from this table rise,
   renewed in body, mind and soul;
   with Christ we die and live again,
   his selfless love has made us whole.

2. With minds alert, upheld by grace,
   to spread the Word in speech and
     deed,
   we follow in the steps of Christ,
   at one with all in hope and need.

3. To fill each human house with love,
   it is the sacrament of care;
   the work that Christ began to do
   we humbly pledge ourselves to share.

4. Then give us courage, living God,
   to choose again the pilgrim way,
   and help us to accept with joy
   the challenge of tomorrow's day.

Fred Kaan (b. 1929)

353

1. Now, my tongue, the myst'ry telling
   of the glorious body sing,
   and the blood, all price excelling,
   which the Gentiles' Lord and King,
   in a virgin's womb once dwelling,
   shed for this world's ransoming.

2. Giv'n for us, for us descending
   of a virgin to proceed,
   he, with us in converse blending,
   scattered here the gospel seed,
   till his sojourn drew to ending
   which he closed with wondrous deed.

3. At the last great supper lying,
   circled by his chosen band,
   meekly with the law complying,
   first he finished its command.
   Then, immortal food supplying,
   gave himself with his own hand.

4. Word made flesh, by word he maketh
   very bread his flesh to be;
   we, in wine, Christ's blood partaketh,
   and if senses fail to see,
   faith alone the true heart waketh,
   to behold the mystery.

Continued overleaf

5. Therefore we, before him bending,
   this great sacrament revere:
   types and shadows have their ending,
   for the newer rite is here;
   faith, our outward sense befriending,
   makes our inward vision clear.

6. Glory let us give and blessing
   to the Father and the Son,
   honour, might and praise addressing,
   while eternal ages run;
   ever too his love confessing,
   who, from both, with both is one.
   (Amen.)

   St. Thomas Aquinas (1227-1274)
   trans. John Mason Neale (1818-1866),
   Edward Caswall (1814-1878) and others

354

1. Now thank we all our God,
   with hearts and hands and voices,
   who wondrous things hath done,
   in whom his world rejoices;
   who from our mother's arms
   hath blessed us on our way
   with countless gifts of love,
   and still is ours today.

2. O may this bounteous God
   through all our life be near us,
   with ever joyful hearts
   and blessèd peace to cheer us;
   and keep us in his grace,
   and guide us when perplexed,
   and free us from all ills
   in this world and the next.

3. All praise and thanks to God
   the Father now be given,
   the Son and him who reigns
   with them in highest heaven,
   the one eternal God,
   whom earth and heav'n adore;
   for thus it was, is now,
   and shall be evermore.

   Martin Rinkart (1586-1649)
   trans. Catherine Winkworth (1827-1878)

355

1. Now the green blade riseth
   from the buried grain,
   wheat that in the dark earth
   many days has lain;
   Love lives again,
   that with the dead has been;
   Love is come again,
   like wheat that springeth green.

2. In the grave they laid him,
   Love by hatred slain,
   thinking that never
   he would wake again,
   laid in the earth
   like grain that sleeps unseen:
   Love is come again,
   like wheat that springeth green.

3. Forth he came at Easter,
   like the risen grain,
   he that for three days
   in the grave had lain;
   quick from the dead,
   my risen Lord is seen:
   Love is come again,
   like wheat that springeth green.

4. When our hearts are wintry,
   grieving or in pain,
   thy touch can call us
   back to life again;
   fields of our hearts,
   that dead and bare have been:
   Love is come again,
   like wheat that springeth green.

   John Macleod Campbell Crum (1872-1958) alt.

356

1. O Breath of Life,
   come sweeping through us,
   revive your Church with life and pow'r;
   O Breath of Life, come cleanse,
      renew us,
   and fit your Church to meet this hour.

2. O Breath of Love,
   come breathe within us,
   renewing thought and will and heart;
   come, love of Christ, afresh to win us,
   revive your Church in ev'ry part!

3. O Wind of God,
   come bend us, break us,
   till humbly we confess our need;
   then, in your tenderness remake us,
   revive, restore – for this we plead.

4. Revive us, Lord;
   is zeal abating
   while harvest fields are vast and white?
   Revive us, Lord, the world is waiting –
   equip thy Church to spread the light.

   Elizabeth Ann Porter Head (1850-1936)

357

1. O come, all ye faithful,
   joyful and triumphant,
   O come ye, O come ye to Bethlehem;
   come and behold him,
   born the king of angels:

   O come, let us adore him,
   O come, let us adore him,
   O come, let us adore him,
   Christ the Lord.

2. God of God,
   Light of Light,
   lo, he abhors not the Virgin's womb;
   very God,
   begotten not created:

3. See how the shepherds,
   summoned to his cradle,
   leaving their flocks,
      draw nigh with lowly fear;
   we too will thither
   bend our joyful footsteps:

4. Lo! star-led chieftains,
   Magi, Christ adoring,
   offer him incense, gold and myrrh;
   we to the Christ-child
   bring our hearts' oblations:

5. Child, for us sinners
   poor and in the manger,
   fain we embrace thee, with love
      and awe;
   who would not love thee,
   loving us so dearly?

6. Sing, choirs of angels,
   sing in exultation,
   sing all ye citizens of heav'n above;
   glory to God
   in the highest:

7. Yea, Lord, we greet thee,
   born this happy morning,
   Jesu, to thee be glory giv'n;
   Word of the Father, now in flesh
      appearing:

   Possibly by John Francis Wade (1711-1786)
   trans. Frederick Oakeley (1802-1880) and others

358

1. O come, O come, Emmanuel,
   and ransom captive Israel,
   that mourns in lonely exile here,
   until the Son of God appear.

   Rejoice, rejoice!
   Emmanuel shall come to thee,
   O Israel.

2. O come, thou rod of Jesse, free
   thine own from Satan's tyranny;
   from depths of hell thy people save,
   and give them vict'ry o'er the grave.

3. O come, thou dayspring, come and
   cheer
   our spirits by thine advent here;
   disperse the gloomy clouds of night,
   and death's dark shadows put to flight.

4. O come, thou key of David, come
   and open wide our heav'nly home;
   make safe the way that leads on high,
   and close the path to misery.

5. O come, O come, thou Lord of might,
   who to thy tribes on Sinai's height
   in ancient times didst give the Law,
   in cloud and majesty and awe.

   from the 'Great O Antiphons' (12th - 13th century)
   trans. John Mason Neale (1818-1866)

359

1. O dearest Lord, thy sacred head
   with thorns was pierced for me;
   O pour thy blessing on my head
   that I may think for thee.

2. O dearest Lord, thy sacred hands
   with nails were pierced for me;
   O shed thy blessing on my hands
   that they may work for thee.

3. O dearest Lord, thy sacred feet
   with nails were pierced for me;
   O pour thy blessing on my feet
   that they may follow thee.

4. O dearest Lord, thy sacred heart
   with spear was pierced for me;
   O pour thy Spirit in my heart
   that I may live for thee.

   Henry Ernest Hardy
   (Father Andrew S.D.C.) (1869-1946)

360

1. O for a closer walk with God,
   a calm and heav'nly frame;
   a light to shine upon the road
   that leads me to the Lamb.

2. What peaceful hours I once enjoyed,
   how sweet their mem'ry still!
   But they have left an aching void
   the world can never fill.

3. The dearest idol I have known,
   whate'er that idol be,
   help me to tear it from thy throne,
   and worship only thee.

4. So shall my walk be close with God,
   calm and serene my frame;
   so purer light shall mark the road
   that leads me to the Lamb.

   William Cowper (1731-1800)

361

1. O for a heart to praise my God,
   a heart from sin set free;
   a heart that's sprinkled with the blood
   so freely shed for me.

2. A heart resigned, submissive, meek,
   my great Redeemer's throne;
   where only Christ is heard to speak,
   where Jesus reigns alone.

3. A humble, lowly, contrite heart,
   believing, true and clean,
   which neither life nor death can part
   from him that dwells within.

4. A heart in ev'ry thought renewed,
   and full of love divine;
   perfect and right and pure and good –
   a copy, Lord, of thine.

5. Thy nature, gracious Lord, impart,
   come quickly from above;
   write thy new name upon my heart,
   thy new best name of love.

Charles Wesley (1707-1788)

2. Jesus! the name that charms our fears,
   that bids our sorrows cease,
   that bids our sorrows cease;
   'tis music in the sinner's ears,
   'tis life and health and peace. (3)

3. He breaks the pow'r of cancelled sin,
   he sets the pris'ner free,
   he sets the pris'ner free;
   his blood can make the foulest clean;
   his blood availed for me. (3)

4. He speaks; and, list'ning to his voice,
   new life the dead receive,
   new life the dead receive,
   the mournful broken hearts rejoice,
   the humble poor believe. (3)

5. Hear him, ye deaf; his praise, ye dumb,
   your loosened tongues employ,
   your loosened tongues employ;
   ye blind, behold your Saviour come;
   and leap, ye lame, for joy! (3)

6. My gracious Master and my God,
   assist me to proclaim,
   assist me to proclaim
   and spread through all the earth abroad
   the honours of thy name. (3)

Charles Wesley (1707-1788)

362

When the tune 'Lyngham' is used

1. O for a thousand tongues to sing
   my dear Redeemer's praise,
   my dear Redeemer's praise,
   the glories of my God and King,
   the triumphs of his grace,
   the triumphs of his grace,
   the triumphs of his grace!

When another tune is used

1. O for a thousand tongues to sing
   my dear Redeemer's praise,
   the glories of my God and King,
   the triumphs of his grace!

2. Jesus! the name that charms our fears,
   that bids our sorrows cease;
   'tis music in the sinner's ears,
   'tis life and health and peace.

Continued overleaf

3. He breaks the pow'r of cancelled sin,
   he sets the pris'ner free;
   his blood can make the foulest clean;
   his blood availed for me.

4. He speaks; and, list'ning to his voice,
   new life the dead receive,
   the mournful broken hearts rejoice,
   the humble poor believe,

5. Hear him, ye deaf; his praise, ye dumb,
   your loosened tongues employ;
   ye blind, behold your Saviour come;
   and leap, ye lame, for joy!

6. My gracious Master and my God,
   assist me to proclaim
   and spread through all the earth abroad
   the honours of thy name.

Charles Wesley (1707-1788)

2. Then hear, O gracious Saviour,
   accept the love we bring,
   that we who know your favour
   may serve you as our king;
   and whether our tomorrows
   be filled with good or ill,
   we'll triumph through our sorrows
   and rise to bless you still:
   to marvel at your beauty
   and glory in your ways,
   and make a joyful duty
   our sacrifice of praise.

Michael Perry (b. 1942)

364

1. O God of Bethel, by whose hand
   thy people still are fed,
   who through this earthly pilgrimage
   hast all our forebears led.

2. Our vows, our prayers, we now present
   before thy throne of grace;
   God of our forebears, be the God
   of their succeeding race.

3. Through each mysterious path of life
   be thou our constant guide;
   give us each day our daily bread,
   and raiment fit provide.

4. O spread thy cov'ring wings around,
   till all our journeys cease,
   and at our Father's loved abode
   our souls arrive in peace.

Philip Doddridge (1702-1751) and
John Logan (1748-1788) alt.

363

1. O God beyond all praising,
   we worship you today,
   and sing the love amazing
   that songs cannot repay;
   for we can only wonder
   at ev'ry gift you send,
   at blessings without number
   and mercies without end:
   we lift our hearts before you
   and wait upon your word,
   we honour and adore you,
   our great and mighty Lord.

365

1. O God of earth and altar,
   bow down and hear our cry,
   our earthly rulers falter,
   our people drift and die;
   the walls of gold entomb us,
   the swords of scorn divide,
   take not thy thunder from us,
   but take away our pride.

2. From all that terror teaches,
   from lies of tongue and pen,
   from all the easy speeches
   that comfort cruel men,
   from sale and profanation
   of honour and the sword,
   from sleep and from damnation,
   deliver us, good Lord!

3. Tie in a living tether
   the prince and priest and thrall,
   bind all our lives together,
   smite us and save us all;
   in ire and exultation
   aflame with faith, and free,
   lift up a living nation,
   a single sword to thee.

   Gilbert Keith Chesterton (1874-1936)

366

1. O God, our help in ages past,
   our hope for years to come,
   our shelter from the stormy blast,
   and our eternal home.

2. Beneath the shadow of thy throne,
   thy saints have dwelt secure;
   sufficient is thine arm alone,
   and our defence is sure.

3. Before the hills in order stood,
   or earth received her frame,
   from everlasting thou art God,
   to endless years the same.

4. A thousand ages in thy sight
   are like an evening gone;
   short as the watch that ends the night
   before the rising sun.

5. Time, like an ever-rolling stream,
   will bear us all away;
   we fade and vanish, as a dream
   dies at the op'ning day.

6. O God, our help in ages past,
   our hope for years to come,
   be thou our guard while troubles last,
   and our eternal home.

   Isaac Watts (1674-1748) alt.

367

1. O God, unseen yet ever near,
   thy presence may we feel;
   and, thus inspired with holy fear,
   before thine altar kneel.

2. Here may thy faithful people know
   the blessings of thy love,
   the streams that through the desert flow,
   the manna from above.

3. We come, obedient to thy word,
   to feast on heav'nly food;
   our meat the body of the Lord,
   our drink his precious blood.

4. Thus may we all thy word obey,
   for we, O God, are thine;
   and go rejoicing on our way,
   renewed with strength divine.

   Edward Osler (1798-1863)

368

1. O happy band of pilgrims,
   if onward ye will tread,
   with Jesus as your fellow,
   to Jesus as your head.

2. The cross that Jesus carried
   he carried as your due:
   the crown that Jesus weareth
   he weareth it for you.

3. The faith by which ye see him,
   the hope in which ye yearn,
   the love that through all troubles
   to him alone will turn.

4. What are they but forerunners
   to lead you to his sight,
   the longed-for distant dawning
   of uncreated light?

5. The trials that beset you,
   the sorrows ye endure,
   are known to Christ your Saviour,
   whose perfect grace will cure.

6. O happy band of pilgrims,
   let fear not dim your eyes,
   remember, your afflictions
   shall lead to such a prize!

John Mason Neale (1818-1866)

369

1. O happy day! that fixed my choice
   on thee, my Saviour and my God!
   Well may this glowing heart rejoice,
   and tell its raptures all abroad.

2. 'Tis done, the work of grace is done!
   I am my Lord's, and he is mine!
   He drew me, and I followed on,
   glad to confess the voice divine.

3. Now rest, my long-divided heart,
   fixed on this blissful centre, rest;
   nor ever from thy Lord depart,
   with him of ev'ry good possessed.

4. High heav'n, that heard the solemn vow,
   that vow renewed shall daily hear;
   till in life's latest hour I bow,
   and bless in death a bond so dear.

*When a tune with a Refrain is used this is
sung after each verse:*

*O happy day! O happy day!
When Jesus washed my sins away;
he taught me how to watch and pray,
and live rejoicing ev'ry day;
O happy day! O happy day!
When Jesus washed my sins away.*

Philip Doddridge (1702-1751) alt.

370

1. O Holy Ghost, thy people bless
   who long to feel thy might,
   and fain would grow in holiness
   as children of the light.

2. To thee we bring, who art the Lord,
   ourselves to be thy throne;
   let ev'ry thought and deed and word
   thy pure dominion own.

3. Life-giving Spirit, o'er us move,
   as on the formless deep;
   give life and order, light and love,
   where now is death or sleep.

4. Great gift of our ascended King,
   his saving truth reveal;
   our tongues inspire his praise to sing,
   our hearts his love to feel.

5. True wind of heav'n, from south or
   north,
   for joy or chast'ning, blow;
   the garden-spices shall spring forth
   if thou wilt bid them flow.

6. O Holy Ghost, of sev'nfold might,
   all graces come from thee;
   grant us to know and serve aright
   One God in Persons Three.

Henry Williams Baker (1821-1877)

371

1. O Holy Spirit, Lord of grace,
   eternal fount of love,
   inflame, we pray, our inmost hearts
   with fire from heav'n above.

2. As thou dost join with holiest bonds
   the Father and the Son,
   so fill thy saints with mutual love
   and link their hearts in one.

3. To God the Father, God the Son
   and God the Holy Ghost,
   be praise eternal from the earth,
   and from the angel-host.

Charles Coffin (1676-1749)
trans. John Chandler (1808-1876) alt.

372

1. O Jesus, I have promised
   to serve thee to the end;
   be thou for ever near me,
   my Master and my friend:
   I shall not fear the battle
   if thou art by my side,
   nor wander from the pathway
   if thou wilt be my guide.

2. O let me feel thee near me:
   the world is ever near;
   I see the sights that dazzle,
   the tempting sounds I hear;
   my foes are ever near me,
   around me and within;
   but, Jesus, draw thou nearer,
   and shield my soul from sin.

3. O let me hear thee speaking
   in accents clear and still,
   above the storms of passion,
   the murmurs of self-will;
   O speak to reassure me,
   to hasten or control;
   O speak and make me listen,
   thou guardian of my soul.

4. O Jesus, thou hast promised,
   to all who follow thee,
   that where thou art in glory
   there shall thy servant be;
   and, Jesus, I have promised
   to serve thee to the end:
   O give me grace to follow,
   my Master and my friend.

5. O let me see thy foot-marks,
   and in them plant mine own;
   my hope to follow duly
   is in thy strength alone:
   O guide me, call me, draw me,
   uphold me to the end;
   and then in heav'n receive me,
   my Saviour and my friend.

John Ernest Bode (1816-1874)

373

1. O King enthroned on high,
   thou Comforter divine,
   blest Spirit of all truth, be nigh
   and make us thine.

2. Thou art the source of life,
   thou art our treasure-store;
   give us thy peace, and end our strife
   for evermore.

3. Descend, O heav'nly Dove,
   abide with us alway;
   and in the fullness of thy love
   cleanse us, we pray.

   Greek hymn (8th century)
   trans. John Brownlie (1857-1925)

374

1. O Lamb of God, most holy,
   salvation's perfect sign,
   by your redeeming passion,
   we share the life divine.
   The cost of our deliv'rance
   in flowing blood is shown,
   and life in all its fullness
   is found in you alone.

2. Upon the cross you carried
   a universe of shame,
   your dying breath atoning
   for centuries of blame.
   So now accept your servant,
   who on your love relied,
   to rest in peace eternal,
   redeemed and purified.

3. O draw us to your presence,
   beyond the sundered veil,
   to stand in silent wonder,
   where words and senses fail.
   In fellowship unbroken
   with all who went before,
   we join with saints and angels
   to worship and adore.

   Michael Forster (b. 1946) based on the German

375

1. O let the Son of God enfold you
   with his Spirit and his love,
   let him fill your heart
   and satisfy your soul.
   O let him have the things that
      hold you,
   and his Spirit, like a dove,
   will descend upon your life
      and make you whole.

   Jesus, O Jesus,
   come and fill your lambs.
   Jesus, O Jesus,
   come and fill your lambs.

2. O come and sing this song with
     gladness
   as your hearts are filled with joy;
   lift your hands in sweet
   surrender to his name.
   O give him all your tears and sadness,
   give him all your years of pain,
   and you'll enter into life in Jesus' name.

John Wimber (b. 1933)
© *1979 Mercy Vineyard Music/Kingsway's Thankyou Music*

376

1. O little one sweet,
     O little one mild,
   thy Father's purpose thou hast fulfilled;
   thou cam'st from heav'n
   to dwell below,
   to share the joys and tears we know.
   O little one sweet,
   O little one mild.

2. O little one sweet,
     O little one mild,
   with joy thou hast the whole world
     filled;
   thou camest here
   from heav'n's domain,
   to bring us comfort in our pain,
   O little one sweet,
   O little one mild.

3. O little one sweet,
     O little one mild,
   in thee Love's beauties are all distilled;
   then light in us
   thy love's bright flame,
   that we may give thee back the same,
   O little one sweet,
   O little one mild.

German, Samuel Scheidt (1650)
trans. Percy Dearmer (1867-1936) alt.

377

1. O little town of Bethlehem,
     how still we see thee lie!
   Above thy deep and dreamless sleep
   the silent stars go by.
   Yet in thy dark streets shineth
   the everlasting light;
   the hopes and fears of all the years
   are met in thee tonight.

2. For Christ is born of Mary;
     and, gathered all above,
   while mortals sleep, the angels keep
   their watch of wond'ring love;
   O morning stars, together
   proclaim the holy birth,
   and praises sing to God the King,
   and peace upon the earth.

3. How silently, how silently,
     the wondrous gift is giv'n!
   So God imparts to human hearts
   the blessings of his heav'n.
   No ear may hear his coming;
   but in this world of sin,
   where meek souls will receive him still,
   the dear Christ enters in.

4. O holy child of Bethlehem,
     descend to us, we pray;
   cast out our sin, and enter in,
   be born in us today.
   We hear the Christmas angels
   the great glad tidings tell:
   O come to us, abide with us,
   our Lord Emmanuel.

Phillips Brooks (1835-1893) alt.

378

1. O Lord, all the world
   belongs to you,
   and you are always
   making all things new.
   What is wrong you forgive,
   and the new life you give
   is what's turning
   the world upside down.

2. The world's only
   loving to its friends,
   but you have brought us
   love that never ends;
   loving enemies too,
   and this loving with you
   is what's turning the world upside down.

3. This world lives divided
   and apart.
   You draw us all together
   and we start,
   in your body, to see
   that in fellowship we
   can be turning the world upside down.

4. The world wants the wealth
   to live in state,
   but you show us a new way
   to be great:
   like a servant you came,
   and if we do the same,
   we'll be turning the world upside down.

5. O Lord, all the world
   belongs to you,
   and you are always
   making all things new.
   Send your Spirit on all
   in your Church whom you call
   to be turning the world upside down.

Patrick Appleford (b. 1925) alt.

379

O Lord, hear my prayer,
O Lord, hear my prayer:
when I call, answer me.
O Lord, hear my prayer,
O Lord, hear my prayer.
Come and listen to me.

Taizé

380

1. O Lord, my God,
   when I, in awesome wonder,
   consider all the worlds
   thy hand has made,
   I see the stars,
   I hear the rolling thunder,
   thy pow'r throughout
   the universe displayed.

   Then sings my soul,
   my Saviour God, to thee:
   how great thou art,
   how great thou art.
   Then sings my soul,
   my Saviour God, to thee:
   how great thou art,
   how great thou art.

2. When through the woods
   and forest glades I wander,
   and hear the birds
   sing sweetly in the trees;
   when I look down
   from lofty mountain grandeur,
   and hear the brook,
   and feel the gentle breeze.

3. And when I think that God,
   his Son not sparing,
   sent him to die,
   I scarce can take it in
   that on the cross,
   my burden gladly bearing,
   he bled and died
   to take away my sin.

4. When Christ shall come
   with shout of acclamation,
   and take me home,
   what joy shall fill my heart;
   then I shall bow
   in humble adoration,
   and there proclaim:
   my God, how great thou art.

Karl Boberg (1859-1940)
trans. Stuart K. Hine (1899-1989)
© 1953 Stuart K. Hine/Kingsway's Thankyou Music

381

1. O Lord of our salvation,
   the pains of all creation
   are borne upon your cross:
   the failure of compassion,
   revealed in starkest fashion,
   exposes all our gold as dross.

2. We hear your voice protesting,
   to love and hope attesting,
   where justice is denied.
   Where innocents are dying,
   where hate is crucifying,
   you call us to your bleeding side.

3. O give us faith to stay here,
   to wait, to watch and pray here,
   and witness to your cry;
   in scarred and tearful faces,
   in countless painful places,
   you give us hope that will not die.

Michael Forster (b. 1946)

382

O Lord, your tenderness,
melting all my bitterness,
O Lord, I receive your love.
O Lord, your loveliness,
changing all my ugliness,
O Lord, I receive your love.
O Lord, I receive your love.
O Lord, I receive your love.

Graham Kendrick (b. 1950)
© 1986 Kingsway's Thankyou Music

383

1. O love how deep, how broad, how high!
   It fills the heart with ecstasy,
   that God, the Son of God, should take
   our mortal form for mortals' sake.

2. He sent no angel to our race
   of higher or of lower place,
   but wore the robe of human frame
   himself, and to this lost world came.

3. For us he was baptised and bore
   his holy fast, and hungered sore;
   for us temptations sharp he knew;
   for us the tempter overthrew.

4. For us to wicked pow'rs betrayed,
   scourged, mocked, in purple robe
     arrayed,
   he bore the shameful cross and death;
   for us at length gave up his breath.

Continued overleaf

5. For us he rose from death again,
   for us he went on high to reign,
   for us he sent his Spirit here
   to guide, to strengthen and to cheer.

6. To him whose boundless love has won
   salvation for us through his Son,
   to God the Father glory be,
   both now and through eternity.

Benjamin Webb (1819-1885) alt.,
from Thomas à Kempis (c. 1379-1471)

385

O most merciful!
O most bountiful!
God the Father almighty!
By the Redeemer's
sweet intercession,
hear us, help us when we cry.

Reginald Heber (1783-1826)

384

1. O Love that wilt not let me go,
   I rest my weary soul in thee;
   I give thee back the life I owe,
   that in thine ocean depths its flow
   may richer, fuller be.

2. O Light that follow'st all my way,
   I yield my flick'ring torch to thee;
   my heart restores its borrowed ray,
   that in thy sunshine's blaze its day
   may brighter, fairer be.

3. O Joy that seekest me through pain,
   I cannot close my heart to thee;
   I trace the rainbow through the rain,
   and feel the promise is not vain
   that morn shall tearless be.

4. O Cross that liftest up my head,
   I dare not ask to fly from thee:
   I lay in dust life's glory dead,
   and from the ground there blossoms red
   life that shall endless be.

George Matheson (1842-1906)

386

1. O my Saviour, lifted
   from the earth for me,
   draw me, in thy mercy,
   nearer unto thee.

2. Lift my earth-bound longings,
   fix them, Lord, above;
   draw me with the magnet
   of thy mighty love.

3. Lord, thine arms are stretching
   ever far and wide,
   to enfold thy children
   to thy loving side.

4. And I come, O Jesus:
   dare I turn away?
   No, thy love hath conquered,
   and I come today.

5. Bringing all my burdens,
   sorrow, sin and care;
   at thy feet I lay them,
   and I leave them there.

William Walsham How (1823-1897)

387

1. O perfect love,
   all human thought transcending,
   lowly we kneel
   in prayer before thy throne,
   that theirs may be
   the love which knows no ending,
   whom thou for evermore
   dost join in one.

2. O perfect life,
   be thou their full assurance
   of tender charity,
   and steadfast faith,
   of patient hope,
   and quiet, brave endurance,
   with childlike trust that fears
   not pain nor death.

3. Grant them the joy
   which brightens earthly sorrow,
   grant them the peace
   which calms all earthly strife;
   and to life's day
   the glorious unknown morrow
   that dawns upon
   eternal love and life.

Dorothy Frances Gurney (1858-1932)

388

1. O praise ye the Lord!
   praise him in the height;
   rejoice in his word,
   ye angels of light;
   ye heavens, adore him,
   by whom ye were made,
   and worship before him,
   in brightness arrayed.

2. O praise ye the Lord!
   praise him upon earth,
   in tuneful accord,
   all you of new birth;
   praise him who hath brought you
   his grace from above,
   praise him who hath taught you
   to sing of his love.

3. O praise ye the Lord!
   all things that give sound;
   each jubilant chord
   re-echo around;
   loud organs his glory
   forth tell in deep tone,
   and, sweet harp, the story
   of what he hath done.

4. O praise ye the Lord!
   thanksgiving and song
   to him be outpoured
   all ages along:
   for love in creation,
   for heaven restored,
   for grace of salvation,
   O praise ye the Lord!

Henry Williams Baker (1821-1877)
based on Psalms 148 and 150 alt.

389

1. O sacred head, surrounded
   by crown of piercing thorn!
   O bleeding head, so wounded,
   so shamed and put to scorn!
   Death's pallid hue comes o'er thee,
   the glow of life decays;
   yet angel-hosts adore thee,
   and tremble as they gaze.

2. Thy comeliness and vigour
   is withered up and gone,
   and in thy wasted figure
   I see death drawing on.
   O agony and dying!
   O love to sinners free!
   Jesu, all grace supplying,
   turn thou thy face on me.

3. In this thy bitter passion,
   good Shepherd, think of me
   with thy most sweet compassion,
   unworthy though I be:
   beneath thy cross abiding
   for ever would I rest,
   in thy dear love confiding,
   and with thy presence blest.

Paul Gerhardt (1607-1676)
based on 'Salve caput cruentatum'
trans. Henry Williams Baker (1821-1877)

390

1. O strength and stay
   upholding all creation,
   who ever dost
   thyself unmoved abide,
   yet day by day
   the light in due gradation
   from hour to hour
   through all its changes guide.

2. Grant to life's day
   a calm unclouded ending,
   an eve untouched
   by shadows of decay,
   the brightness of
   a holy death-bed blending
   with dawning glories
   of th'eternal day.

3. Hear us, O Father,
   gracious and forgiving,
   through Jesus Christ
   thy co-eternal Word,
   who with the Holy Ghost
   by all things living
   now and to endless ages
   art adored.

St. Ambrose (c. 340-397) trans. John Ellerton (1826-1893)
and Fenton John Anthony Hort (1828-1892)

391

1. O thou, who at thy
   Eucharist didst pray
   that all thy Church
   might be for ever one,
   grant us at ev'ry
   eucharist to say,
   with longing heart and soul,
   'Thy will be done.'
   O may we all one bread,
   one body be,
   through this blest
   sacrament of unity.

2. For all thy Church,
   O Lord, we intercede;
   make thou our sad
   divisions soon to cease;
   draw us the nearer
   each to each, we plead,
   by drawing all to thee,
   O Prince of Peace:
   thus may we all one bread,
   one body be,
   through this blest
   sacrament of unity.

3. We pray thee too
   for wand'rers from thy fold;
   O bring them back,
   good Shepherd of the sheep,
   back to the faith
   which saints believed of old,
   back to the Church
   which still that faith doth keep:
   soon may we all one bread,
   one body be,
   through this blest
   sacrament of unity.

4. So, Lord, at length
   when sacraments shall cease,
   may we be one
   with all thy Church above,
   one with thy saints
   in one unbroken peace,
   one with thy saints
   in one unbounded love:
   more blessèd still,
   in peace and love to be
   one with the Trinity
   in unity.

William Harry Turton (1856-1938) based on John 17

392

1. O thou who camest from above
   the fire celestial to impart,
   kindle a flame of sacred love
   on the mean altar of my heart.

2. There let it for thy glory burn
   with inextinguishable blaze,
   and trembling to its source return
   in humble prayer and fervent praise.

3. Jesus, confirm my heart's desire
   to work and speak and think for thee;
   still let me guard the holy fire
   and still stir up the gift in me.

4. Ready for all thy perfect will,
   my acts of faith and love repeat,
   till death thy endless mercies seal,
   and make the sacrifice complete.

Charles Wesley (1707-1788) based on Leviticus 6:13

393

1. O worship the King
   all glorious above;
   O gratefully sing
   his pow'r and his love:
   our shield and defender,
   the Ancient of Days,
   pavillioned in splendour,
   and girded with praise.

Continued overleaf

2. O tell of his might,
   O sing of his grace,
   whose robe is the light,
   whose canopy space;
   his chariots of wrath
   the deep thunder-clouds form,
   and dark is his path
   on the wings of the storm.

3. This earth, with its store
   of wonders untold,
   almighty, thy pow'r
   hath founded of old:
   hath stablished it fast
   by a changeless decree,
   and round it hath cast,
   like a mantle, the sea.

4. Thy bountiful care
   what tongue can recite?
   It breathes in the air,
   it shines in the light;
   it streams from the hills,
   it descends to the plain,
   and sweetly distils
   in the dew and the rain.

5. Frail children of dust,
   and feeble as frail,
   in thee do we trust,
   nor find thee to fail;
   thy mercies how tender,
   how firm to the end!
   Our maker, defender,
   redeemer, and friend.

6. O measureless might,
   ineffable love,
   while angels delight
   to hymn thee above,
   thy humbler creation,
   though feeble their lays,
   with true adoration
   shall sing to thy praise.

   Robert Grant (1799-1838) based on Psalm 104

394

1. O worship the Lord
   in the beauty of holiness;
   bow down before him,
   his glory proclaim;
   with gold of obedience,
   and incense of lowliness,
   kneel and adore him:
   the Lord is his name.

2. Low at his feet lay
   thy burden of carefulness:
   high on his heart
   he will bear it for thee,
   comfort thy sorrows,
   and answer thy prayerfulness,
   guiding thy steps
   as may best for thee be.

3. Fear not to enter
   his courts in the slenderness
   of the poor wealth
   thou wouldst reckon as thine:
   truth in its beauty,
   and love in its tenderness,
   these are the off'rings
   to lay on his shrine.

4. These, though we bring them
   in trembling and fearfulness,
   he will accept
   for the name that is dear;
   mornings of joy give
   for ev'nings of tearfulness,
   trust for our trembling
   and hope for our fear.

5. O worship the Lord
in the beauty of holiness;
bow down before him,
his glory proclaim;
with gold of obedience
and incense of lowliness,
kneel and adore him:
the Lord is his name.

John Samuel Bewley Monsell (1811-1875)

395

1. Of the Father's love begotten,
ere the worlds began to be,
he is Alpha and Omega,
he the source, the ending he,
of the things that are, that have been,
and that future years shall see,
evermore and evermore.

2. At his word they were created;
he commanded; it was done:
heav'n and earth and depths of ocean
in their threefold order one;
all that grows beneath the shining
of the light of moon and sun,
evermore and evermore.

3. O that birth for ever blessèd,
when the Virgin, full of grace,
by the Holy Ghost conceiving,
bare the Saviour of our race,
and the babe, the world's Redeemer,
first revealed his sacred face,
evermore and evermore.

4. O ye heights of heav'n, adore him;
angel hosts, his praises sing;
pow'rs, dominions, bow before him,
and extol our God and King:
let no tongue on earth be silent,
ev'ry voice in concert ring,
evermore and evermore.

5. This is he whom seers and sages
sang of old with one accord;
whom the writings of the prophets
promised in their faithful word;
now he shines, the long-expected:
let our songs declare his worth,
evermore and evermore.

6. Christ, to thee, with God the Father,
and, O Holy Ghost, to thee,
hymn and chant and high
    thanksgiving,
and unwearied praises be;
honour, glory, and dominion,
and eternal victory,
evermore and evermore.

Aurelius Clemens Prudentius (348-413)
trans. John Mason Neale (1818-1866) alt.

396

1. Oft in danger, oft in woe,
onward, Christians, onward go;
bear the toil, endure the strife,
strengthened with the bread of life.

2. Onward through the desert night,
keeping faith and vision bright;
face the challenge of the hour
trusting in your Saviour's pow'r.

3. Let not sorrow dim your eye,
soon shall ev'ry tear be dry;
let not fears your course impede,
great your strength if great your need.

4. Let your drooping hearts be glad;
march in faith and honour clad;
march, nor think the journey long,
march to hope's eternal song.

5. Onward then, undaunted, move;
more than faithful God will prove;
though the raging waters flow,
Christian pilgrims, onward go.

Henry Kirke White (1785-1806) and others

397

Oh! Oh! Oh! how good is the Lord,
Oh! Oh! Oh! how good is the Lord,
Oh! Oh! Oh! how good is the Lord,
I never will forget
what he has done for me.

1. He gives me salvation,
   how good is the Lord,
   he gives me salvation,
   how good is the Lord,
   he gives me salvation,
   how good is the Lord,
   I never will forget
   what he has done for me.

2. He gives me his blessings . . .

3. He gives me his Spirit . . .

4. He gives me his healing . . .

5. He gives me his glory . . .

Other verses may be added, as appropriate
Unknown

398

1. Oh, the love of my Lord
   is the essence
   of all that I love here on earth.
   All the beauty I see
   he has given to me,
   and his giving
   is gentle as silence.

2. Ev'ry day, ev'ry hour,
   ev'ry moment
   have been blessed by the strength of
   his love.
   At the turn of each tide
   he is there at my side,
   and his touch
   is as gentle as silence.

3. There've been times when
   I've turned from his presence,
   and I've walked other paths, other ways;
   but I've called on his name
   in the dark of my shame,
   and his mercy
   was gentle as silence.

Estelle White (b. 1925)

399

1. On a hill far away
   stood an old rugged cross,
   the emblem of suff'ring and shame;
   and I loved that old cross
   where the dearest and best
   for a world of lost sinners was slain.

   So I'll cherish the old rugged cross,
   till my trophies at last I lay down;
   I will cling to the old rugged cross
   and exchange it some day for a crown.

2. O, that old rugged cross,
   so despised by the world,
   has a wondrous attraction for me:
   for the dear Lamb of God
   left his glory above
   to bear it to dark Calvary.

3. In the old rugged cross,
   stained with blood so divine,
   a wondrous beauty I see.
   For 'twas on that old cross
   Jesus suffered and died
   to pardon and sanctify me.

4. To the old rugged cross
   I will ever be true,
   its shame and reproach gladly bear.
   Then he'll call me some day
   to my home far away;
   there his glory for ever I'll share.

George Bennard (1873-1958)
© The Rodeheaver Co/Word Music Inc/
Word Music (UK)/CopyCare Ltd

400

1. On Christmas night all Christians sing,
   to hear the news the angels bring,
   on Christmas night all Christians sing,
   to hear the news the angels bring,
   news of great joy, news of great mirth,
   news of our merciful King's birth.

2. Then why should we on earth be
        so sad,
   since our Redeemer made us glad,
   then why should we on earth be
        so sad,
   since our Redeemer made us glad,
   when from our sin he set us free,
   all for to gain our liberty?

3. When sin departs before his grace,
   then life and health come in its place,
   when sin departs before his grace,
   then life and health come in its place,
   angels and earth with joy may sing,
   all for to see the new-born King.

4. All out of darkness we have light,
   which made the angels sing this night:
   all out of darkness we have light,
   which made the angels sing this night:
   'Glory to God and peace to men,
   now and for evermore. Amen.'

Traditional English carol alt.

401

1. On Jordan's bank the Baptist's cry
   announces that the Lord is nigh;
   awake, and hearken, for he brings
   glad tidings of the King of kings.

2. Then cleansed be ev'ry breast from sin;
   make straight the way for God within;
   prepare we in our hearts a home,
   where such a mighty guest may come.

3. For thou art our salvation, Lord,
   our refuge and our great reward;
   without thy grace we waste away,
   like flow'rs that wither and decay.

4. To heal the sick stretch out thine hand,
   and bid the fallen sinner stand;
   shine forth and let thy light restore
   earth's own true loveliness once more.

5. All praise, eternal Son, to thee
   whose advent doth thy people free,
   whom with the Father we adore
   and Holy Ghost for evermore.

Charles Coffin (1676-1749)
trans. John Chandler (1806-1876) alt.

402

1. On this day, the first of days,
   God the Father's name we praise,
   who, creation's Lord and spring,
   did the world from darkness bring.

2. On this day his only Son
   over death the triumph won;
   on this day the Spirit came
   with his gifts of living flame.

3. On this day his people raise
   one pure sacrifice of praise,
   and, with all the saints above,
   tell of Christ's redeeming love.

4. Praise, O God, to thee be giv'n,
   praise on earth and praise in heav'n,
   praise to thy eternal Son,
   who this day our vict'ry won.

18th century trans. Henry Williams Baker (1821-1877)
adapted by the editors of 'English Praise'

3. And through all his wondrous
      childhood
   day by day like us he grew;
   he was little, weak and helpless,
   tears and smiles like us he knew;
   and he feeleth for our sadness,
   and he shareth in our gladness.

4. Still among the poor and lowly
   hope in Christ is brought to birth,
   with the promise of salvation
   for the nations of the earth;
   still in him our life is found
   and our hope of heav'n is crowned.

5. And our eyes at last shall see him
   through his own redeeming love,
   for that child so dear and gentle
   is our Lord in heav'n above;
   and he leads his children on
   to the place where he is gone.

vs. 1-3 and 5: Cecil Frances Alexander (1818-1895) alt.
v. 4: Michael Forster (b. 1946)

403

1. Once in royal David's city
   stood a lowly cattle shed,
   where a mother laid her baby
   in a manger for his bed:
   Mary was that mother mild,
   Jesus Christ her little child.

2. He came down to earth from heaven,
   who is God and Lord of all,
   and his shelter was a stable,
   and his cradle was a stall;
   with the poor and mean and lowly,
   lived on earth our Saviour holy.

404

1. Once, only once, and once for all,
   his precious life he gave;
   before the Cross our spirits fall,
   and own it strong to save.

2. 'One off'ring, single and complete,'
   with lips and heart we say;
   but what he never can repeat
   he shows forth day by day.

3. For, as the priest of Aaron's line
   within the holiest stood,
   and sprinkled all the mercy-shrine
   with sacrificial blood;

4. So he who once atonement wrought,
   our Priest of endless pow'r,
   presents himself for those he bought
   in that dark noontide hour.

5. And so we show thy death, O Lord,
   till thou again appear;
   and feel, when we approach thy board,
   we have an altar here.

6. All glory to the Father be,
   all glory to the Son,
   all glory, Holy Ghost, to thee,
   while endless ages run.

   William Bright (1824-1901)

405

1. One more step along the world I go,
   one more step along the world I go.
   From the old things to the new
   keep me travelling along with you.

   And it's from the old
   I travel to the new,
   keep me travelling
   along with you.

2. Round the corners of the world I turn,
   more and more about the world
      I learn.
   All the new things that I see
   you'll be looking at along with me.

3. As I travel through the bad and good,
   keep me travelling the way I should.
   Where I see no way to go,
   you'll be telling me the way, I know.

4. Give me courage when the world
      is rough,
   keep me loving though the world
      is tough.
   Leap and sing in all I do,
   keep me travelling along with you.

5. You are older than the world can be,
   you are younger than the life in me.
   Ever old and ever new,
   keep me travelling along with you.

   Sydney Carter (b. 1915)

406

1. One shall tell another,
   and all shall tell their friends,
   husbands, wives and children
   shall come following on.
   From house to house in fam'lies
   shall more be gathered in;
   and lights will shine in ev'ry street,
   so warm and welcoming.

   Come on in and taste the new wine,
   the wine of the kingdom,
   the wine of the kingdom of God:
   here is healing and forgiveness,
   the wine of the kingdom,
   the wine of the kingdom of God.

2. Compassion of the Father
   is ready now to flow;
   through acts of love and mercy
   we must let it show.
   He turns now from his anger
   to show a smiling face,
   and longs that all should stand beneath
   the fountain of his grace.

Continued overleaf

3. He longs to do much more than
   our faith has yet allowed,
   to thrill us and surprise us
   with his sov'reign pow'r.
   Where darkness has been darkest,
   the brightest light will shine;
   his invitation comes to us –
   it's yours and it is mine.

Graham Kendrick (b. 1950)
© 1981 Kingsway's Thankyou Music

407

1. Only by grace can we enter,
   only by grace can we stand;
   not by our human endeavour,
   but by the blood of the Lamb.
   Into your presence you call us,
   you call us to come.
   Into your presence you draw us,
   and now by your grace we come,
   now by your grace we come.

2. Lord, if you mark our transgressions,
   who would stand?
   Thanks to your grace we are cleansed
   by the blood of the Lamb.
   Lord, if you mark our transgressions,
   who would stand?
   Thanks to your grace we are cleansed
   by the blood of the Lamb.

Repeat verse 1

Gerrit Gustafson
© 1990 Integrity's Hosanna! Music/
Kingsway's Thankyou Music

408

1. Onward, Christian pilgrims,
   Christ will be our light;
   see, the heav'nly vision
   breaks upon our sight!
   Out of death's enslavement
   Christ has set us free,
   on then to salvation,
   hope and liberty.

   Onward, Christian pilgrims,
   Christ will be our light;
   see, the heav'nly vision
   breaks upon our sight!

2. Onward, Christian pilgrims,
   up the rocky way,
   where the dying Saviour
   bids us watch and pray.
   Through the darkened valley
   walk with those who mourn,
   share the pain and anger,
   share the promised dawn!

3. Onward, Christian pilgrims,
   in the early dawn;
   death's great seal is broken,
   life and hope reborn!
   Faith in resurrection
   strengthens pilgrims' hearts,
   ev'ry load is lightened,
   ev'ry fear departs.

4. Onward, Christian pilgrims,
   hearts and voices raise,
   till the whole creation
   echoes perfect praise:
   swords are turned to ploughshares,
   pride and envy cease,
   truth embraces justice,
   hope resolves in peace.

Michael Forster (b. 1946)

409

Open our eyes, Lord,
we want to see Jesus,
to reach out and touch him
and say that we love him;
open our ears, Lord,
and help us to listen;
O, open our eyes, Lord,
we want to see Jesus!

Robert Cull (b. 1949)
© 1976 Maranatha! Music/CopyCare Ltd

410

1. Our blest Redeemer, ere he breathed
   his tender last farewell,
   a Guide, a Comforter, bequeathed
   with us to dwell.

2. He came in tongues of living flame,
   to teach, convince, subdue;
   all-pow'rful as the wind he came,
   as viewless too.

3. He came sweet influence to impart,
   a gracious, willing guest,
   while he can find one humble heart
   wherein to rest.

4. And his that gentle voice we hear,
   soft as the breath of ev'n,
   that checks each fault, that calms each
     fear,
   and speaks of heav'n.

5. And ev'ry virtue we possess,
   and ev'ry vict'ry won,
   and ev'ry thought of holiness,
   are his alone.

6. Spirit of purity and grace,
   our weakness, pitying, see:
   O make our hearts thy dwelling-place,
   and worthier thee.

Harriet Auber (1773-1862)

411

1. Our Father, who art in heaven,
   hallowèd be thy name.
   Thy kingdom come, thy will be done,
   hallowèd be thy name,
   hallowèd be thy name.

2. On earth as it is in heaven.
   Give us this day our daily bread.

3. Forgive us our trespasses,
   as we forgive those who trespass
     against us.

4. Lead us not into temptation,
   but deliver us from all that is evil.

5. For thine is the kingdom, the power
     and the glory,
   for ever and for ever and ever.

6. Amen, amen, it shall be so.
   Amen, amen, it shall be so.

Traditional Caribbean,
based on Matthew 6:9-13 and Luke 11:2-4

412

1. Peace is flowing like a river,
   flowing out through you and me,
   spreading out into the desert,
   setting all the captives free.

   Let it flow through me,
   let it flow through me,
   let the mighty peace of God
   flow out through me.
   Let it flow through me,
   let it flow through me,
   let the mighty peace of God
   flow out through me.

2. Love is flowing like a river,
   flowing out through you and me,
   spreading out into the desert,
   setting all the captives free.

3. Joy is flowing like a river,
   flowing out through you and me,
   spreading out into the desert,
   setting all the captives free.

4. Faith is flowing like a river,
   flowing out through you and me,
   spreading out into the desert,
   setting all the captives free.

5. Hope is flowing like a river,
   flowing out through you and me,
   spreading out into the desert,
   setting all the captives free.

Unknown

413

1. Peace, perfect peace,
   in this dark world of sin?
   The blood of Jesus
   whispers peace within.

2. Peace, perfect peace,
   by thronging duties pressed?
   To do the will of Jesus,
   this is rest.

3. Peace, perfect peace,
   with sorrows surging round?
   In Jesus' presence
   naught but calm is found.

4. Peace, perfect peace,
   with loved ones far away?
   In Jesus' keeping
   we are safe, and they.

5. Peace, perfect peace,
   our future all unknown?
   Jesus we know,
   and he is on the throne.

6. Peace, perfect peace,
   death shad'wing us and ours?
   Jesus has vanquished death
   and all its pow'rs.

7. It is enough: earth's struggles
   soon shall cease,
   and Jesus call us
   to heav'n's perfect peace.

Edward Henry Bickersteth (1825-1906)

414

1. Peace, perfect peace,
   is the gift of Christ our Lord.
   Peace, perfect peace,
   is the gift of Christ our Lord.
   Thus, says the Lord,
   will the world know my friends.
   Peace, perfect peace,
   is the gift of Christ our Lord.

2. Love, perfect love,
   is the gift of Christ our Lord.
   Love, perfect love,
   is the gift of Christ our Lord.
   Thus, says the Lord,
   will the world know my friends.
   Love, perfect love,
   is the gift of Christ our Lord.

3. Faith, perfect faith,
   is the gift of Christ our Lord.
   Faith, perfect faith,
   is the gift of Christ our Lord.
   Thus, says the Lord,
   will the world know my friends.
   Faith, perfect faith,
   is the gift of Christ our Lord.

4. Hope, perfect hope,
   is the gift of Christ our Lord.
   Hope, perfect hope,
   is the gift of Christ our Lord.
   Thus, says the Lord,
   will the world know my friends.
   Hope, perfect hope,
   is the gift of Christ our Lord.

5. Joy, perfect joy,
   is the gift of Christ our Lord.
   Joy, perfect joy,
   is the gift of Christ our Lord.
   Thus, says the Lord,
   will the world know my friends.
   Joy, perfect joy,
   is the gift of Christ our Lord.

Kevin Mayhew (b. 1942)

415

Peace to you.
We bless you now
in the name of the Lord.
Peace to you.
We bless you now
in the name of the Prince of Peace.
Peace to you.

Graham Kendrick (b. 1950)
© 1988 Make Way Music Ltd

416

Peter and John went to pray,
they met a lame man on the way.
He asked for alms
and held out his palms
and this is what Peter did say:
'Silver and gold have I none,
but such as I have give I thee,
in the name of Jesus Christ
of Nazareth, rise up and walk!'
He went walking and leaping
and praising God,
walking and leaping
and praising God.
'In the name of Jesus Christ
of Nazareth, rise up and walk.'

Unknown, based on Acts 3

417

Praise God from whom all blessings flow,
praise him, all creatures here below,
praise him above ye heav'nly host,
praise Father, Son and Holy Ghost.

Thomas Ken (1637-1710)

418

Praise him on the trumpet,
the psalt'ry and harp;
praise him on the timbrel and the dance;
praise him with stringed instruments
  too;
praise him on the loud cymbals,
praise him on the loud cymbals;
let ev'rything that has breath praise the
  Lord!

Hallelujah, praise the Lord;
hallelujah, praise the Lord:
let ev'rything that has breath
praise the Lord!
Hallelujah, praise the Lord;
hallelujah, praise the Lord:
let ev'rything that has breath
praise the Lord!

John Kennett
© 1981 Kingsway's Thankyou Music

419

1. Praise him, praise him,
   all his children praise him!
   He is love, he is love.
   Praise him, praise him,
   all his children praise him!
   He is love, he is love.

2. Thank him, thank him,
   all his children thank him!
   He is love, he is love.
   Thank him, thank him,
   all his children thank him!
   He is love, he is love.

3. Love him, love him,
   all his children love him!
   He is love, he is love.
   Love him, love him,
   all his children love him!
   He is love, he is love.

4. Crown him, crown him,
   all his children crown him!
   He is love, he is love.
   Crown him, crown him,
   all his children crown him!
   He is love, he is love.

Percy Dearmer (1867-1936)
based on Carey Bonner (1859-1938)

420

1. Praise him, praise him!
   Jesus, our blessèd Redeemer!
   Sing, O earth,
   his wonderful love proclaim!
   Hail him, hail him!
   highest archangels in glory;
   strength and honour
   give to his holy name!
   Like a shepherd,
   Jesus will guard his children,
   in his arms he carries
   them all day long.

Praise him, praise him!
tell of his excellent greatness;
praise him, praise him
ever in joyful song!

2. Praise him, praise him!
   Jesus, our blessèd Redeemer!
   For our sins
   he suffered, and bled, and died!
   He – our rock,
   our hope of eternal salvation,
   hail him, hail him!
   Jesus the crucified!
   Sound his praises
   – Jesus who bore our sorrows,
   love unbounded, wonderful,
   deep and strong.

3. Praise him, praise him!
   Jesus, our blessèd Redeemer!
   Heav'nly portals,
   loud with hosannas ring!
   Jesus, Saviour,
   reigneth for ever and ever:
   crown him, crown him!
   Prophet, and Priest, and King!
   Christ is coming,
   over the world victorious,
   pow'r and glory
   unto the Lord belong.

   Frances Jane van Alstyne
   (Fanny J. Crosby) (1820-1915)

421

1. Praise him, praise him,
   praise him in the morning,
   praise him in the noontime.
   Praise him, praise him,
   praise him when the sun goes down.

2. Love him, love him,
   love him in the morning,
   love him in the noontime.
   Love him, love him,
   love him when the sun goes down.

3. Trust him, trust him,
   trust him in the morning,
   trust him in the noontime.
   Trust him, trust him,
   trust him when the sun goes down.

4. Serve him, serve him,
   serve him in the morning,
   serve him in the noontime.
   Serve him, serve him,
   serve him when the sun goes down.

5. Jesus, Jesus,
   Jesus in the morning,
   Jesus in the noontime.
   Jesus, Jesus,
   Jesus when the sun goes down.

   Unknown

422

1. Praise, my soul, the King of heaven!
   To his feet thy tribute bring;
   ransomed, healed, restored, forgiven,
   who like me his praise should sing?
   Praise him! Praise him!
   Praise him! Praise him!
   Praise the everlasting King!

Continued overleaf

2. Praise him for his grace and favour
   to our fathers in distress;
   praise him still the same as ever,
   slow to chide and swift to bless.
   Praise him! Praise him!
   Praise him! Praise him!
   Glorious in his faithfulness!

3. Father-like he tends and spares us;
   well our feeble frame he knows;
   in his hands he gently bears us,
   rescues us from all our foes.
   Praise him! Praise him!
   Praise him! Praise him!
   Widely as his mercy flows!

4. Angels, help us to adore him;
   ye behold him face to face;
   sun and moon, bow down before him,
   dwellers all in time and space.
   Praise him! Praise him!
   Praise him! Praise him!
   Praise with us the God of grace!

   Henry Francis Lyte (1793-1847) alt.
   based on Psalm 103

4. Praise him that he gave the rain
   to mature the swelling grain:

5. And hath bid the fruitful field
   crops of precious increase yield:

6. Praise him for our harvest-store;
   he hath filled the garner-floor:

7. And for richer food than this,
   pledge of everlasting bliss:

8. Glory to our bounteous King;
   glory let creation sing:
   glory to the Father, Son
   and blest Spirit, Three in One.

   Henry Williams Baker (1821-1877)

423

1. Praise, O praise our God and King;
   hymns of adoration sing:

   for his mercies still endure
   ever faithful, ever sure.

2. Praise him that he made the sun
   day by day his course to run:

3. And the silver moon by night,
   shining with her gentle light:

424

1. Praise the Lord, rise up rejoicing,
   worship, thanks, devotion voicing:
   glory be to God on high!
   Christ, your cross and passion sharing,
   by this Eucharist declaring
   yours th'eternal victory.

2. Scattered flock, one Shepherd sharing,
   lost and lonely, one voice hearing,
   ears are open to your word;
   by your blood new life receiving,
   in your body firm, believing,
   we are yours, and you the Lord.

3. Send us forth alert and living,
   sins forgiven, wrongs forgiving,
   in your Spirit strong and free.
   Finding love in all creation,
   bringing peace in ev'ry nation,
   may we faithful foll'wers be.

   Howard Charles Adie Gaunt (1902-1983)

425

1. Praise the Lord, ye heav'ns, adore him!
   Praise him, angels in the height;
   sun and moon, rejoice before him,
   praise him, all ye stars and light.
   Praise the Lord, for he hath spoken;
   worlds his mighty voice obeyed:
   laws, which never shall be broken,
   for their guidance he hath made.

2. Praise the Lord, for he is glorious:
   never shall his promise fail.
   God hath made his saints victorious;
   sin and death shall not prevail.
   Praise the God of our salvation,
   hosts on high, his pow'r proclaim;
   heav'n and earth and all creation,
   laud and magnify his name!

3. Worship, honour, glory, blessing,
   Lord, we offer to thy name;
   young and old, thy praise expressing,
   join their Saviour to proclaim.
   As the saints in heav'n adore thee,
   we would bow before thy throne;
   as thine angels serve before thee,
   so on earth thy will be done.

   vs. 1 and 2: from 'Foundling Hospital Collection' (1796)
   v. 3: Edward Osler (1798-1863)

426

1. Praise to the Holiest in the height,
   and in the depth be praise;
   in all his words most wonderful,
   most sure in all his ways.

2. O loving wisdom of our God!
   when all was sin and shame,
   a second Adam to the fight,
   and to the rescue came.

3. O wisest love! that flesh and blood,
   which did in Adam fail,
   should strive afresh against the foe,
   should strive and should prevail.

4. And that a higher gift than grace
   should flesh and blood refine,
   God's presence and his very self,
   and essence all-divine.

5. And in the garden secretly,
   and on the cross on high,
   should teach his brethren, and inspire
   to suffer and to die.

6. Praise to the Holiest in the height,
   and in the depth be praise;
   in all his words most wonderful,
   most sure in all his ways.

   John Henry Newman (1801-1890)

427

1. Praise to the Lord,
   the Almighty, the King of creation;
   O my soul, praise him,
   for he is thy health and salvation:
   all ye who hear,
   now to his temple draw near,
   joining in glad adoration.

2. Praise to the Lord,
   who o'er all things so wondrously
      reigneth,
   shieldeth thee gently from harm,
   or when fainting sustaineth:
   hast thou not seen
   how thy heart's wishes have been
   granted in what he ordaineth?

3. Praise to the Lord,
   who doth prosper thy work and
      defend thee;
   surely his goodness and mercy
   shall daily attend thee:
   ponder anew
   what the Almighty can do,
   if to the end he befriend thee.

4. Praise to the Lord,
   O let all that is in me adore him!
   All that hath life and breath,
   come now with praises before him!
   Let the Amen
   sound from his people again:
   gladly for ay we adore him.

Joachim Neander (1650-1680)
trans. Catherine Winkworth (1827-1878)

428

1. Purify my heart,
   let me be as gold
   and precious silver.
   Purify my heart,
   let me be as gold, pure gold.

   Refiner's fire,
   my heart's one desire
   is to be holy,
   set apart for you, Lord.
   I choose to be holy,
   set apart for you, my master,
   ready to do your will.

2. Purify my heart,
   cleanse me from within
   and make me holy.
   Purify my heart,
   cleanse me from my sin, deep within.

Brian Doerksen
© 1990 Mercy Vineyard Music/Kingsway's Thankyou Music

429

1. Put thou thy trust in God,
   in duty's path go on;
   walk in his strength with faith and hope,
   so shall thy work be done.

2. Commit thy ways to him,
   thy works into his hands,
   and rest on his unchanging word,
   who heav'n and earth commands.

3. Though years on years roll on,
   his cov'nant shall endure;
   though clouds and darkness hide
      his path,
   the promised grace is sure.

4. Give to the winds thy fears;
   hope, and be undismayed:
   God hears thy sighs and counts thy
      tears;
   God shall lift up thy head.

5. Through waves and clouds and storms
   his pow'r will clear thy way:
   wait thou his time; the darkest night
   shall end in brightest day.

6. Leave to his sov'reign sway
   to choose and to command;
   so shalt thou, wond'ring, own his way,
   how wise, how strong his hand.

   Paul Gerhardt (1607-1676)
   trans. John Wesley (1703-1791) and others

430

1. Rejoice in the Lord always
   and again I say rejoice.
   Rejoice in the Lord always
   and again I say rejoice.
   Rejoice, rejoice
   and again I say rejoice.
   Rejoice, rejoice
   and again I say rejoice.

   Based on Philippians 4:4

431

1. Rejoice, O land, in God thy might;
   his will obey, him serve aright;
   for thee the saints uplift their voice:
   fear not, O land, in God rejoice.

2. Glad shalt thou be, with blessing
      crowned,
   with joy and peace thou shalt abound;
   yea, love with thee shall make his home
   until thou see God's kingdom come.

3. He shall forgive thy sins untold:
   remember thou his love of old;
   walk in his way, his word adore,
   and keep his truth for evermore.

   Robert Bridges (1844-1930)

432

1. Rejoice, the Lord is King!
   Your Lord and King adore;
   mortals, give thanks and sing,
   and triumph evermore.

   Lift up your heart, lift up your voice;
   rejoice, again I say, rejoice.

2. Jesus the Saviour reigns,
   the God of truth and love;
   when he had purged our stains,
   he took his seat above.

3. His kingdom cannot fail;
   he rules o'er earth and heav'n;
   the keys of death and hell
   are to our Jesus giv'n.

4. He sits at God's right hand
   till all his foes submit,
   and bow to his command,
   and fall beneath his feet.

   Charles Wesley (1707-1788)

433

1. Rejoice, the year upon its way
   has brought again that blessèd day
   when on the Church by Christ our
       Lord
   the Holy Spirit was outpoured.

2. From out the heav'ns a rushing noise
   came like the tempest's sudden voice,
   and mingled with th'Apostles' prayer,
   proclaiming loud that God was there.

3. Like quiv'ring tongues of light
       and flame,
   upon each one the Spirit came:
   tongues, that the earth might hear
       their call,
   and fire, that love might burn in all.

4. And so to all were spread abroad
   the wonders of the works of God;
   they knew the prophet's word fulfilled,
   and owned the gift which God had
       willed.

5. Look down, most gracious God,
       this day
   upon thy people as we pray;
   and Christ the Lord upon us pour
   the Spirit's gift for evermore.
   Amen.

Based on the Latin (c. 4th century) trans. the Editors of
'The New English Hymnal'

434

1. Restore, O Lord,
   the honour of your name,
   in works of sov'reign pow'r
   come shake the earth again,
   that all may see
   and come with rev'rent fear
   to the living God
   whose kingdom shall outlast the years.

2. Restore, O Lord,
   in all the earth your fame,
   and in our time revive
   the Church that bears your name.
   And in your anger,
   Lord, remember mercy,
   O living God
   whose mercy shall outlast the years.

3. Bend us, O Lord,
   where we are hard and cold,
   in your refiner's fire
   come purify the gold.
   Though suff'ring comes
   and evil crouches near,
   still our living God
   is reigning, he is reigning here.

4. Restore, O Lord,
   the honour of your name,
   in works of sov'reign pow'r
   come shake the earth again,
   that all may see
   and come with rev'rent fear
   to the living God
   whose kingdom shall outlast the years.

Graham Kendrick (b. 1950) and Chris Rolinson
© 1981 Kingsway's Thankyou Music

435

1. Ride on, ride on in majesty!
   Hark, all the tribes hosanna cry;
   thy humble beast pursues his road
   with palms and scattered garments
     strowed.

2. Ride on, ride on in majesty!
   In lowly pomp ride on to die;
   O Christ, thy triumphs now begin
   o'er captive death and conquered sin.

3. Ride on, ride on in majesty!
   The wingèd squadrons of the sky
   look down with sad and wond'ring eyes
   to see th'approaching sacrifice.

4. Ride on, ride on in majesty!
   Thy last and fiercest strife is nigh;
   the Father, on his sapphire throne,
   awaits his own anointed Son.

5. Ride on, ride on in majesty!
   In lowly pomp ride on to die;
   bow thy meek head to mortal pain,
   then take, O God, thy pow'r, and reign.

Henry Hart Milman (1791-1868) alt.

436

Rise and shine,
and give God his glory, glory.
Rise and shine,
and give God his glory, glory.
Rise and shine,
and give God his glory, glory,
children of the Lord.

1. The Lord said to Noah:
   'There's gonna be a floody, floody.'
   Lord said to Noah:
   'There's gonna be a floody, floody.
   Get those children
   out of the muddy, muddy,
   children of the Lord.'

2. So Noah, he built him,
   he built him an arky, arky,
   Noah, he built him,
   he built him an arky, arky,
   built it out of
   hickory barky, barky,
   children of the Lord.

3. The animals, they came on,
   they came on, by twosies, twosies,
   animals, they came on,
   they came on, by twosies, twosies,
   elephants and
   kangaroosies, roosies,
   children of the Lord.

4. It rained and poured
   for forty daysies, daysies,
   rained and poured
   for forty daysies, daysies,
   nearly drove those
   animals crazyies, crazyies,
   children of the Lord.

5. The sun came out
   and dried up the landy, landy,
   sun came out
   and dried up the landy, landy,
   everything was
   fine and dandy, dandy,
   children of the Lord.

6. If you get to heaven
   before I do-sies, do-sies,
   you get to heaven
   before I do-sies, do-sies,
   tell those angels,
   I'm comin' too-sies, too-sies,
   children of the Lord.

Based on Genesis 6:4

437

1. Rock of ages, cleft for me,
   let me hide myself in thee;
   let the water and the blood,
   from thy riven side which flowed,
   be of sin the double cure:
   cleanse me from its guilt and pow'r.

2. Not the labours of my hands
   can fulfil thy law's demands;
   could my zeal no respite know,
   could my tears for ever flow,
   all for sin could not atone:
   thou must save, and thou alone.

3. Nothing in my hands I bring,
   simply to thy cross I cling;
   naked, come to thee for dress;
   helpless, look to thee for grace;
   tainted, to the fountain fly;
   wash me, Saviour, or I die.

4. While I draw this fleeting breath,
   when mine eyelids close in death,
   when I soar through tracts unknown,
   see thee on thy judgement throne;
   Rock of ages, cleft for me,
   let me hide myself in thee.

Augustus Montague Toplady (1740-1778) alt.

438

1. Saviour, again
   to thy dear name we raise
   with one accord
   our parting hymn of praise;
   we stand to bless thee
   ere our worship cease;
   then, lowly kneeling,
   wait thy word of peace.

2. Grant us thy peace
   upon our homeward way;
   with thee began,
   with thee shall end, the day:
   guard thou the lips from sin,
   the hearts from shame,
   that in this house
   have called upon thy name.

3. Grant us thy peace,
   Lord, through the coming night;
   turn thou for us
   its darkness into light;
   from harm and danger
   keep thy children free,
   for dark and light
   are both alike to thee.

4. Grant us thy peace
   throughout our earthly life,
   our balm in sorrow,
   and our stay in strife;
   then, when thy voice
   shall bid our conflict cease,
   call us, O Lord,
   to thine eternal peace.

John Ellerton (1826-1893)

439

1. See amid the winter's snow,
   born for us on earth below,
   see the tender Lamb appears,
   promised from eternal years.

   Hail, thou ever-blessèd morn,
   hail, redemption's happy dawn!
   Sing through all Jerusalem,
   Christ is born in Bethlehem.

2. Lo, within a manger lies
   he who built the starry skies;
   he who, throned in heights sublime,
   sits amid the cherubim.

3. Say, ye holy shepherds, say,
   what your joyful news today?
   Wherefore have ye left your sheep
   on the lonely mountain steep?

4. 'As we watched at dead of night,
   lo, we saw a wondrous light;
   angels, singing peace on earth,
   told us of the Saviour's birth.'

5. Sacred infant, all divine,
   what a tender love was thine,
   thus to come from highest bliss,
   down to such a world as this!

6. Virgin mother, Mary blest,
   by the joys that fill thy breast,
   pray for us, that we may prove
   worthy of the Saviour's love.

   Edward Caswall (1814-1878)

440

1. See him lying on a bed of straw:
   a draughty stable with an open door.
   Mary cradling the babe she bore:
   the Prince of Glory is his name.

   O now carry me to Bethlehem
   to see the Lord of love again:
   just as poor as was the stable then,
   the Prince of Glory when he came!

2. Star of silver, sweep across the skies,
   show where Jesus in the manger lies;
   shepherds, swiftly from your stupor
     rise
   to see the Saviour of the world!

3. Angels, sing again the song you sang,
   sing the glory of God's gracious plan;
   sing that Bethl'em's little baby can
   be the saviour of us all.

4. Mine are riches, from your poverty;
   from your innocence, eternity;
   mine, forgiveness by your death
     for me,
   child of sorrow for my joy.

   Michael Perry (b. 1942)

441

1. See the conqu'ror mounts in triumph,
   see the King in royal state
   riding on the clouds his chariot
   to his heav'nly palace gate;
   hark, the choirs of angel-voices
   joyful alleluias sing,
   and the portals high are lifted
   to receive their heav'nly King.

2. Who is this that comes in glory
   with the trump of jubilee?
   Lord of battles, God of armies,
   he has gained the victory;
   he who on the cross did suffer,
   he who from the grave arose,
   he has vanquished sin and Satan,
   he by death has spoiled his foes.

3. Thou hast raised our human nature
   in the clouds of God's right hand;
   there we sit in heav'nly places,
   there with thee in glory stand;
   Jesus reigns, adored by angels,
   takes our flesh to heaven's throne;
   mighty Lord, in thine ascension,
   we by faith behold our own.

4. Glory be to God the Father;
   glory be to God the Son,
   dying, ris'n, ascending for us,
   who the heav'nly realm has won;
   glory to the Holy Spirit;
   to One God in persons Three;
   glory both in earth and heaven,
   glory, endless glory, be.

   Christopher Wordsworth (1807-1885) alt.

442

1. Seek ye first the kingdom of God,
   and his righteousness,
   and all these things shall be added
     unto you;
   allelu, alleluia.

   Alleluia, alleluia, alleluia,
   allelu, alleluia.

2. You shall not live by bread alone,
   but by ev'ry word
   that proceeds from the mouth of God;
   allelu, alleluia.

3. Ask and it shall be given unto you,
   seek and ye shall find;
   knock, and it shall be opened unto you;
   allelu, alleluia.

   v. 1: Karen Lafferty (b. 1948)
   vs. 2 & 3: unknown, based on Matthew 6:33; 7:7
   © 1972 Maranatha! Music/CopyCare Ltd

443

1. Shall we not love thee, Mother dear,
   whom Jesus loves so well,
   and to his glory year by year
   thy praise and honour tell?

2. Thee did he choose from whom to take
   true flesh, his flesh to be;
   in it to suffer for our sake,
   and by it make us free.

3. O wondrous depth of love divine,
   that he should bend so low;
   and, Mary, O what joy was thine
   the Saviour's love to know.

4. Joy to be mother of the Lord,
   yet thine the truer bliss,
   in ev'ry thought and deed and word
   to be for ever his.

5. Now in the realm of life above
   close to thy Son thou art,
   while on thy soul glad streams of love
   flow from his sacred heart.

6. Jesu, the Virgin's holy Son,
   praise we thy mother blest;
   grant when our earthly course is run,
   life with the saints at rest.

   Henry Williams Baker (1821-1877)

444

1. Silent night, holy night.
   All is calm, all is bright,
   round yon virgin mother and child;
   holy infant, so tender and mild,
   sleep in heavenly peace,
   sleep in heavenly peace.

2. Silent night, holy night.
   Shepherds quake at the sight,
   glories stream from heaven afar,
   heav'nly hosts sing alleluia:
   Christ, the Saviour is born,
   Christ, the Saviour is born.

3. Silent night, holy night.
   Son of God, love's pure light,
   radiant beams from thy holy face,
   with the dawn of redeeming grace:
   Jesus, Lord, at thy birth,
   Jesus, Lord, at thy birth.

   Joseph Mohr (1792-1848)
   trans. John Freeman Young (1820-1885)

445

1. Sing lullaby!
   Lullaby baby, now reclining,
   sing lullaby!
   Hush, do not wake the infant king.
   Angels are watching,
   stars are shining
   over the place where he is lying:
   sing lullaby!

2. Sing lullaby!
   Lullaby baby, now a-sleeping,
   sing lullaby!
   Hush, do not wake the infant king.
   Soon will come sorrow
   with the morning,
   soon will come bitter grief and
       weeping:
   sing lullaby!

3. Sing lullaby!
   Lullaby baby, now a-dozing,
   sing lullaby!
   Hush, do not wake the infant king.
   Soon comes the cross,
   the nails, the piercing,
   then in the grave at last reposing:
   sing lullaby!

4. Sing lullaby!
   Lullaby! is the babe awaking?
   Sing lullaby.
   Hush, do not stir the infant king.
   Dreaming of Easter,
   gladsome morning,
   conquering death, its bondage
       breaking:
   sing lullaby!

   Sabine Baring-Gould (1834-1924)

446

1. Sing, my tongue, the glorious battle,
   sing the last the dread affray;
   o'er the Cross, the victor's trophy,
   sound the high triumphal lay;
   how, the pains of death enduring,
   earth's Redeemer won the day.

2. When at length th'appointed fullness
   of the sacred time was come,
   he was sent, the world's creator,
   from the Father's heav'nly home,
   and was found in human fashion,
   offspring of the Virgin's womb.

3. Now the thirty years are ended
   which on earth he willed to see,
   willingly he meets his Passion,
   born to set his people free;
   on the cross the Lamb is lifted,
   there the sacrifice to be.

4. There the nails and spear he suffers,
   vinegar and gall and reed;
   from his sacred body piercèd
   blood and water both proceed:
   precious flood, which all creation
   from the stain of sin hath freed.

PART TWO

5. Faithful Cross, above all other,
   one and only noble tree!
   None in foliage, none in blossom,
   none in fruit thy peer may be;
   sweetest wood and sweetest iron,
   sweetest weight is hung on thee!

6. Bend, O lofty tree, thy branches,
   thy too rigid sinews bend;
   and awhile the stubborn hardness,
   which thy birth bestowed, suspend;
   and the limbs of heav'n's high monarch
   gently on thine arms extend.

7. Thou alone wast counted worthy
   this world's ransom to sustain,
   that by thee a wrecked creation
   might its ark and haven gain,
   with the sacred blood anointed
   of the Lamb that hath been slain.

8. Praise and honour to the Father,
   praise and honour to the Son,
   praise and honour to the Spirit,
   ever Three and ever One,
   One in might and One in glory,
   while eternal ages run.
   (Amen.)

Venantius Fortunatus (c. 530-609)
trans. John Mason Neale (1818-1866)

447

1. Sing to God new songs of worship,
   all his deeds are marvellous;
   he has brought salvation to us
   with his hand and holy arm:
   he has shown to all the nations
   righteousness and saving pow'r;
   he recalled his truth and mercy
   to his people Israel.

2. Sing to God new songs of worship,
   earth has seen his victory;
   let the lands of earth be joyful
   praising him with thankfulness:
   sound upon the harp his praises,
   play to him with melody;
   let the trumpets sound his triumph,
   show your joy to God the king!

3. Sing to God new songs of worship,
   let the sea now make a noise;
   all on earth and in the waters
   sound your praises to the Lord:
   let the hills be joyful together,
   let the rivers clap their hands,
   for with righteousness and justice
   he will come to judge the earth.

   Michael Baughen (b. 1930) from Psalm 98

448

1. Sing we of the blessèd Mother
   who received the angel's word,
   and obedient to his summons
   bore in love the infant Lord;
   sing we of the joys of Mary
   at whose breast that child was fed
   who is Son of God eternal
   and the everlasting Bread.

2. Sing we, too, of Mary's sorrows,
   of the sword that pierced her through,
   when beneath the cross of Jesus
   she his weight of suff'ring knew,
   looked upon her Son and Saviour
   reigning high on Calv'ry's tree,
   saw the price of our redemption
   paid to set the sinner free.

3. Sing again the joys of Mary
   when she saw the risen Lord,
   and, in prayer with Christ's apostles,
   waited on his promised word:
   from on high the blazing glory
   of the Spirit's presence came,
   heav'nly breath of God's own being,
   manifest through wind and flame.

4. Sing the greatest joy of Mary
   when on earth her work was done,
   and the Lord of all creation
   brought her to his heav'nly home:
   virgin mother, Mary blessèd,
   raised on high and crowned with
     grace,
   may your Son, the world's redeemer,
   grant us all to see his face.

   George Bourne Timms (b. 1910)

449

1. Soldiers of Christ, arise,
   and put your armour on,
   strong in the strength which God
     supplies
   through his eternal Son.

2. Strong in the Lord of hosts,
   and in his mighty pow'r;
   who in the strength of Jesus trusts
   is more than conqueror.

3. Stand then in his great might,
   with all his strength endued;
   and take, to arm you for the fight,
   the panoply of God.

4. To keep your armour bright,
   attend with constant care,
   still walking in your Captain's sight
   and watching unto prayer.

5. From strength to strength go on,
   wrestle and fight and pray;
   tread all the pow'rs of darkness down,
   and win the well-fought day.

6. That, having all things done,
   and all your conflicts past,
   ye may o'ercome, through Christ alone,
   and stand entire at last.

   Charles Wesley (1707-1788)
   based on Ephesians 6:10-18

450

1. Soldiers who are Christ's below,
   strong in faith resist the foe:
   boundless is the pledged reward
   unto them who serve the Lord.
   Alleluia.

2. 'Tis no palm of fading leaves
   that the conqu'ror's hand receives;
   joys are ours, serene and pure,
   light that ever shall endure.
   Alleluia.

3. For the souls that overcome
   waits the beauteous heav'nly home,
   where the blessèd evermore
   tread on high the starry floor.
   Alleluia.

4. Passing soon and little worth
   are the things that tempt on earth;
   heav'nward lift thy soul's regard:
   God himself is thy reward.
   Alleluia.

5. Father, who the crown dost give,
   Saviour, by whose death we live,
   Spirit, who our hearts dost raise,
   Three in One, thy name we praise.
   Alleluia.

Latin hymn (18th century)
trans. John H. Clark (1839-1888) alt.

451

1. Songs of thankfulness and praise,
   Jesus, Lord to thee we raise,
   manifested by the star
   to the sages from afar;
   branch of royal David's stem,
   in thy birth at Bethlehem;
   anthems be to thee addressed:
   God in man made manifest.

2. Manifest at Jordan's stream,
   prophet, priest and King supreme,
   and at Cana wedding-guest,
   in thy Godhead manifest,
   manifest in pow'r divine,
   changing water into wine;
   anthems be to thee addressed:
   God in man made manifest.

3. Manifest in making whole,
   palsied limbs and fainting soul,
   manifest in valiant fight,
   quelling all the devil's might,
   manifest in gracious will,
   ever bringing good from ill;
   anthems be to thee addressed:
   God in man made manifest.

4. Sun and moon shall darkened be,
   stars shall fall, the heav'ns shall flee;
   Christ will then like lightning shine,
   all will see his glorious sign.
   All will then the trumpet hear,
   all will see the judge appear;
   thou by all wilt be confessed:
   God in man made manifest.

5. Grant us grace to see thee, Lord,
   mirrored in thy holy word;
   may we imitate thee now,
   and be pure, as pure art thou;
   that we like to thee may be
   at thy great Epiphany,
   and may praise thee, ever blest,
   God in man made manifest.

Christopher Wordsworth (1807-1885)

452

1. Soul of my Saviour,
   sanctify my breast;
   Body of Christ,
   be thou my saving guest;
   Blood of my Saviour,
   bathe me in thy tide,
   wash me with water
   flowing from thy side.

2. Strength and protection
   may thy passion be;
   O blessèd Jesus,
   hear and answer me;
   deep in thy wounds, Lord,
   hide and shelter me;
   so shall I never,
   never part from thee.

3. Guard and defend me
   from the foe malign;
   in death's dread moments
   make me only thine;
   call me, and bid me
   come to thee on high,
   where I may praise thee
   with thy saints for ay.

   Ascribed to Pope John XXII (1249-1334)
   trans. unknown

453

1. Spirit of mercy, truth and love,
   O shed thine influence from above,
   and still from age to age convey
   the wonders of this sacred day.

2. In ev'ry clime, by ev'ry tongue,
   be God's surpassing glory sung;
   let all the list'ning earth be taught
   the acts our great Redeemer wrought.

3. Unfailing comfort, heav'nly guide,
   still o'er thy holy Church preside;
   let humankind thy blessings prove,
   Spirit of mercy, truth and love.

   'Foundling Hospital Collection' (1774) alt.

454

Spirit of the living God,
fall afresh on me.
Spirit of the living God,
fall afresh on me.
Melt me, mould me,
fill me, use me.
Spirit of the living God,
fall afresh on me.

Daniel Iverson (1890-1972)
© 1963 Birdwing Music/Alliance Media Ltd/CopyCare Ltd

455

Spirit of the living God,
fall afresh on me;
Spirit of the living God,
fall afresh on me;
fill me anew, fill me anew;
Spirit of the Lord,
fall afresh on me.

Paul Armstrong
© 1984 Restoration Music Ltd/Sovereign Lifestyle Music Ltd

456

1. Stand up and bless the Lord,
   ye people of his choice;
   stand up and bless the Lord your God
   with heart and soul and voice.

2. Though high above all praise,
   above all blessing high,
   who would not fear his holy name,
   and laud and magnify?

3. O for the living flame
   from his own altar brought,
   to touch our lips, our mind inspire,
   and wing to heav'n our thought.

4. God is our strength and song,
   and his salvation ours;
   then be his love in Christ proclaimed
   with all our ransomed pow'rs.

5. Stand up and bless the Lord,
   the Lord your God adore;
   stand up and bless his glorious name
   henceforth for evermore.

James Montgomery (1771-1854)

457

1. Stand up, stand up for Jesus,
   stand up before his cross,
   an instrument of torture
   inflicting pain and loss;
   transformed by his obedience
   to God's redeeming plan,
   the cross was overpowered
   by Christ, both God and man.

2. Stand up, stand up for Jesus,
   be counted as his own;
   his gospel of forgiveness
   he cannot spread alone.
   The love which draws us to him,
   he calls us out to share;
   he calls us to the margins
   to be his presence there.

3. Stand up, stand up for Jesus,
   in faith and hope be strong,
   stand firm for right and justice,
   opposed to sin and wrong.
   Give comfort to the wounded,
   and care for those in pain,
   for Christ, in those who suffer,
   is crucified again.

4. Stand up, stand up for Jesus,
   who reigns as King of kings,
   be ready for the challenge
   of faith his kingship brings.
   He will not force obedience,
   he gives to each the choice
   to turn from all that's holy,
   or in his love rejoice.

5. Stand up, stand up for Jesus,
   give courage to the weak,
   be unashamed to praise him,
   be bold his name to speak.
   Confront the cross unflinching,
   Christ's love has set us free;
   he conquered death for ever
   and lives eternally.

Jean Holloway (b. 1939)

458

Stay with me,
remain here with me,
watching and praying,
watching and praying.

Taizé Community

459

Steal away, steal away,
steal away to Jesus.
Steal away, steal away home,
I ain't got long to stay here.

1. My Lord, he calls me,
   he calls me by the thunder.
   The trumpet sounds within my soul;
   I ain't got long to stay here.

2. Green trees are bending,
   the sinner stands a-trembling.
   The trumpet sounds within my soul;
   I ain't got long to stay here.

3. My Lord, he calls me,
   he calls me by the lightning.
   The trumpet sounds within my soul;
   I ain't got long to stay here.

Spiritual

460

1. Strengthen for service, Lord, the hands
   that holy things have taken;
   let ears that now have heard thy songs
   to clamour never waken.

2. Lord, may the tongues which 'Holy'
   sang
   keep free from all deceiving;
   the eyes which saw thy love be bright,
   thy blessèd hope perceiving.

3. The feet that tread thy holy courts
   from light do thou not banish;
   the bodies by thy Body fed
   with thy new life replenish.

Syriac Liturgy, perhaps by Ephraim the Syrian
(c. 306-373), trans. Charles William Humphreys
(1840-1921) and Percy Dearmer (1867-1936)

461

1. Such love, pure as the whitest snow;
   such love weeps for the shame I know;
   such love, paying the debt I owe;
   O Jesus, such love.

2. Such love, stilling my restlessness;
   such love, filling my emptiness;
   such love, showing me holiness;
   O Jesus, such love.

3. Such love springs from eternity;
   such love, streaming through history;
   such love, fountain of life to me;
   O Jesus, such love.

Graham Kendrick (b. 1950)
© 1988 Make Way Music Ltd

462

1. Sun of my soul, thou Saviour dear,
   it is not night if thou be near:
   O may no earth-born cloud arise
   to hide thee from thy servant's eyes.

2. When the soft dews of kindly sleep
   my wearied eyelids gently steep,
   be my last thought, how sweet to rest
   for ever on my Saviour's breast.

3. Abide with me from morn till eve,
   for without thee I cannot live;
   abide with me when night is nigh,
   for without thee I dare not die.

4. Watch by the sick; enrich the poor
   with blessings from thy boundless
   store;
   be ev'ry mourner's sleep tonight
   like infant's slumbers, pure and light.

John Keble (1792-1866)

463

1. Sweet sacrament divine,
   hid in thy earthly home,
   lo, round thy lowly shrine,
   with suppliant hearts we come;
   Jesus, to thee our voice we raise,
   in songs of love and heartfelt praise,
   sweet sacrament divine,
   sweet sacrament divine.

2. Sweet sacrament of peace,
   dear home of ev'ry heart,
   where restless yearnings cease,
   and sorrows all depart;
   there in thine ear all trustfully
   we tell our tale of misery,
   sweet sacrament of peace,
   sweet sacrament of peace.

3. Sweet sacrament of rest,
   ark from the ocean's roar,
   within thy shelter blest
   soon may we reach the shore;
   save us, for still the tempest raves,
   save, lest we sink beneath the waves,
   sweet sacrament of rest,
   sweet sacrament of rest.

4. Sweet sacrament divine,
   earth's light and jubilee,
   in thy far depths doth shine
   thy Godhead's majesty;
   sweet light, so shine on us, we pray,
   that worthless joys may fade away,
   sweet sacrament divine,
   sweet sacrament divine.

   Francis Stanfield (1835-1914) alt.

464

1. Take my life, and let it be
   consecrated, Lord, to thee;
   take my moments and my days,
   let them flow in ceaseless praise.

2. Take my hands, and let them move
   at the impulse of thy love;
   take my feet, and let them be
   swift and beautiful for thee.

3. Take my voice, and let me sing
   always, only, for my King;
   take my lips, and let them be
   filled with messages from thee.

4. Take my silver and my gold;
   not a mite would I withhold;
   take my intellect, and use
   ev'ry pow'r as thou shalt choose.

5. Take my will, and make it thine:
   it shall be no longer mine;
   take my heart: it is thine own;
   it shall be thy royal throne.

6. Take my love; my Lord, I pour
   at thy feet its treasure-store;
   take myself, and I will be
   ever, only, all for thee.

   Frances Ridley Havergal (1836-1879)

465

1. Take up thy cross, the Saviour said,
   if thou wouldst my disciple be;
   deny thyself, the world forsake,
   and humbly follow after me.

2. Take up thy cross – let not its weight
   fill thy weak spirit with alarm:
   his strength shall bear thy spirit up,
   and brace thy heart, and nerve thine arm.

3. Take up thy cross, nor heed the shame,
   nor let thy foolish pride rebel:
   thy Lord for thee the Cross endured,
   to save thy soul from death and hell.

4. Take up thy cross then in his strength,
   and calmly ev'ry danger brave;
   'twill guide thee to a better home,
   and lead to vict'ry o'er the grave.

5. Take up thy cross, and follow Christ,
   nor think till death to lay it down;
   for only those who bear the cross
   may hope to wear the glorious crown.

6. To thee, great Lord, the One in Three,
   all praise for evermore ascend:
   O grant us in our home to see
   the heav'nly life that knows no end.

Charles William Everest (1814-1877)
based on Mark 8, alt.

466

1. Teach me, my God and King,
   in all things thee to see;
   and what I do in anything
   to do it as for thee.

2. A man that looks on glass,
   on it may stay his eye;
   or, if he pleaseth, through it pass,
   and then the heav'n espy.

3. All may of thee partake;
   nothing can be so mean
   which, with this tincture, 'For thy sake',
   will not grow bright and clean.

4. A servant with this clause
   makes drudgery divine;
   who sweeps a room, as for thy laws,
   makes that and the action fine.

5. This is the famous stone
   that turneth all to gold;
   for that which God doth touch and own
   cannot for less be told.

George Herbert (1593-1633)

467

1. Tell out, my soul,
   the greatness of the Lord:
   unnumbered blessings,
   give my spirit voice;
   tender to me
   the promise of his word;
   in God my Saviour
   shall my heart rejoice.

2. Tell out, my soul,
   the greatness of his name:
   make known his might,
   the deeds his arm has done;
   his mercy sure,
   from age to age the same;
   his holy name,
   the Lord, the mighty one.

3. Tell out, my soul,
   the greatness of his might:
   pow'rs and dominions
   lay their glory by;
   proud hearts and stubborn
   wills are put to flight,
   the hungry fed,
   the humble lifted high.

4. Tell out, my soul,
   the glories of his word:
   firm is his promise,
   and his mercy sure.
   Tell out, my soul,
   the greatness of the Lord
   to children's children
   and for evermore.

Timothy Dudley-Smith (b. 1926)
based on Luke 1:46-55

468

1. Thank you, Lord, for this new day,
   thank you, Lord, for this new day,
   thank you, Lord, for this new day,
   right where we are.

   Alleluia, praise the Lord,
   alleluia, praise the Lord,
   alleluia, praise the Lord,
   right where we are.

2. Thank you, Lord, for food to eat,
   thank you, Lord, for food to eat,
   thank you, Lord, for food to eat,
   right where we are.

3. Thank you, Lord, for clothes to wear,
   thank you, Lord, for clothes to wear,
   thank you, Lord, for clothes to wear,
   right where we are.

4. Thank you, Lord, for all your gifts,
   thank you, Lord, for all your gifts,
   thank you, Lord, for all your gifts,
   right where we are.

Diane Davis Andrew,
adapted by Geoffrey Marshall-Taylor
© 1971 Celebration/Kingsway's Thankyou Music

469

Thanks for the fellowship
found at this meal,
thanks for a day refreshed;
thanks to the Lord
for his presence we feel,
thanks for the food he blessed.

Joyfully sing praise to the Lord,
praise to the risen Son,
alleluia, ever adored,
pray that his will be done.
As he was known
in the breaking of bread,
now is he known again;
and by his hand
have the hungry been fed,
thanks be to Christ. Amen!

Jean Holloway (b. 1939)

470

1. The advent of our King
   our prayers must now employ,
   and we must hymns of welcome sing
   in strains of holy joy.

2. The everlasting Son
   incarnate deigns to be;
   himself a servant's form puts on,
   to set his servants free.

3. Daughter of Sion, rise
   to meet thy lowly King;
   nor let thy faithless heart despise
   the peace he comes to bring.

4. As Judge, on clouds of light,
   he soon will come again,
   and his true members all unite
   with him in heav'n to reign.

5. All glory to the Son
   who comes to set us free,
   with Father, Spirit, ever One,
   through all eternity.

Charles Coffin (1676-1749)
trans. John Chandler (1806-1876) alt.

471

1. The angel Gabriel
   from heaven came,
   his wings as drifted snow,
   his eyes as flame.
   'All hail', said he,
   'thou lowly maiden, Mary,
   most highly favoured lady.' Gloria!

2. 'For known a blessèd Mother
   thou shalt be.
   All generations laud
   and honour thee.
   Thy Son shall be Emmanuel,
   by seers foretold,
   most highly favoured lady.' Gloria!

3. Then gentle Mary meekly
   bowed her head.
   'To me be as it pleaseth God,'
   she said.
   'My soul shall laud and magnify
   his holy name.'
   Most highly favoured lady! Gloria!

4. Of her, Emmanuel,
   the Christ, was born
   in Bethlehem,
   all on a Christmas morn;
   and Christian folk throughout
   the world will ever say:
   'Most highly favoured lady.' Gloria!

   Sabine Baring-Gould (1834-1924)

472

1. The Church of God a kingdom is,
   where Christ in pow'r doth reign;
   where spirits yearn till, seen in bliss,
   their Lord shall come again.

2. Glad companies of saints possess
   this Church below, above;
   and God's perpetual calm doth bless
   their paradise of love.

3. An altar stands within the shrine
   whereon, once sacrificed,
   is set, immaculate, divine,
   the Lamb of God, the Christ.

4. There rich and poor, from countless
         lands,
   praise Christ on mystic rood;
   there nations reach forth holy hands
   to take God's holy food.

5. There pure life-giving streams o'erflow
   the sower's garden-ground;
   and faith and hope fair blossoms show,
   and fruits of love abound.

6. O King, O Christ, this endless grace
   to all your people bring,
   to see the vision of your face
   in joy, O Christ, our King.

   Lionel Muirhead (1845-1925) alt.

473

1. The Church's one foundation
   is Jesus Christ, her Lord;
   she is his new creation,
   by water and the word;
   from heav'n he came and sought her
   to be his holy bride,
   with his own blood he bought her,
   and for her life he died.

   Continued overleaf

2. Elect from ev'ry nation,
   yet one o'er all the earth,
   her charter of salvation,
   one Lord, one faith, one birth;
   one holy name she blesses,
   partakes one holy food,
   and to one hope she presses,
   with ev'ry grace endued.

3. 'Mid toil and tribulation,
   and tumult of her war,
   she waits the consummation
   of peace for evermore;
   till with the vision glorious
   her longing eyes are blest,
   and the great Church victorious
   shall be the Church at rest.

4. Yet she on earth hath union
   with God the Three in One,
   and mystic sweet communion
   with those whose rest is won:
   O happy ones and holy! Lord,
   give us grace that we
   like them, the meek and lowly,
   on high may dwell with thee.

   Samuel John Stone (1839-1900)

474

1. The day of resurrection!
   Earth, tell it out abroad;
   the passover of gladness,
   the passover of God!
   From death to life eternal,
   from earth unto the sky,
   our Christ hath brought us over
   with hymns of victory.

2. Our hearts be pure from evil,
   that we may see aright
   the Lord in rays eternal
   of resurrection-light;
   and list'ning to his accents,
   may hear so calm and plain
   his own 'All hail' and, hearing,
   may raise the victor strain.

3. Now let the heav'ns be joyful,
   and earth her song begin,
   the round world keep high triumph,
   and all that is therein;
   let all things, seen and unseen,
   their notes of gladness blend,
   for Christ the Lord hath risen,
   our joy that hath no end.

   St. John of Damascus (c. 750)
   trans. John Mason Neale (1818-1866)

475

1. The day thou gavest, Lord, is ended:
   the darkness falls at thy behest;
   to thee our morning hymns ascended,
   thy praise shall sanctify our rest.

2. We thank thee that thy Church
      unsleeping,
   while earth rolls onward into light,
   through all the world her watch is
      keeping,
   and rests not now by day or night.

3. As o'er each continent and island
   the dawn leads on another day,
   the voice of prayer is never silent,
   nor dies the strain of praise away.

4. The sun that bids us rest is waking
   our brethren 'neath the western sky,
   and hour by hour fresh lips are making
   thy wondrous doings heard on high.

5. So be it, Lord; thy throne shall never,
   like earth's proud empires, pass away;
   thy kingdom stands, and grows for ever,
   till all thy creatures own thy sway.

John Ellerton (1826-1893)

476

1. Th'eternal gifts of Christ the King,
   th'apostles' glory, let us sing;
   and all, with hearts of gladness, raise
   due hymns of thankful love and praise.

2. Theirs is the steadfast faith of saints,
   and hope that never yields nor faints,
   and love of Christ in perfect glow
   that lays the prince of this world low.

3. In them the Father's glory shone,
   in them the will of God the Son,
   in them exults the Holy Ghost,
   through them rejoice the heav'nly host.

4. To thee, Redeemer, now we cry,
   that thou wouldst join to them on high
   thy servants, who this grace implore,
   for ever and for evermore.

St. Ambrose (c. 340-397)
trans. John Mason Neale (1818-1866) alt.

477

1. The first Nowell the angel did say
   was to certain poor shepherds in fields
   as they lay;
   in fields where they lay keeping their
   sheep,
   on a cold winter's night that was so
   deep.

Nowell, Nowell, Nowell, Nowell,
born is the King of Israel!

2. They lookèd up and saw a star,
   shining in the east, beyond them far,
   and to the earth it gave great light,
   and so it continued both day and night.

3. And by the light of that same star,
   three wise men came from country far;
   to seek for a king was their intent,
   and to follow the star wherever it went.

4. This star drew nigh to the north-west,
   o'er Bethlehem it took its rest,
   and there it did both stop and stay
   right over the place where Jesus lay.

5. Then entered in those wise men three,
   full rev'rently upon their knee,
   and offered there in his presence,
   their gold and myrrh and frankincense.

6. Then let us all with one accord
   sing praises to our heav'nly Lord,
   that hath made heav'n and earth of
   naught,
   and with his blood mankind hath
   bought.

from William Sandys' 'Christmas Carols,
Ancient and Modern' (1833)

478

1. The God of Abraham praise,
   who reigns enthroned above,
   Ancient of everlasting Days,
   and God of love:
   Jehovah, great I AM,
   by earth and heav'n confessed;
   we bow and bless the sacred name,
   for ever blest.

2. The God of Abraham praise,
   at whose supreme command
   from earth we rise, and seek the joys
   at his right hand:
   we all on earth forsake,
   its wisdom, fame and pow'r;
   and him our only portion make,
   our shield and tow'r.

3. The God of Abraham praise,
   whose all-sufficient grace
   shall guide us all our happy days,
   in all our ways:
   he is our faithful friend;
   he is our gracious God;
   and he will save us to the end,
   through Jesus' blood.

4. He by himself has sworn –
   we on his oath depend –
   we shall, on eagles' wings upborne,
   to heav'n ascend:
   we shall behold his face,
   we shall his pow'r adore,
   and sing the wonders of his grace
   for evermore.

5. The whole triumphant host
   give thanks to God on high:
   'Hail, Father, Son and Holy Ghost!'
   they ever cry:
   Hail, Abraham's God and ours!
   We join the heav'nly throng,
   and celebrate with all our pow'rs
   in endless song.

Thomas Olivers (1725-1799)
based on the Hebrew Yigdal alt.

479

1. The God of love my shepherd is,
   and he that doth me feed;
   while he is mine and I am his,
   what can I want or need?

2. He leads me to the tender grass,
   where I both feed and rest;
   then to the streams that gently pass:
   in both I have the best.

3. Or if I stray, he doth convert,
   and bring my mind in frame,
   and all this not for my desert,
   but for his holy name.

4. Yea, in death's shady black abode
   well may I walk, not fear;
   for thou art with me, and thy rod
   to guide, thy staff to bear.

5. Surely thy sweet and wondrous love
   shall measure all my days;
   and, as it never shall remove,
   so neither shall my praise.

George Herbert (1593-1633) based on Psalm 23

480

1. The head that once was crowned with
   thorns
   is crowned with glory now:
   a royal diadem adorns
   the mighty victor's brow.

2. The highest place that heav'n affords
   is his, is his by right.
   The King of kings and Lord of lords,
   and heav'n's eternal light.

3. The joy of all who dwell above,
   the joy of all below,
   to whom he manifests his love,
   and grants his name to know.

4. To them the cross, with all its shame,
   with all its grace is giv'n;
   their name an everlasting name,
   their joy the joy of heav'n.

5. They suffer with their Lord below,
   they reign with him above,
   their profit and their joy to know
   the myst'ry of his love.

6. The cross he bore is life and health,
   though shame and death to him;
   his people's hope, his people's wealth,
   their everlasting theme.

Thomas Kelly (1769-1855)

481

1. The holly and the ivy,
   when they are both full grown,
   of all the trees that are in the wood
   the holly bears the crown.

   *The rising of the sun
   and the running of the deer,
   the playing of the merry organ,
   sweet singing in the choir.*

2. The holly bears a blossom,
   white as the lily flow'r,
   and Mary bore sweet Jesus Christ
   to be our sweet Saviour.

3. The holly bears a berry,
   as red as any blood,
   and Mary bore sweet Jesus Christ
   to do poor sinners good.

4. The holly bears a prickle,
   as sharp as any thorn,
   and Mary bore sweet Jesus Christ
   on Christmas day in the morn.

5. The holly bears a bark,
   as bitter as any gall,
   and Mary bore sweet Jesus Christ
   for to redeem us all.

6. The holly and the ivy,
   when they are both full grown,
   of all the trees that are in the wood
   the holly bears the crown.

Traditional

482

1. The ink is black, the page is white,
together we learn to read and write,
to read and write;
and now a child can understand
this is the law of all the land,
all the land;
the ink is black, the page is white,
together we learn to read and write,
to read and write.

2. The slate is black, the chalk is white,
the words stand out so clear and
bright,
so clear and bright;
and now at last we plainly see
the alphabet of liberty,
liberty;
the slate is black, the chalk is white,
together we learn to read and write,
to read and write.

3. A child is black, a child is white,
the whole world looks upon the sight,
upon the sight;
for very well the whole world knows,
this is the way that freedom grows,
freedom grows;
a child is black, a child is white,
together we learn to read and write,
to read and write.

4. The world is black, the world is white,
it turns by day and then by night,
and then by night;
it turns so each and ev'ry one
can take his station in the sun,
in the sun;
the world is black, the world is white,
together we learn to read and write,
to read and write.

David Arkin

483

1. The King is among us,
his spirit is here,
let's draw near and worship,
let songs fill the air.

2. He looks down upon us,
delight in his face,
enjoying his children's love,
enthralled by our praise.

3. For each child is special,
accepted and loved,
a love gift from Jesus
to his Father above.

4. And now he is giving
his gifts to us all,
for no one is worthless
and each one is called.

5. The Spirit's anointing
on all flesh comes down,
and we shall be channels
for works like his own.

6. We come now believing
your promise of pow'r,
for we are your people
and this is your hour.

7. The King is among us,
his Spirit is here,
let's draw near and worship,
let songs fill the air.

Graham Kendrick (b. 1950)
© 1981 Kingsway's Thankyou Music

484

1. The King of love my shepherd is,
   whose goodness faileth never;
   I nothing lack if I am his
   and he is mine for ever.

2. Where streams of living waters flow
   my ransomed soul he leadeth,
   and where the verdant pastures grow
   with food celestial feedeth.

3. Perverse and foolish oft I strayed,
   but yet in love he sought me,
   and on his shoulder gently laid,
   and home, rejoicing, brought me.

4. In death's dark vale I fear no ill
   with thee, dear Lord, beside me;
   thy rod and staff my comfort still,
   thy cross before to guide me.

5. Thou spread'st a table in my sight,
   thy unction grace bestoweth:
   and O what transport of delight
   from thy pure chalice floweth!

6. And so through all the length of days
   thy goodness faileth never;
   good Shepherd, may I sing thy praise
   within thy house for ever.

Henry Williams Baker (1821-1877)
based on Psalm 23

485

1. The Lord is King! lift up thy voice,
   O earth, and all ye heav'ns, rejoice;
   from world to world the joy shall ring:
   'The Lord omnipotent is King!'

2. He reigns! ye saints, exalt your strains;
   your God is King, your Saviour reigns;
   and he is at the Father's side,
   the Man of Love, the Crucified.

3. Alike pervaded by his eye
   all parts of his dominion lie:
   this world of ours and worlds unseen,
   and thin the boundary between.

4. One Lord one empire all secures;
   he reigns, and endless life is yours;
   through earth and heav'n one song
      shall ring:
   'The Lord omnipotent is King!'

Josiah Conder (1789-1855) alt.

486

The Lord is my light,
my light and salvation;
in God I trust,
in God I trust.

Based on Psalm 27

487

The Lord is my song,
the Lord is my praise:
all my hope comes from God.
The Lord is my song,
the Lord is my praise:
God, the well-spring of life.

Taizé Community

488

1. The Lord is ris'n indeed:
   now is his work performed;
   now is the mighty captive freed,
   and death's strong castle stormed.

2. The Lord is ris'n indeed:
   then hell has lost his prey;
   with him is ris'n the ransomed seed
   to reign in endless day.

3. The Lord is ris'n indeed:
   he lives, to die no more;
   he lives, the sinner's cause to plead,
   whose curse and shame he bore.

4. The Lord is ris'n indeed:
   attending angels, hear!
   up to the courts of heav'n with speed
   the joyful tidings bear.

5. Then take your golden lyres
   and strike each cheerful chord;
   join, all ye bright celestial choirs,
   to sing our risen Lord.

Thomas Kelly (1769-1855)

489

1. The Lord will come and not be slow,
   his footsteps cannot err;
   before him righteousness shall go,
   his royal harbinger.

2. Truth from the earth, like to a flow'r,
   shall bud and blossom free;
   and justice, from her heav'nly bow'r,
   bless all humanity.

3. The nations all whom thou hast made
   shall come, and all shall frame
   to bow them low before thee, Lord,
   and glorify thy name.

4. For great thou art, and wonders great
   by thy strong hand are done:
   thou in thy everlasting seat
   remainest God alone.

John Milton (1608-1674)
based on Psalms 82, 85 and 86, alt.

490

When the tune 'Crimond' is used

1. The Lord's my shepherd, I'll not want,
   He makes me down to lie
   in pastures green. He leadeth me
   the quiet waters by.

2. My soul he doth restore again,
   and me to walk doth make
   within the paths of righteousness,
   e'en for his own name's sake.

3. Yea, though I walk in death's dark vale,
   yet will I fear none ill.
   For thou art with me, and thy rod
   and staff me comfort still.

4. My table thou hast furnishèd
   in presence of my foes:
   my head thou dost with oil anoint,
   and my cup overflows.

5. Goodness and mercy all my life
   shall surely follow me.
   And in God's house for evermore
   my dwelling-place shall be.

Psalm 23 from 'The Scottish Psalter' (1650)

When the Tune 'Brother James's Air' is used

1. The Lord's my shepherd, I'll not want.
   He makes me down to lie
   in pastures green. He leadeth me
   the quiet waters by.
   He leadeth me, he leadeth me
   the quiet waters by.

2. My soul he doth restore again,
   and me to walk doth make
   within the paths of righteousness,
   e'en for his own name's sake.
   within the paths of righteousness,
   e'en for his own name's sake.

3. Yea, though I walk in death's dark vale,
   yet will I fear none ill.
   For thou art with me, and thy rod
   and staff me comfort still.
   For thou art with me, and thy rod
   and staff me comfort still.

4. My table thou hast furnishèd
   in presence of my foes:
   my head thou dost with oil anoint,
   and my cup overflows.
   my head thou dost with oil anoint,
   and my cup overflows.

5. Goodness and mercy all my life
   shall surely follow me.
   And in God's house for evermore
   my dwelling-place shall be.
   And in God's house for evermore
   my dwelling-place shall be.

   Psalm 23 from 'The Scottish Psalter' (1650)

491

1. The race that long in darkness pined
   has seen a glorious light;
   the people dwell in day, who dwelt
   in death's surrounding night.

2. To hail thy rise, thou better Sun,
   the gath'ring nations come,
   joyous as when the reapers bear
   the harvest treasures home.

3. To us a child of hope is born,
   to us a Son is giv'n;
   him shall the tribes of earth obey,
   him all the hosts of heav'n.

4. His name shall be the Prince of Peace,
   for evermore adored;
   the Wonderful, the Counsellor,
   the great and mighty Lord.

5. His pow'r increasing still shall spread,
   his reign no end shall know;
   justice shall guard his throne above,
   and peace abound below.

   John Morison (1750-1798) based on Isaiah 9:2-7

492

1. The royal banners forward go,
   the cross shines forth in mystic glow;
   where he in flesh, our flesh who made,
   our sentence bore, our ransom paid.

   Continued overleaf

2. There whilst he hung, his sacred side
   by soldier's spear was opened wide,
   to cleanse us in the precious flood
   of water mingled with his blood.

3. Fulfilled is now what David told
   in true prophetic song of old,
   how God the sinner's king should be;
   for God is reigning from the tree.

4. O tree of glory, tree most fair,
   ordained those holy limbs to bear,
   how bright in purple robe it stood,
   the purple of a Saviour's blood!

5. To thee, eternal Three in One,
   let homage meet by all be done,
   as by the cross thou dost restore,
   so rule and guide us evermore.
   Amen.

   Venantius Fortunatus (530-609)
   trans. John Mason Neale (1818-1866) and others

493

1. The spacious firmament on high,
   with all the blue ethereal sky,
   and spangled heav'ns, a shining frame,
   their great Original proclaim.
   The unwearied sun from day to day
   does his Creator's pow'r display,
   and publishes to ev'ry land
   the works of an almighty hand,
   the works of an almighty hand.

2. Soon as the evening shades prevail
   the moon takes up the wondrous tale,
   and nightly to the list'ning earth
   repeats the story of her birth;
   whilst all the stars that round her burn,
   and all the planets in their turn,
   confirm the tidings, as they roll,
   and spread the truth from pole to pole,
   and spread the truth from pole to pole.

3. What though in solemn silence all
   move round the dark terrestrial ball;
   what though nor lit'ral voice nor sound
   amid their radiant orbs be found;
   in reason's ear they all rejoice,
   and utter forth a glorious voice,
   for ever singing as they shine,
   'The hand that made us is divine,
   the hand that made us is divine.'

   Joseph Addison (1672-1719) based on Psalm 19:1-6, alt.

494

1. The Spirit lives to set us free,
   walk, walk in the light.
   He binds us all in unity,
   walk, walk in the light.

   Walk in the light,
   walk in the light,
   walk in the light,
   walk in the light of the Lord.

2. Jesus promised life to all,
   walk, walk in the light.
   The dead were wakened by his call,
   walk, walk in the light.

3. He died in pain on Calvary,
   walk, walk in the light,
   to save the lost like you and me,
   walk, walk in the light.

4. We know his death was not the end,
   walk, walk in the light.
   He gave his Spirit to be our friend,
   walk, walk in the light.

5. By Jesus' love our wounds are healed,
   walk, walk in the light.
   The Father's kindness is revealed,
   walk, walk in the light.

6. The Spirit lives in you and me,
   walk, walk in the light.
   His light will shine for all to see,
   walk, walk in the light.

Damian Lundy (b. 1944)

495

1. The strife is o'er, the battle done;
   now is the Victor's triumph won;
   O let the song of praise be sung:
   Alleluia.

2. Death's mightiest pow'rs have done
      their worst,
   and Jesus hath his foes dispersed;
   let shouts of praise and joy outburst:
   Alleluia.

3. On the third morn he rose again
   glorious in majesty to reign;
   O let us swell the joyful strain:
   Alleluia.

4. Lord, by the stripes which wounded
      thee
   from death's dread sting thy servants
      free,
   that we may live, and sing to thee:
   Alleluia.

Latin hymn (17th century)
trans. Francis Pott (1832-1909)

496

1. The Virgin Mary
   had a baby boy,
   the Virgin Mary
   had a baby boy,
   the Virgin Mary
   had a baby boy,
   and they said that his
   name was Jesus.

   He came from the glory,
   he came from the glorious kingdom.
   He came from the glory,
   he came from the glorious kingdom.
   O yes, believer.
   O yes, believer.
   He came from the glory,
   he came from the glorious kingdom.

2. The angels sang
   when the baby was born, (3)
   and proclaimed him
   the Saviour Jesus.

3. The wise men saw
   where the baby was born, (3)
   and they saw that his
   name was Jesus.

Traditional West Indian

497

1. Thee we adore,
   O hidden Saviour, thee,
   who in thy sacrament
   art pleased to be;
   both flesh and spirit
   in thy presence fail,
   yet here thy presence
   we devoutly hail.

2. O blest memorial
   of our dying Lord,
   who living bread
   to all doth here afford;
   O may our souls
   for ever feed on thee,
   and thou, O Christ,
   for ever precious be.

3. Fountain of goodness,
   Jesus, Lord and God,
   cleanse us, unclean,
   with thy most cleansing blood;
   increase our faith and love,
   that we may know
   the hope and peace
   which from thy presence flow.

4. O Christ, whom now
   beneath a veil we see,
   may what we thirst for
   soon our portion be:
   to gaze on thee unveiled,
   and see thy face,
   the vision of thy glory
   and thy grace.

St. Thomas Aquinas (1227-1274)
trans. James Russell Woodford (1820-1885) alt.

498

1. There are hundreds of sparrows,
   thousands, millions,
   they're two a penny,
   far too many there must be;
   there are hundreds and thousands,
   millions of sparrows,
   but God knows ev'ry one
   and God knows me.

2. There are hundreds of flowers,
   thousands, millions,
   and flowers fair
   the meadows wear for all to see;
   there are hundreds and thousands,
   millions of flowers,
   but God knows ev'ry one
   and God knows me.

3. There are hundreds of planets,
   thousands, millions,
   way out in space
   each has a place by God's decree;
   there are hundreds and thousands,
   millions of planets,
   but God knows ev'ry one
   and God knows me.

4. There are hundreds of children,
   thousands, millions,
   and yet their names
   are written on God's memory,
   there are hundreds and thousands,
   millions of children,
   but God knows ev'ry one
   and God knows me.

John Gowans

499

1. There is a green hill far away,
   without a city wall,
   where the dear Lord was crucified
   who died to save us all.

2. We may not know, we cannot tell,
   what pains he had to bear,
   but we believe it was for us
   he hung and suffered there.

3. He died that we might be forgiv'n,
   he died to make us good;
   that we might go at last to heav'n,
   saved by his precious blood.

4. There was no other good enough
   to pay the price of sin;
   he only could unlock the gate
   of heav'n, and let us in.

5. O dearly, dearly has he loved,
   and we must love him too,
   and trust in his redeeming blood,
   and try his works to do.

   Cecil Frances Alexander (1818-1895)

500

1. There is a Redeemer,
   Jesus, God's own Son,
   precious Lamb of God, Messiah,
   Holy One.

   Thank you, O my Father,
   for giving us your Son,
   and leaving your Spirit
   till the work on earth is done.

2. Jesus, my Redeemer,
   name above all names,
   precious Lamb of God, Messiah,
   O for sinners slain.

3. When I stand in glory,
   I will see his face,
   and there I'll serve my King for ever,
   in that holy place.

   Melody Green, based on Scripture
   © Birdwing Music/BMG Songs Inc/
   Alliance Media Ltd/CopyCare Ltd

501

1. There's a wideness in God's mercy,
   like the wideness of the sea;
   there's a kindness in his justice,
   which is more than liberty.
   There is no place where earth's sorrows
   are more felt than up in heav'n;
   there is no place where earth's failings
   have such kindly judgement giv'n.

2. But we make his love too narrow
   by false limits of our own;
   and we magnify his strictness
   with a zeal he will not own.
   There is plentiful redemption
   in the blood that has been shed,
   there is joy for all the members
   in the sorrows of the Head.

3. For the love of God is broader
   than the scope of human mind,
   and the heart of the Eternal
   is most wonderfully kind.
   If our love were but more simple,
   we should take him at his word;
   and our hearts would find assurance
   in the promise of the Lord.

   Frederick William Faber (1814-1863) alt.

502

1. Thine arm, O Lord, in days of old
   was strong to heal and save;
   it triumphed o'er disease and death,
   o'er darkness and the grave:
   to thee they went, the blind, the dumb,
   the palsied and the lame,
   the outcasts with their grievances,
   the sick with fevered frame.

2. And lo, thy touch brought life and
       health,
   gave speech and strength and sight;
   and youth renewed and frenzy calmed
   owned thee, the Lord of light:
   and now, O Lord, be near to bless,
   almighty as before,
   in crowded street, by restless couch,
   as by that ancient shore.

3. Be thou our great deliv'rer still,
   thou Lord of life and death;
   restore and quicken, soothe and bless,
   with thine almighty breath:
   to hands that work, and eyes that see,
   give wisdom's heav'nly lore,
   that whole and sick, and weak and
       strong,
   may praise thee evermore.

   Edward Hayes Plumptre (1821-1891) alt.

503

1. Thine be the glory,
   risen, conqu'ring Son,
   endless is the vict'ry
   thou o'er death hast won;
   angels in bright raiment
   rolled the stone away,
   kept the folded grave-clothes
   where thy body lay.

*Thine be the glory,
risen, conqu'ring Son,
endless is the vict'ry
thou o'er death hast won.*

2. Lo! Jesus meets us,
   risen from the tomb;
   lovingly he greets us,
   scatters fear and gloom.
   Let the Church with gladness
   hymns of triumph sing,
   for her Lord now liveth;
   death hast lost its sting.

3. No more we doubt thee,
   glorious Prince of Life;
   life is naught without thee:
   aid us in our strife.
   Make us more than conqu'rors
   through thy deathless love;
   bring us safe through Jordan
   to thy home above.

   *Edmond Louis Budry (1854-1932)
   trans. Richard Birch Hoyle (1875-1939)*

504

1. Thine for ever! God of love,
   hear us from thy throne above;
   thine for ever may we be
   here and in eternity.

2. Thine for ever! Lord of life,
   shield us through our earthly strife;
   thou the life, the truth, the way,
   guide us to the realms of day.

3. Thine for ever! O how blest
   they who find in thee their rest!
   Saviour, guardian, heav'nly friend,
   O defend us to the end.

4. Thine for ever! Shepherd, keep
   us thy frail and trembling sheep;
   safe within thy tender care,
   let us all thy goodness share.

5. Thine for ever! thou our guide,
   all our wants by thee supplied,
   all our sins by thee forgiv'n,
   lead us, Lord, from earth to heav'n.

   Mary Fawler Maude (1819-1913) alt.

505

1. Think of a world
   without any flowers,
   think of a world
   without any trees,
   think of a sky
   without any sunshine,
   think of the air
   without any breeze.
   We thank you, Lord,
   for flow'rs and trees and sunshine,
   we thank you, Lord,
   and praise your holy name.

2. Think of a world
   without any animals,
   think of a field
   without any herd,
   think of a stream
   without any fishes,
   think of a dawn
   without any bird.
   We thank you, Lord,
   for all your living creatures,
   we thank you, Lord,
   and praise your holy name.

3. Think of a world
   without any people,
   think of a street
   with no-one living there,
   think of a town
   without any houses,
   no-one to love
   and nobody to care.
   We thank you, Lord,
   for families and friendships,
   we thank you, Lord,
   and praise your holy name.

   Doreen Newport (b. 1927)

506

1. This is my body, broken for you,
   bringing you wholeness, making you
     free.
   Take it and eat it, and when you do,
   do it in love for me.

2. This is my blood, poured out for you,
   bringing forgiveness, making you free.
   Take it and drink it, and when you do,
   do it in love for me.

3. Back to my Father soon I shall go.
   Do not forget me; then you will see
   I am still with you, and you will know
   you're very close to me.

4. Filled with my Spirit, how you will grow!
   You are my branches; I am the tree.
   If you are faithful, others will know
   you are alive in me.

5. Love one another: I have loved you,
   and I have shown you how to be free;
   serve one another, and when you do,
   do it in love for me.

   vs. 1 & 2: Jimmy Owens,
   vs. 3-5: Damian Lundy (b. 1944)
   © 1978 Bud John Songs/Alliance Media Ltd/CopyCare Ltd

507

1. This is my will, my one command,
   that love should dwell among you all.
   This is my will, that you should love
   as I have shown that I love you.

2. No greater love can be than this:
   to choose to die to save one's friends.
   You are my friends if you obey
   what I command that you should do.

3. I call you now no longer slaves;
   no slave knows all his master does.
   I call you friends, for all I hear
   my Father say you hear from me.

4. You chose not me, but I chose you,
   that you should go and bear much
     fruit.
   I chose you out that you in me
   should bear much fruit that will abide.

5. All that you ask my Father dear
   for my name's sake you shall receive.
   This is my will, my one command,
   that love should dwell in each, in all.

James Quinn (b. 1919)

508

1. This is the day, this is the day
   that the Lord has made,
   that the Lord has made;
   we will rejoice, we will rejoice
   and glad in it, and be glad in it.
   This is the day that the Lord has made;
   we will rejoice and be glad in it.
   This is the day, this is the day
   that the Lord has made.

2. This is the day, this is the day
   when he rose again,
   when he rose again;
   we will rejoice, we will rejoice
   and be glad in it, and be glad in it.
   This is the day when he rose again;
   we will rejoice and be glad in it.
   This is the day, this is the day
   when he rose again.

3. This is the day, this is the day
   when the Spirit came,
   when the Spirit came;
   we will rejoice, we will rejoice
   and be glad in it, and be glad in it.
   This is the day when the Spirit came;
   we will rejoice and be glad in it.
   This is the day, this is the day
   when the Spirit came.

Les Garrett (b. 1944) based on Psalm 118
© 1967 Scripture in Song/CopyCare Ltd

509

1. This joyful Eastertide,
   away with sin and sorrow,
   my love, the Crucified,
   hath sprung to life this morrow.

   Had Christ, that once was slain,
   ne'er burst his three-day prison,
   our faith had been in vain:
   but now hath Christ arisen,
   arisen, arisen, arisen.

2. My flesh in hope shall rest,
   and for a season slumber:
   till trump from east to west
   shall wake the dead in number.

3. Death's flood hath lost its chill,
   since Jesus crossed the river:
   lover of souls, from ill
   my passing soul deliver.

   George Ratcliffe Woodward (1848-1934)

510

This little light of mine,
I'm gonna let it shine.
This little light of mine,
I'm gonna let it shine.
This little light of mine,
I'm gonna let it shine,
let it shine, let it shine,
let it shine.

1. The light that shines
   is the light of love,
   lights the darkness
   from above,
   it shines on me
   and it shines on you,
   and shows what the
   power of love can do.
   I'm gonna shine my light
   both far and near,
   I'm gonna shine my light
   both bright and clear.
   Where there's a dark
   corner in this land,
   I'm gonna let my
   little light shine.

2. On Monday he gave
   me the gift of love.
   Tuesday peace came
   from above.
   On Wednesday he told me
   to have more faith.
   On Thursday he gave me
   a little more grace.
   Friday he told me
   just to watch and pray.
   Saturday he told me
   just what to say.
   On Sunday he gave me
   the pow'r divine to let
   my little light shine.

   Traditional

511

This world you have made
is a beautiful place;
it tells the pow'r of your love.
We rejoice in the beauty
of your world,
from the seas
to the heavens above.

1. The morning whispers of purity;
   the evening of your peace;
   the thunder booms your exuberance
   in the awesome pow'r you release.

2. The tenderness of a new-born child;
   the gentleness of the rain;
   simplicity in a single cell;
   and complexity in a brain.

3. Your stillness rests in a silent pool;
   infinity drifts in space;
   your grandeur straddles the mountain
      tops;
   and we see your face in each face.

   Susan Sayers (b. 1946)

512

1. Thou art the Way: by thee alone
   from sin and death we flee;
   and all who would the Father seek
   must seek him, Lord, by thee.

2. Thou art the Truth: thy word alone
   true wisdom can impart;
   thou only canst inform the mind
   and purify the heart.

3. Thou art the Life: the rending tomb
   proclaims thy conqu'ring arm;
   and those who put their trust in thee
   nor death nor hell shall harm.

4. Thou art the Way, the Truth, the Life:
   grant us that Way to know,
   that Truth to keep, that Life to win,
   whose joys eternal flow.

George Washington Doane (1799-1859)
based on John 14

2. Heaven's arches rang
   when the angels sang
   and proclaimed thee of royal degree,
   but in lowliest birth
   didst thou come to earth
   and in deepest humility.

3. Though the fox found rest,
   and the bird its nest
   in the shade of the cedar tree,
   yet the world found no bed
   for the Saviour's head
   in the desert of Galilee.

4. Though thou camest, Lord,
   with the living word
   that should set all thy people free,
   yet with treachery,
   scorn and a crown of thorn
   did they bear thee to Calvary.

5. When the heav'ns shall ring
   and the angels sing
   at thy coming to victory.
   let thy voice call me home,
   saying 'Heav'n has room,
   there is room at my side for thee.'

Emily Elizabeth Steele Elliott (1836-1897) based on
Luke 2:7, adapted by Michael Forster (b. 1946)

513

1. Thou didst leave thy throne
   and thy kingly crown
   when thou camest to earth for me,
   but in Bethlehem's home
   was there found no room
   for thy holy nativity.

O come to my heart, Lord Jesus,
there is room in my heart for thee.

514

1. Thou, whose almighty word
   chaos and darkness heard,
   and took their flight;
   hear us, we humbly pray,
   and where the gospel-day
   sheds not its glorious ray,
   let there be light.

2. Thou, who didst come to bring
on thy redeeming wing,
healing and sight,
health to the sick in mind,
sight to the inly blind,
O now to all mankind
let there be light.

3. Spirit of truth and love,
life-giving, holy Dove,
speed forth thy flight;
move on the water's face,
bearing the lamp of grace,
and in earth's darkest place
let there be light.

4. Holy and blessèd Three,
glorious Trinity,
Wisdom, Love, Might;
boundless as ocean's tide
rolling in fullest pride,
through the earth far and wide
let there be light.

John Marriott (1780-1825)

515

1. Three in One, and One in Three,
ruler of the earth and sea,
hear us while we lift to thee
holy chant and psalm.

2. Light of lights! with morning-shine
lift on us thy light divine;
and let charity benign
breathe on us her balm.

3. Light of lights! when falls the ev'n,
let it close on sin forgiv'n,
fold us in the peace of heav'n;
shed a holy calm.

4. Three in One, and One in Three,
dimly here we worship thee;
with the saints hereafter we
hope to bear the palm.

Gilbert Rorison (1821-1869)

516

1. Through all the changing scenes of life,
in trouble and in joy,
the praises of my God shall still
my heart and tongue employ.

2. O magnify the Lord with me,
with me exalt his name;
when in distress to him I called,
he to my rescue came.

3. The hosts of God encamp around
the dwellings of the just;
deliv'rance he affords to all
who on his succour trust.

4. O make but trial of his love:
experience will decide
how blest are they, and only they,
who in his truth confide.

5. Fear him, ye saints, and you will then
have nothing else to fear;
make you his service your delight,
your wants shall be his care.

6. To Father, Son and Holy Ghost,
the God whom we adore,
be glory as it was, is now,
and shall be evermore.

Psalm 34 in 'New Version' (Tate and Brady, 1696)

517

1. Through the night of doubt and sorrow
   onward goes the pilgrim band,
   singing songs of expectation,
   marching to the promised land.

2. Clear before us, through the darkness,
   gleams and burns the guiding light;
   so we march in hope united,
   stepping fearless through the night.

3. One the light of God's own presence
   o'er his ransomed people shed,
   chasing far the gloom and terror,
   bright'ning all the path we tread.

4. One the object of our journey,
   one the faith which never tires,
   one the earnest looking forward,
   one the hope our God inspires.

5. One the strain that lips of thousands
   lift as from the heart of one:
   one the conflict, one the peril,
   one the march in God begun.

6. One the gladness of rejoicing
   on the far eternal shore,
   where the one almighty Father
   reigns in love for evermore.

7. Onward, therefore, fellow pilgrims,
   onward with the Cross our aid;
   bear its shame and fight its battle,
   till we rest beneath its shade.

8. Soon shall come the great awaking,
   soon the rending of the tomb;
   then the scatt'ring of all shadows,
   and the end of toil and gloom.

Bernhardt Severin Ingemann (1789-1862)
trans. Sabine Baring-Gould (1834-1924) alt.

518

1. Thy hand, O God, has guided
   thy flock, from age to age;
   the wondrous tale is written,
   full clear, on ev'ry page;
   our forebears owned thy goodness,
   and we their deeds record;
   and both of this bear witness:
   one Church, one Faith, one Lord.

2. Thy heralds brought glad tidings
   to greatest, as to least;
   they bade them rise, and hasten
   to share the great King's feast;
   and this was all their teaching,
   in ev'ry deed and word,
   to all alike proclaiming:
   one Church, one Faith, one Lord.

3. Through many a day of darkness,
   through many a scene of strife,
   the faithful few fought bravely
   to guard the nation's life.
   Their gospel of redemption,
   sin pardoned, hope restored,
   was all in this enfolded:
   one Church, one Faith, one Lord.

4. And we, shall we be faithless?
   Shall hearts fail, hands hang down?
   Shall we evade the conflict,
   and cast away our crown?
   Not so: in God's deep counsels
   some better thing is stored:
   we will maintain, unflinching,
   one Church, one Faith, one Lord.

5. Thy mercy will not fail us,
   nor leave thy work undone;
   with thy right hand to help us,
   the vict'ry shall be won;
   and then by all creation,
   thy name shall be adored.
   And this shall be their anthem:
   one Church, one Faith, one Lord.

   Edward Hayes Plumptre (1821-1891) alt.

6. O'er lands both near and far
   thick darkness broodeth yet:
   arise, O morning star,
   arise, and never set.

   Lewis Hensley (1824-1905) alt.

519

1. Thy kingdom come, O God,
   thy rule, O Christ, begin;
   break with thine iron rod
   the tyrannies of sin.

2. Where is thy reign of peace
   and purity and love?
   When shall all hatred cease,
   as in the realms above?

3. When comes the promised time
   that war shall be no more,
   and lust, oppression, crime
   shall flee thy face before?

4. We pray thee, Lord, arise,
   and come in thy great might;
   revive our longing eyes,
   which languish for thy sight.

5. Some scorn thy sacred name,
   and wolves devour thy fold;
   by many deeds of shame
   we learn that love grows cold.

520

1. Thy kingdom come! on bended knee
   the passing ages pray;
   and faithful souls have yearned to see
   on earth that kingdom's day.

2. But the slow watches of the night
   not less to God belong;
   and for the everlasting right
   the silent stars are strong.

3. And lo, already on the hills
   the flags of dawn appear;
   gird up your loins, ye prophet souls,
   proclaim the day is near.

4. The day in whose clear-shining light
   all wrong shall stand revealed,
   when justice shall be throned in might,
   and ev'ry hurt be healed.

5. When knowledge, hand in hand with
        peace,
   shall walk the earth abroad:
   the day of perfect righteousness,
   the promised day of God.

   Frederick Lucian Hosmer (1840-1929)

521

1. Thy way, not mine, O Lord,
   however dark it be;
   lead me by thine own hand,
   choose out the path for me.

2. Smooth let it be or rough,
   it will be still the best;
   winding or straight, it leads
   right onward to thy rest.

3. I dare not choose my lot;
   I would not if I might:
   choose thou for me, my God,
   so shall I walk aright.

4. The kingdom that I seek
   is thine, so let the way
   that leads to it be thine,
   else I must surely stray.

5. Take thou my cup, and it
   with joy or sorrow fill,
   as best to thee may seem;
   choose thou my good and ill.

6. Choose thou for me my friends,
   my sickness or my health;
   choose thou my cares for me,
   my poverty or wealth.

7. Not mine, not mine, the choice
   in things or great or small;
   be thou my guide, my strength,
   my wisdom, and my all.

Horatius Bonar (1808-1889)

522

1. To God be the glory!
   great things he hath done;
   so loved he the world
   that he gave us his Son;
   who yielded his life
   an atonement for sin,
   and opened the life-gate
   that all may go in.

   Praise the Lord, praise the Lord!
   let the earth hear his voice;
   praise the Lord, praise the Lord!
   let the people rejoice:
   O come to the Father,
   through Jesus the Son,
   and give him the glory;
   great things he hath done.

2. O perfect redemption,
   the purchase of blood!
   to ev'ry believer
   the promise of God;
   the vilest offender
   who truly believes,
   that moment from Jesus
   a pardon receives.

3. Great things he hath taught us,
   great things he hath done,
   and great our rejoicing
   through Jesus the Son;
   but purer, and higher,
   and greater will be
   our wonder, our rapture,
   when Jesus we see.

Frances Jane van Alstyne
(Fanny J. Crosby) (1820-1915)

523

1. To the name of our salvation
   laud and honour let us pay,
   which for many a generation
   hid in God's foreknowledge lay,
   but with holy exultation
   we may sing aloud today.

2. Jesus is the name we treasure,
   name beyond what words can tell;
   name of gladness, name of pleasure,
   ear and heart delighting well;
   name of sweetness passing measure,
   saving us from sin and hell.

3. 'Tis the name for adoration,
   name for songs of victory;
   name for holy meditation
   in the vale of misery;
   name for joyful veneration
   by the citizens on high.

4. 'Tis the name that whoso preacheth
   speaks like music to the ear;
   who in prayer this name beseecheth
   sweetest comfort findeth near;
   who its perfect wisdom reacheth
   heav'nly joy posesseth here.

5. Jesus is the name exalted
   over ev'ry other name;
   in this name, whene'er assaulted,
   we can put our foes to shame:
   strength to them who else had halted,
   eyes to blind, and feet to lame.

6. Therefore we in love adoring
   this most blessèd name revere,
   holy Jesus, thee imploring
   so to write it in us here,
   that hereafter, heav'nward soaring,
   we may sing with angels there.

'Gloriosi Salvatoris' (15th century)
trans. John Mason Neale (1818-1866) alt.

524

1. To thee, O Lord, our hearts we raise
   in hymns of adoration;
   to thee bring sacrifice of praise
   with shouts of exultation:
   bright robes of gold the fields adorn,
   the hills with joy are ringing,
   the valleys stand so thick with corn
   that even they are singing.

2. And now, on this our festal day,
   thy bounteous hand confessing,
   upon thine altar, Lord, we lay
   the first-fruits of thy blessing:
   by thee our souls are truly fed
   with gifts of grace supernal;
   thou who dost give us earthly bread,
   give us the bread eternal.

3. We bear the burden of the day,
   and often toil seems dreary;
   but labour ends with sunset ray,
   and rest comes for the weary:
   may we, the angel-reaping o'er,
   stand at the last accepted,
   Christ's golden sheaves for evermore
   to garners bright elected.

4. O blessèd is that land of God,
   where saints abide for ever;
   where golden fields spread far and
     broad,
   where flows the crystal river:
   the strains of all its holy throng
   with ours today are blending;
   thrice blessèd is that harvest-song
   which never hath an ending.

William Chatterton Dix (1837-1898) alt.

525

Ubi caritas et amor.
Ubi caritas Deus ibi est.

1. Your love, O Jesus Christ,
   has gathered us together.

2. May your love, O Jesus Christ,
   be foremost in our lives.

3. Let us love one another
   as God has loved us.

4. Let us be one in love together
   in the one bread of Christ.

5. The love of God in Jesus Christ
   bears eternal joy.

6. The love of God in Jesus Christ
   will never have an end.

Taizé Community

526

1. Unto us a boy is born!
   King of all creation;
   came he to a world forlorn,
   the Lord of ev'ry nation,
   the Lord of ev'ry nation.

2. Cradled in a stall was he,
   watched by cows and asses;
   but the very beasts could see
   that he the world surpasses,
   that he the world surpasses.

3. Then the fearful Herod cried,
   'Pow'r is mine in Jewry!'
   So the blameless children died
   the victims of his fury,
   the victims of his fury.

4. Now may Mary's Son, who came
   long ago to love us,
   lead us all with hearts aflame
   unto the joys above us,
   unto the joys above us.

5. Omega and Alpha he!
   Let the organ thunder,
   while the choir with peals of glee
   shall rend the air asunder,
   shall rend the air asunder.

15th century trans. Percy Dearmer (1867-1936) alt.

527

1. Virgin-born, we bow before thee:
   blessèd was the womb that bore thee;
   Mary, maid and mother mild,
   blessèd was she in her child.

2. Blessèd was the breast that fed thee;
   blessèd was the hand that led thee;
   blessèd was the parent's eye
   that watched thy slumb'ring infancy.

3. Blessèd she by all creation,
   who brought forth the world's salvation,
   blessèd they, for ever blest,
   who love thee most and serve thee best.

4. Virgin-born, we bow before thee:
   blessèd was the womb that bore thee;
   Mary, maid and mother mild,
   blessèd was she in her child.

Reginald Heber (1783-1826)

528

Wait for the Lord, whose day is near.
Wait for the Lord: keep watch, take
heart!

1. Prepare the way for the Lord.
   Make a straight path for him.

2. The glory of the Lord
   shall be revealed.

3. All the earth will see the Lord.

4. Rejoice in the Lord always:
   he is at hand.

5. Seek first the kingdom of God,
   seek and you shall find.

6. Joy and gladness for all
   who seek the Lord.

7. I waited for the Lord:
   he heard my cry.

8. Our eyes are fixed
   on the Lord our God.

9. O Lord, show us your way.
   Guide us in your truth.

10. Prepare the way of the Lord.

Taizé Community, based on Scripture

529

1. Wake, O wake! with tidings thrilling
   the watchmen all
   the air are filling:
   arise, Jerusalem, arise!
   Midnight strikes! no more delaying,
   'The hour has come!'
   we hear them saying.
   Where are ye all, ye maidens wise?
   The Bridegroom comes in sight,
   raise high your torches bright!
   Alleluia!
   The wedding song
   swells loud and strong:
   go forth and join the festal throng.

2. Sion hears the watchmen shouting,
   her heart leaps up
   with joy undoubting,
   she stands and waits with eager eyes;
   see her Friend from heav'n descending,
   adorned with truth
   and grace unending!
   her light burns clear, her star doth rise.
   Now come, thou precious Crown,
   Lord Jesu, God's own son!
   Hosanna!
   Let us prepare
   to follow there,
   where in thy supper we may share.

3. Ev'ry soul in thee rejoices;
   from earthly and
   angelic voices
   be glory giv'n to thee alone!
   Now the gates of pearl receive us,
   thy presence never more
   shall leave us,
   we stand with angels round thy throne.
   Earth cannot give below
   the bliss thou dost bestow.
   Alleluia!
   Grant us to raise,
   to length of days,
   the triumph-chorus of thy praise.

Philipp Nicolai (1556-1608)
trans. Francis Crawford Burkitt (1864-1935) alt.

530

1. We believe in God the Father,
maker of the universe,
and in Christ his Son our Saviour,
come to us by virgin birth.
We believe he died to save us,
bore our sins, was crucified;
then from death he rose victorious,
ascended to the Father's side.

Jesus, Lord of all, Lord of all; (4)
name above all names,
name above all names!

2. We believe he sends his Spirit
on his Church with gifts of pow'r;
God, his word of truth affirming,
sends us to the nations now.
He will come again in glory,
judge the living and the dead:
ev'ry knee shall bow before him,
then must ev'ry tongue confess.

Graham Kendrick (b. 1950)
© 1986 Kingsway's Thankyou Music

531

1. We hail thy presence glorious,
O Christ our great High Priest,
o'er sin and death victorious,
at thy thanksgiving feast:
as thou art interceding
for us in heav'n above,
thy Church on earth is pleading
thy perfect work of love.

2. Through thee in ev'ry nation
thine own their hearts upraise,
off'ring one pure oblation,
one sacrifice of praise:
with thee in blest communion
the living and the dead
are joined in closest union,
one Body with one Head.

3. O living bread from heaven,
Jesu, our Saviour good,
who thine own self hast given
to be our souls' true food;
for us thy body broken
hung on the cross of shame:
this bread its hallowed token
we break in thy dear name.

4. O stream of love unending,
poured from the one true vine,
with our weak nature blending
the strength of life divine;
our thankful faith confessing
in thy life-blood outpoured,
we drink this cup of blessing
and praise thy name, O Lord.

5. May we, thy word believing,
thee through thy gifts receive,
that, thou within us living,
we all to God may live;
draw us from earth to heaven
till sin and sorrow cease,
forgiving and forgiven,
in love and joy and peace.

Richard Godfrey Parsons (1882-1948)

532

1. We have a gospel to proclaim,
   good news for all throughout the earth;
   the gospel of a Saviour's name:
   we sing his glory, tell his worth.

2. Tell of his birth at Bethlehem,
   not in a royal house or hall,
   but in a stable dark and dim,
   the Word made flesh, a light for all.

3. Tell of his death at Calvary,
   hated by those he came to save;
   in lonely suff'ring on the cross:
   for all he loved, his life he gave.

4. Tell of that glorious Easter morn,
   empty the tomb, for he was free;
   he broke the pow'r of death and hell
   that we might share his victory.

5. Tell of his reign at God's right hand,
   by all creation glorified.
   He sends his Spirit on his Church
   to live for him, the Lamb who died.

6. Now we rejoice to name him King:
   Jesus is Lord of all the earth.
   This gospel-message we proclaim:
   we sing his glory, tell his worth.

Edward Joseph Burns (b. 1938)

533

1. We love the place, O God,
   wherein thine honour dwells;
   the joy of thine abode
   all earthly joy excels.

2. It is the house of prayer,
   wherein thy servants meet;
   and thou, O Lord, art there
   thy chosen flock to greet.

3. We love the sacred font;
   for there the holy Dove
   to pour is ever wont
   his blessing from above.

4. We love thine altar, Lord;
   O what on earth so dear?
   For there, in faith adored,
   we find thy presence near.

5. We love the word of life,
   the word that tells of peace,
   of comfort in the strife,
   and joys that never cease.

6. We love to sing below
   for mercies freely giv'n;
   but O, we long to know
   the triumph-song of heav'n.

7. Lord Jesus, give us grace
   on earth to love thee more,
   in heav'n to see thy face,
   and with thy saints adore.

William Bullock (1798-1874) and
Henry Williams Baker (1821-1877)

534

1. We plough the fields and scatter
   the good seed on the land,
   but it is fed and watered
   by God's almighty hand:
   he sends the snow in winter,
   the warmth to swell the grain,
   the breezes and the sunshine,
   and soft, refreshing rain.

   All good gifts around us
   are sent from heav'n above;
   then thank the Lord,
   O thank the Lord,
   for all his love.

2. He only is the maker
   of all things near and far;
   he paints the wayside flower,
   he lights the evening star;
   he fills the earth with beauty,
   by him the birds are fed;
   much more to us, his children,
   he gives our daily bread.

3. We thank thee then, O Father,
   for all things bright and good:
   the seed-time and the harvest,
   our life, our health, our food.
   Accept the gifts we offer
   for all thy love imparts,
   and, what thou most desirest,
   our humble, thankful hearts.

Matthias Claudius (1740-1815)
trans. Jane Montgomery Campbell (1817-1878) alt.

535

1. We pray thee, heav'nly Father,
   to hear us in thy love,
   and pour upon thy children
   the unction from above;
   that so in love abiding,
   from all defilement free,
   we may in pureness offer
   our Eucharist to thee.

2. Be thou our guide and helper,
   O Jesus Christ, we pray;
   so may we well approach thee,
   if thou wilt be the Way:
   thou, very Truth, hast promised
   to help us in our strife,
   food of the weary pilgrim,
   eternal source of life.

3. And thou, creator Spirit,
   look on us, we are thine;
   renew in us thy graces,
   upon our darkness shine;
   that, with thy benediction
   upon our souls outpoured,
   we may receive in gladness
   the body of the Lord.

4. O Trinity of Persons,
   O Unity most high,
   on thee alone relying
   thy servants would draw nigh:
   unworthy in our weakness,
   on thee our hope is stayed,
   and blessed by thy forgiveness
   we will not be afraid.

Vincent Stuckey Stratton Coles (1845-1929)

536

1. We sing the praise of him who died,
   of him who died upon the cross;
   the sinner's hope, though all deride,
   will turn to gain this bitter loss.

2. Inscribed upon the cross we see
   in shining letters, 'God is love';
   he bears our sins upon the tree;
   he brings us mercy from above.

3. The cross! it takes our guilt away:
   it holds the fainting spirit up;
   it cheers with hope the gloomy day,
   and sweetens ev'ry bitter cup.

4. It makes the coward spirit brave
   to face the darkness of the night;
   it takes the terror from the grave,
   and gilds the bed of death with light.

5. The balm of life, the cure of woe,
   the measure and the pledge of love,
   the sinner's refuge here below,
   the angels' theme in heav'n above.

   Thomas Kelly (1769-1855) alt.

537

1. We three kings of Orient are;
   bearing gifts we traverse afar;
   field and fountain, moor and
     mountain,
   following yonder star.

   O star of wonder, star of night,
   star with royal beauty bright,
   westward leading, still proceeding,
   guide us to thy perfect light.

2. Born a King on Bethlehem plain,
   gold I bring, to crown him again,
   King for ever, ceasing never,
   over us all to reign.

3. Frankincense to offer have I,
   incense owns a Deity nigh,
   prayer and praising, gladly raising,
   worship him, God most high.

4. Myrrh is mine, its bitter perfume
   breathes a life of gathering gloom;
   sorrowing, sighing, bleeding, dying,
   sealed in the stone-cold tomb.

5. Glorious now behold him arise,
   King and God and sacrifice;
   alleluia, alleluia,
   earth to heav'n replies.

   John Henry Hopkins (1820-1891) alt.

538

1. We will lay our burden down,
   we will lay our burden down,
   we will lay our burden down
   in the hands of the risen Lord.

2. We will light the flame of love,
   we will light the flame of love,
   we will light the flame of love,
   as the hands of the risen Lord.

3. We will show both hurt and hope,
   we will show both hurt and hope,
   we will show both hurt and hope,
   like the hands of the risen Lord.

4. We will walk the path of peace,
   we will walk the path of peace,
   we will walk the path of peace,
   hand in hand with the risen Lord.

   John L. Bell (b. 1949) and Graham Maule (b. 1958)

539

1. We'll walk the land with hearts on fire;
and ev'ry step will be a prayer.
Hope is rising, new day dawning;
sound of singing fills the air.

2. Two thousand years, and still the flame
is burning bright across the land.
Hearts are waiting, longing, aching,
for awakening once again.

Let the flame burn brighter
in the heart of the darkness,
turning night to glorious day.
Let the song grow louder,
as our love grows stronger;
let it shine!

3. We'll walk for truth, speak out for love;
in Jesus' name we shall be strong,
to lift the fallen, to save the children,
to fill the nation with your song.

Graham Kendrick (b. 1950)
© 1989 Make Way Music Ltd

540

1. Were you there when
they crucified my Lord?
Were you there when
they crucified my Lord?
O, sometimes it causes me
to tremble, tremble, tremble.
Were you there when
they crucified my Lord?

2. Were you there when
they nailed him to a tree?
Were you there when
they nailed him to a tree?
O, sometimes it causes me
to tremble, tremble, tremble.
Were you there when
they nailed him to a tree?

3. Were you there when
they pierced him in the side?
Were you there when
they pierced him in the side?
O, sometimes it causes me
to tremble, tremble, tremble.
Were you there when
they pierced him in the side?

4. Were you there when
they laid him in the tomb?
Were you there when
they laid him in the tomb?
O, sometimes it causes me
to tremble, tremble, tremble.
Were you there when
they laid him in the tomb?

5. Were you there when
he rose to glorious life?
Were you there when
he rose to glorious life?
O, sometimes it causes me
to tremble, tremble, tremble.
Were you there when
he rose to glorious life?

Spiritual alt.

541

1. What a friend we have in Jesus,
   all our sins and griefs to bear!
   What a privilege to carry
   ev'rything to him in prayer!
   O what peace we often forfeit,
   O what needless pain we bear,
   all because we do not carry
   ev'rything to God in prayer!

2. Have we trials and temptations?
   Is there trouble anywhere?
   We should never be discouraged:
   take it to the Lord in prayer!
   Can we find a friend so faithful,
   who will all our sorrows share?
   Jesus knows our ev'ry weakness –
   take it to the Lord in prayer!

3. Are we weak and heavy-laden,
   cumbered with a load of care?
   Jesus only is our refuge,
   take it to the Lord in prayer!
   Do thy friends despise, forsake thee?
   Take it to the Lord in prayer!
   In his arms he'll take and shield thee,
   thou wilt find a solace there.

Joseph Medlicott Scriven (1819-1886)

542

1. What child is this who, laid to rest,
   on Mary's lap is sleeping?
   Whom angels greet
   with anthems sweet,
   while shepherds watch are keeping?
   This, this is Christ the King,
   whom shepherds guard and angels
     sing:
   come, greet the infant Lord,
   the babe, the Son of Mary!

2. Why lies he in such mean estate,
   where ox and ass are feeding?
   Good Christians, fear:
   for sinners here
   the silent Word is pleading.
   Nails, spear, shall pierce him through,
   the cross be borne for me, for you:
   hail, hail the Word made flesh,
   the babe, the Son of Mary!

3. So bring him incense, gold and myrrh,
   come rich and poor, to own him.
   The King of kings
   salvation brings,
   let loving hearts enthrone him.
   Raise, raise the song on high,
   the Virgin sings her lullaby:
   joy, joy for Christ is born,
   the babe, the Son of Mary!

William Chatterton Dix (1837-1898) alt.

543

1. When a knight won his spurs,
   in the stories of old,
   he was gentle and brave,
   he was gallant and bold;
   with a shield on his arm
   and a lance in his hand,
   for God and for valour
   he rode through the land.

2. No charger have I,
   and no sword by my side,
   yet still to adventure
   and battle I ride,
   though back into storyland
   giants have fled,
   and the knights are no more
   and the dragons are dead.

Continued overleaf

3. Let faith be my shield
   and let joy be my steed
   'gainst the dragons of anger,
   the ogres of greed;
   and let me set free,
   with the sword of my youth,
   from the castle of darkness,
   the pow'r of the truth.

   Jan Struther (1901-1953)

6. Through ev'ry period of my life
   thy goodness I'll pursue,
   and after death in distant worlds
   the glorious theme renew.

7. Through all eternity to thee
   a joyful song I'll raise;
   for O! eternity's too short
   to utter all thy praise.

   Joseph Addison (1672-1719) alt.

544

1. When all thy mercies, O my God,
   my rising soul surveys,
   transported with the view, I'm lost
   in wonder, love and praise.

2. Unnumbered comforts to my soul
   thy tender care bestowed,
   before my infant heart conceived
   from whom those comforts flowed.

3. When in such slipp'ry paths I ran
   in childhood's careless days,
   thine arm unseen conveyed me safe,
   to walk in adult ways.

4. When worn with sickness oft hast thou
   with health renewed my face;
   and when in sins and sorrows sunk,
   revived my soul with grace.

5. Ten thousand thousand precious gifts
   my daily thanks employ,
   and not the least a cheerful heart
   which tastes those gifts with joy.

545

1. When God Almighty came to earth,
   he took the pain of Jesus' birth,
   he took the flight of refugee,
   and whispered: 'Humbly follow me.'

2. When God Almighty went to work,
   carpenter's sweat he didn't shirk,
   profit and loss he didn't flee,
   and whispered: 'Humbly follow me.'

3. When God Almighty walked the street,
   the critic's curse he had to meet,
   the cynic's smile he had to see,
   and whispered: 'Humbly follow me.'

4. When God Almighty met his folk,
   of peace and truth he boldly spoke
   to set the slave and tyrant free,
   and whispered: 'Humbly follow me.'

5. When God Almighty took his place
   to save the sometimes human race,
   he took it boldly on a tree,
   and whispered: 'Humbly follow me.'

6. When God Almighty comes again,
   he'll meet us incognito as then;
   and though no words may voice his
        plea,
   he'll whisper: 'Are you following me?'

John L. Bell (b. 1949) and Graham Maule (b. 1958)

546

When I feel the touch
of your hand upon my life,
it causes me to sing a song,
that I love you, Lord.
So from deep within
my spirit singeth unto you,
you are my King, you are my God,
and I love you, Lord.

Keri Jones and David Matthew
© 1978 Springtide/Word Music (UK)/CopyCare Ltd

547

When I look into your holiness,
when I gaze into your loveliness,
when all things that surround
become shadows in the light of you.
When I've found the joy
of reaching your heart,
when my will becomes
enthrall'd in your love,
when all things that surround
become shadows in the light of you:
I worship you, I worship you,
the reason I live is to worship you.
I worship you, I worship you,
the reason I live is to worship you.

Wayne and Cathy Perrin
© 1980 Integrity's Hosanna! Music/Kingsway's
Thankyou Music

548

1. When I needed a neighbour,
   were you there, were you there?
   When I needed a neighbour,
   were you there?

   And the creed and the colour
   and the name won't matter,
   were you there?

2. I was hungry and thirsty,
   were you there, were you there?
   I was hungry and thirsty,
   were you there?

3. I was cold, I was naked,
   were you there, were you there?
   I was cold, I was naked,
   were you there?

4. When I needed a shelter,
   were you there, were you there?
   When I needed a shelter,
   were you there?

5. When I needed a healer,
   were you there, were you there?
   When I needed a healer,
   were you there?

6. Wherever you travel,
   I'll be there, I'll be there,
   wherever you travel,
   I'll be there.

   And the creed and the colour
   and the name won't matter,
   I'll be there.

Sydney Carter (b. 1915)

549

1. When I survey the wondrous cross
   on which the Prince of Glory died,
   my richest gain I count but loss,
   and pour contempt on all my pride.

2. Forbid it, Lord, that I should boast,
   save in the death of Christ, my God:
   all the vain things that charm me most,
   I sacrifice them to his blood.

3. See from his head, his hands, his feet,
   sorrow and love flow mingling down:
   did e'er such love and sorrow meet,
   or thorns compose so rich a crown?

4. Were the whole realm of nature mine,
   that were an off'ring far too small;
   love so amazing, so divine,
   demands my soul, my life, my all.

   Isaac Watts (1674-1748)

550

1. When, in our music,
   God is glorified,
   and adoration leaves
   no room for pride,
   it is as though
   the whole creation cried:
   Alleluia.

2. How often, making music,
   we have found
   a new dimension
   in the world of sound,
   as worship moved us
   to a more profound
   Alleluia!

3. So has the Church,
   in liturgy and song,
   in faith and love,
   through centuries of wrong,
   borne witness to the truth
   in ev'ry tongue:
   Alleluia!

4. And did not Jesus sing
   a psalm that night
   when utmost evil strove
   against the Light?
   Then let us sing,
   for whom he won the fight:
   Alleluia!

5. Let ev'ry instrument
   be tuned for praise!
   Let all rejoice
   who have a voice to raise!
   And may God give us
   faith to sing always:
   Alleluia!

   Fred Pratt Green (b. 1903)

551

1. When morning gilds the skies,
   my heart awaking cries,
   may Jesus Christ be praised.
   Alike at work and prayer
   to Jesus I repair;
   may Jesus Christ be praised.

2. The night becomes as day,
   when from the heart we say:
   may Jesus Christ be praised.
   The pow'rs of darkness fear,
   when this sweet chant they hear:
   may Jesus Christ be praised.

3. In heav'n's eternal bliss
   the loveliest strain is this:
   may Jesus Christ be praised.
   Let air, and sea, and sky
   from depth to height reply:
   may Jesus Christ be praised.

4. Be this, while life is mine,
   my canticle divine:
   may Jesus Christ be praised.
   Be this th'eternal song
   through all the ages on:
   may Jesus Christ be praised.

German (19th century)
trans. Edward Caswall (1814-1878)

552

1. When our God came to earth,
   not for him noble birth:
   he affirmed human worth
   from a humble manger,
   just another stranger.

   Let the poor rejoice!
   Let the mute give voice!
   Love is shown,
   God is known,
   Christ is born of Mary.

2. Not for kings was the word
   which the poor shepherds heard:
   hope renewed, grace conferred,
   and the hillside ringing
   with the angels' singing.

3. Bethlehem, humble town
   where the babe wears the crown,
   turns the world upside down:
   God so unexpected,
   homeless and rejected.

4. Let us sing Mary's song,
   bringing hope, righting wrong,
   heard with fear by the strong,
   poor and humble raising,
   God of justice praising.

Michael Forster (b. 1946)

553

1. When we walk with the Lord
   in the light of his word,
   what a glory he sheds on our way!
   While we do his good will,
   he abides with us still,
   and with all who will trust and obey.

   Trust and obey,
   for there's no other way
   to be happy in Jesus,
   but to trust and obey.

2. Not a burden we bear,
   not a sorrow we share,
   but our toil he doth richly repay;
   not a grief nor a loss,
   not a frown nor a cross,
   but is blest if we trust and obey.

3. But we never can prove
   the delights of his love
   until all on the altar we lay;
   for the favour he shows,
   and the joy he bestows,
   are for them who will trust and obey.

4. Then in fellowship sweet
   we will sit at his feet,
   or we'll walk by his side in the way.
   What he says he will do,
   where he sends we will go,
   never fear, only trust and obey.

John Henry Sammis (1846-1919)

554

1. While shepherds watched their flocks
      by night,
   all seated on the ground,
   the angel of the Lord came down,
   and glory shone around.

2. 'Fear not,' said he (for mighty dread
   had seized their troubled mind);
   'glad tidings of great joy I bring
   to you and all mankind.

3. 'To you in David's town this day
   is born of David's line
   a Saviour, who is Christ the Lord;
   and this shall be the sign:

4. 'The heav'nly babe you there shall find
   to human view displayed,
   all meanly wrapped in swathing bands,
   and in a manger laid.'

5. Thus spake the seraph, and forthwith
   appeared a shining throng
   of angels praising God, who thus
   addressed their joyful song:

6. 'All glory be to God on high,
   and to the earth be peace;
   good will henceforth from heav'n to
      men
   begin and never cease.'

   Nahum Tate (1652-1715)

555

1. Who are these like stars appearing,
   these, before God's throne who stand?
   Each a golden crown is wearing:
   who are all this glorious band?
   Alleluia, hark, they sing,
   praising loud their heav'nly King.

2. Who are these in dazzling brightness,
   clothed in God's own righteousness,
   these, whose robes of purest whiteness
   shall their lustre still possess,
   still untouched by time's rude hand –
   whence came all this glorious band?

3. These are they who have contended
   for their Saviour's honour long,
   wrestling on till life was ended,
   following not the sinful throng;
   these, who well the fight sustained,
   triumph by the Lamb have gained.

4. These are they whose hearts were riven,
   sore with woe and anguish tried,
   who in prayer full oft have striven
   with the God they glorified;
   now, their painful conflict o'er,
   God has bid them weep no more.

5. These, th' Almighty contemplating,
   did as priests before him stand,
   soul and body always waiting
   day and night at his command:
   now in God's most holy place
   blest they stand before his face.

   *Heinrich Theobald Schenck (1656-1727) trans. Frances
   Elizabeth Cox (1812-1897) based on Revelation 7:13*

556

1. Who is this so weak and helpless,
   child of lowly Hebrew maid,
   rudely in a stable sheltered,
   coldly in a manger laid?
   'Tis the Lord of all creation,
   who this wondrous path hath trod;
   he is God from everlasting,
   and to everlasting God.

2. Who is this – a Man of Sorrows,
   walking sadly life's hard way;
   homeless, weary, sighing, weeping
   over sin and Satan's sway?
   'Tis our God, our glorious Saviour,
   who beyond our mortal sight
   now for us a place prepareth
   free from grief and full of light.

3. Who is this – behold him raining
   drops of blood upon the ground?
   Who is this – despised, rejected,
   mocked, insulted, beaten, bound?
   'Tis our God, who gifts and graces
   on his Church now poureth down;
   all his faithful ones empow'ring
   to partake in cross and crown.

4. Who is this that hangeth dying,
   with the thieves on either side?
   Nails his hands and feet are tearing,
   and the spear hath pierced his side.
   'Tis the God who ever liveth
   'mid the shining ones on high,
   in the glorious golden city
   reigning everlastingly.

William Walsham How (1823-1897) alt.

557

1. Who put the colours
   in the rainbow?
   Who put the salt into the sea?
   Who put the cold
   into the snowflake?
   Who made you and me?
   Who put the hump
   upon the camel?
   Who put the neck on the giraffe?
   Who put the tail
   upon the monkey?
   Who made hyenas laugh?
   Who made whales and snails and
      quails?
   Who made hogs and dogs and frogs?
   Who made bats and rats and cats?
   Who made ev'rything?

2. Who put the gold
   into the sunshine?
   Who put the sparkle in the stars?
   Who put the silver
   in the moonlight?
   Who made Earth and Mars?
   Who put the scent
   into the roses?
   Who taught the honey bee to dance?
   Who put the tree
   inside the acorn?
   It surely can't be chance!
   Who made seas and leaves and trees?
   Who made snow and winds that blow?
   Who made streams and rivers flow?
   God made all of these!

Paul Booth

558

1. Who would think that what was needed
   to transform and save the earth
   might not be a plan or army,
   proud in purpose, proved in worth?
   Who would think, despite derision,
   that a child should lead the way?
   God surprises earth with heaven,
   coming here on Christmas day.

2. Shepherds watch and wise men wonder,
   monarchs scorn and angels sing;
   such a place as none would reckon
   hosts a holy helpless thing;
   stable beasts and by-passed strangers
   watch a baby laid in hay:
   God surprises earth with heaven,
   coming here on Christmas day.

3. Centuries of skill and science
   span the past from which we move,
   yet experience questions whether,
   with such progress, we improve.
   While the human lot we ponder,
   lest our hopes and humour fray,
   God surprises earth with heaven,
   coming here on Christmas day.

John L. Bell (b. 1949) and Graham Maule (b. 1958)

559

Wide, wide as the ocean,
high as the heavens above;
deep, deep as the deepest sea
is my Saviour's love.
I, though so unworthy,
still am a child of his care,
for his word teaches me that
his love reaches me ev'rywhere.

C. Austin Miles
© The Rodeheaver Co/Word Music Inc./
Word Music (UK)/CopyCare Ltd

560

1. Will you come and follow me
   if I but call your name?
   Will you go where you don't know,
   and never be the same?
   Will you let my love be shown,
   will you let my name be known,
   will you let my life be grown
   in you, and you in me?

2. Will you leave yourself behind
   if I but call your name?
   Will you care for cruel and kind,
   and never be the same?
   Will you risk the hostile stare
   should your life attract or scare,
   will you let me answer prayer
   in you, and you in me?

3. Will you let the blinded see
   if I but call your name?
   Will you set the pris'ners free,
   and never be the same?
   Will you kiss the leper clean
   and do such as this unseen,
   and admit to what I mean
   in you, and you in me?

4. Will you love the 'you' you hide
   if I but call your name?
   Will you quell the fear inside,
   and never be the same?
   Will you use the faith you've found
   to reshape the world around
   through my sight and touch and sound
   in you, and you in me?

5. Lord, your summons echoes true
   when you but call my name.
   Let me turn and follow you,
   and never be the same.
   In your company I'll go
   where your love and footsteps show.
   Thus I'll move and live and grow
   in you, and you in me.

   John L. Bell (b. 1949) and Graham Maule (b. 1958)

561

1. Will your anchor hold
   in the storms of life,
   when the clouds unfold
   their wings of strife?
   When the strong tides lift,
   and the cables strain,
   will your anchor drift,
   or firm remain?

   *We have an anchor
   that keeps the soul
   steadfast and sure
   while the billows roll;
   fastened to the rock
   which cannot move,
   grounded firm and deep
   in the Saviour's love!*

2. Will your anchor hold
   in the straits of fear,
   when the breakers roar
   and the reef is near?
   While the surges rage,
   and the wild winds blow,
   shall the angry waves
   then your bark o'erflow?

3. Will your anchor hold
   in the floods of death,
   when the waters cold
   chill your latest breath?
   On the rising tide
   you can never fail,
   while your anchor holds
   within the veil.

4. Will your eyes behold
   through the morning light,
   the city of gold
   and the harbour bright?
   Will you anchor safe
   by the heav'nly shore,
   when life's storms are past
   for evermore?

   Priscilla Jane Owens (1829-1899)

562

Within our darkest night,
you kindle the fire
that never dies away,
that never dies away.
Within our darkest night,
you kindle the fire
that never dies away,
that never dies away.

Taizé Community

563

1. Ye choirs of new Jerusalem,
   your sweetest notes employ,
   the Paschal victory to hymn
   in strains of holy joy.

2. For Judah's Lion burst his chains,
   and crushed the serpent's head;
   and brought with him, from death's
      domain,
   the long-imprisoned dead.

3. From hell's devouring jaws the prey
   alone our leader bore;
   his ransomed hosts pursue their way
   where he hath gone before.

4. Triumphant in his glory now
   his sceptre ruleth all:
   earth, heav'n and hell before him bow,
   and at his footstool fall.

5. While joyful thus his praise we sing,
   his mercy we implore,
   into his palace bright to bring,
   and keep us evermore.

6. All glory to the Father be,
   all glory to the Son,
   all glory, Holy Ghost, to thee,
   while endless ages run.
   Alleluia. Amen.

St. Fulbert of Chartres (d. 1028)
trans. Robert Campbell (1814-1868)

564

1. Ye holy angels bright,
   who wait at God's right hand,
   or through the realms of light
   fly at your Lord's command,
   assist our song,
   for else the theme
   too high doth seem
   for mortal tongue.

2. Ye blessèd souls at rest,
   who ran this earthly race,
   and now, from sin released,
   behold the Saviour's face,
   God's praises sound,
   as in his sight
   with sweet delight
   ye do abound.

3. Ye saints, who toil below,
   adore your heav'nly King,
   and onward as ye go
   some joyful anthem sing;
   take what he gives
   and praise him still,
   through good or ill,
   who ever lives.

4. My soul, bear thou thy part,
   triumph in God above:
   and with a well-tuned heart
   sing thou the songs of love;
   let all thy days
   till life shall end,
   whate'er he send,
   be filled with praise.

Richard Baxter (1615-1691)
and John Hampden Gurney (1802-1862)

565

1. Ye servants of God,
   your Master proclaim,
   and publish abroad
   his wonderful name;
   the name all victorious
   of Jesus extol:
   his kingdom is glorious,
   and rules over all.

2. God ruleth on high,
   almighty to save;
   and still he is nigh:
   his presence we have:
   the great congregation
   his triumph shall sing,
   ascribing salvation
   to Jesus our King.

3. Salvation to God
   who sits on the throne!
   let all cry aloud,
   and honour the Son.
   The praises of Jesus
   the angels proclaim,
   fall down on their faces,
   and worship the Lamb.

4. Then let us adore,
   and give him his right:
   all glory and pow'r,
   all wisdom and might,
   and honour and blessing,
   with angels above,
   and thanks never-ceasing,
   and infinite love.

   Charles Wesley (1707-1788)

566

1. Ye servants of the Lord,
   each for his coming wait,
   observant of his heav'nly word,
   and watchful at his gate.

2. Let all your lamps be bright,
   and trim the golden flame;
   gird up your loins as in his sight,
   for awesome is his name.

3. Watch! 'tis your Lord's command,
   and while we speak, he's near;
   mark the first signal of his hand,
   and ready all appear.

4. O happy servants they,
   in such a posture found,
   who share their Saviour's triumph day,
   with joy and honour crowned.

5. Christ shall the banquet spread
   with his own royal hand,
   and raise each faithful servant's head
   amid th'angelic band.

   Philip Doddridge (1702-1751) alt.

567

1. Ye watchers and ye holy ones,
   bright seraphs, cherubim and thrones,
   raise the glad strain, alleluia.
   Cry out, dominions, princedoms,
     pow'rs,
   virtues, archangels, angels' choirs,

   *Alleluia, alleluia, alleluia,
   alleluia, alleluia!*

Continued overleaf

2. O higher than the cherubim,
more glorious than the seraphim,
lead their praises, alleluia.
O Mary, bearer of the Word,
most gracious, magnify the Lord:

Alleluia, alleluia, alleluia,
alleluia, alleluia!

3. Respond, ye souls in endless rest,
ye patriarchs and prophets blest,
alleluia, alleluia.
Ye holy twelve, ye martyrs strong,
all saints triumphant, raise the song:

4. O friends, in gladness let us sing,
supernal anthems echoing,
alleluia, alleluia.
To God the Father, God the Son
and God the Spirit, Three in One:

Athelstan Riley (1858-1945) alt.

568

1. Ye who own the faith of Jesus
sing the wonders that were done,
when the love of God the Father
o'er our sin the vict'ry won,
when he made the Virgin Mary
mother of his only Son.

Hail Mary, hail Mary,
hail Mary, full of grace.

2. Blessèd were the chosen people
out of whom the Lord did come,
blessèd was the land of promise
fashioned for his earthly home;
but more blessèd was the mother,
she who bore him in her womb.

3. Wherefore let all faithful people
tell the honour of her name,
let the Church in her foreshadowed
part in her thanksgiving claim;
what Christ's mother sang in gladness
let Christ's people sing the same.

4. Let us weave our supplications,
she with us and we with her,
for advancement of the faithful,
for each faithful worshipper,
for the doubting, for the sinful,
for each heedless wanderer.

5. May the mother's intercessions
on our homes a blessing win,
that the children all be prospered,
strong and fair and pure within,
following our Lord's own footsteps,
firm in faith and free from sin.

6. For the sick and for the agèd,
for our dear ones far away,
for the hearts that mourn in secret,
all who need our prayers today,
for the faithful gone before us,
may the Holy Virgin pray.

7. Praise, O Mary, praise the Father,
praise thy Saviour and thy Son,
praise the everlasting Spirit,
who hath made thee ark and throne;
o'er all creatures high exalted,
lowly praise the Three in One.

Vincent Stuckey Stratton Coles (1845-1929)

569

You are beautiful
beyond description,
too marvellous for words,
too wonderful for comprehension
like nothing ever seen or heard.
Who can grasp your infinite wisdom?
Who can fathom
the depth of your love?
You are beautiful
beyond description,
Majesty enthroned above.
And I stand,
I stand in awe of you;
I stand, I stand in awe of you.
Holy God,
to whom all praise is due,
I stand in awe of you.

Mark Altrogge
© *1987 People of Destiny Int./Word Music Inc./
Word Music (UK)/CopyCare Ltd*

570

You are the King of Glory,
you are the Prince of Peace,
you are the Lord of heav'n and earth,
you're the Son of righteousness.
Angels bow down before you,
worship and adore,
for you have the words
of eternal life,
you are Jesus Christ the Lord.
Hosanna to the Son of David!
Hosanna to the King of kings!
Glory in the highest heaven,
for Jesus the Messiah reigns!

Mavis Ford
© *1978 Springtide/Word Music (UK)/CopyCare Ltd*

571

You shall go out with joy
and be led forth with peace,
and the mountains and the hills
shall break forth before you.
There'll be shouts of joy
and the trees of the field
shall clap,
shall clap their hands.
And the trees of the field
shall clap their hands,
and the trees of the field
shall clap their hands,
and the trees of the field
shall clap their hands,
and you'll go out with joy.

Stuart Dauermann (b. 1944) based on Isaiah 55:12
© *1975 Lillenas Publishing Co/Kingsway's Thankyou Music*

Indexes

Authors, Translators and Sources of Words

Index of Uses

TIMES AND SEASONS

*Hymns generally applicable to the
main seasons are included here. For
suggestions more specifically related
to the Lectionary, see the ASB Index*

MORNING

EVENING

ADVENT

Scriptural Index

Index of Hymns for the ASB Lectionary

EPIPHANY 4

EPIPHANY 5

EPIPHANY 6

9 BEFORE EASTER

8 BEFORE EASTER

Index of First Lines

Acknowledgements

The publishers wish to express their gratitude to the following for permission to use copyright material in this book:

The Executors of L.T.J. Arlott, 11 Victoria Street, Alderney, Channel Islands GY9 3AN for *God whose farm is all creation*.

Ateliers et Presses de Taizé, F-71250, Taizé-Communauté, France for *Adoramus te, Domine, Bless the Lord, Gloria, In the Lord I'll be ever thankful, Jesus, remember me, Kyrie, Laudate Dominum, Nada te turbe, O Lord, hear my prayer, Stay with me, The Lord is my light, The Lord is my song, Ubi caritas, Wait for the Lord* and *Within our darkest night*.

Mr Paul Booth for *Who put the colours in the rainbow?*

The Rev'd. E Burns for *We have a gospel to proclaim*.

The Canterbury Press, St Mary's Works, St Mary's Plain, Norwich, Norfolk NR3 3BH for *Christ the fair glory, Good Christians all rejoice, Lord of beauty, thine the splendour, Lift high the cross* and *Rejoice, the year upon its way*.

Cassell Plc, Wellington House, 125 Strand, London WC2R 0BB for *Forth in the peace of Christ we go* © Geoffrey Chapman, *O dearest Lord, thy sacred head* © Mowbray and *This is my will* © Geoffrey Chapman. Also for *God is love* © Copyright revived 1996 Mowbray.

Chatto & Windus Ltd, 20 Vauxhall Bridge Road, London SW1V 2SA for *Be thou my vision* © Copyright revived 1996.

The Church Pension Fund, 445 Fifth Avenue, New York 10016-0109 USA for *All praise to thee* from 'The Hymnal' 1982 © The Church Pension Fund.

CopyCare Ltd, PO Box 77, Hailsham, East Sussex BN27 3EF for *Allelluia* (Donald Fishel) © 1973 Word of God Music/The Copyright Company, *As we are gathered* © 1979 Springtide/Word Music (UK), *Brother, let me be your servant* © 1977 Scripture in Song, *Father, we adore you* © 1972 Maranatha! Music, *Father, we love you* © 1976 Maranatha! Music, *God forgave my sin* © 1972 Bud John Songs/Alliance Media Ltd, *Great is the Lord and most worthy of praise* © 1985 Body Songs, *He is exalted* © 1985 Straightway Music/Alliance Media Ltd, *Holy, holy, holy* © Bud John Songs/ Alliance Media Ltd, *I love you, Lord* © 1978 Maranatha! Music, *I will enter his gates* © 1976 Maranatha! Music, *Jesus is Lord* © 1982 Springtide/Word Music (UK), *Jesus name above all names* © 1974 Scripture in Song, *On a hill far away* © The Rodeheaver Co/Word Music Inc/Word Music (UK), *Open our eyes, Lord* © 1976 Maranatha! Music, *Spirit of the living God* © 1963 Birdwing Music/Alliance Media Ltd, *This is my body* © 1978 Bud John Songs/Alliance Media Ltd, *This is the day* © 1967 Scripture in Song, *When I feel the touch* © 1978 Springtide/Word Music (UK), *Wide, wide as the ocean* © The Rodeheaver Co/Word Music Inc/Word Music (UK), *Hosanna to the Son of David* © 1978 Springtide/Word Music (UK), *I stand in awe* © 1987 People of Destiny Int/Word Music Inc/Word Music (UK), *Seek ye first* © 1972 Maranatha! Music, *I will sing the wondrous story* © Harper Collins Religious, and *There is a Redeemer* © 1982 Birdwing Music/BMG Songs Inc/Alliance Media Ltd.

Mrs M. Cross for *Father, Lord of all creation*.

J. Curwen & Son, 8/9 Frith Street, London W1V 5TZ for *All creatures of our God and King*. Also, *In our day of thanksgiving* © copyright revived 1996.

Dr. E.F. Downs for *God of grace and God of glory*.

The Rt. Rev'd. Timothy Dudley-Smith, 9 Ashlands, Ford, Salisbury, Wilts SP4 6DY for *Faithful vigil ended, Fill your hearts with joy, Jesus, Prince and Saviour, Lord, for the years* and *Tell out, my soul*.

Durham Music Ltd, 1a Farm Place, London W8 7SX for *The Ink is Black* © 1970 Templeton Publishing Co Inc.

Faber Music Ltd, 3 Queen Square, London WC1N 3AU for *Holy Spirit, come, confirm us* © 1971 Faber Music Ltd, reprinted from 'New Catholic Hymnal'.

GIA Publications Inc, 7404 S. Mason Avenue, Chicago, IL 60638, USA for *I am the bread of life* © 1966 GIA Publications Inc.

The Rev'd. M.J. Hancock for *Filled with the Spirit's power, For Mary, mother of our Lord* and *Awake, awake, fling off the night*.

David Higham Associates Ltd, 5-8 Lower John Street, Golden Square, London W1R 4HA for *Morning has broken* from 'The Children's Bells', published by Oxford University Press.

Hope Publishing Co, 380 South Main Place, Carol Stream, IL 60188, USA for *Great is thy faithfulness* © 1923 renewal 1951 Hope Publishing Co, *How lovely, Lord, how lovely* © 1986 Hope Publishing Co and *New songs of celebration render* © 1974 Hope Publishing Co. All rights reserved. Used by permission.

The Iona Community, Community House, Pearce Institute, Govan, Glasgow G51 3UU for *Among us and before us, Bread is blessed and broken, Christ's is the world*, and *We will lay our burden down*, all © 1989 WGRG from the 'Love from below' collection; *Cloth for the cradle, Dance and sing, Heaven shall not wait,*